Sustainable Happiness

Richard Haycock

BALBOA.
PRESS
A DIVISION OF HAY HOUSE

Balboa Press books may be ordered through booksellers or by contacting:

Balboa Press
A Division of Hay House
1663 Liberty Drive
Bloomington, IN 47403
www.balboapress.com.au
1 (877) 407-4847

Print information available on the last page.

ISBN: 978-1-5043-1128-1 (sc)
ISBN: 978-1-5043-1129-8 (e)

Balboa Press rev. date: 11/28/2017

Thanks Mum and Dad
For Everyone
Love Richard

Contents

Preface

Gudday from New Zealand beautiful people, this book is my best endeavour to articulate a subject that is mystifying the minds of millions. This subject contains two areas which are intrinsically connected. These are, how to attain and sustain happiness, and why it is that people behave in ways that cause pain and suffering to themselves and others. There is no separation here.

This book is a study read, and one in which there is an expectation that you will try to join the dots between everything I have written here and your life. Reach for understanding.

Due to the depth of this work, a perfectly sequential approach to this writing is not entirely possible nor appropriate, because everything I wish to say ties together to paint a broad and dynamic picture. Therefore, this book will require referral back to previously written concepts, where you have interpreted your own personal experience from this broader perspective.

Often when we talk about any subject let alone our human emotional world, there are many misunderstandings. We all have different interpretations and beliefs hence these confusions.

Most self-help books are asking you to think. This one not only asks you to think deeply it asks for a 180 degree turn in our naturally developed yet flawed interpretations of our emotional responses. Hence, understanding this interpretation, this perspective can feel counter intuitive when trying to embody it to begin with. It can turn you around inside trying to understand, but when you do, when it clicks you attain a freedom unsurpassed. The emotional responsibility gained with this interpretation, is your first step towards a truly Sustainable Happiness, a more vibrant, alive, clear minded you!

Our emotional world, our state of being as an individual directly affects the society we live in far more powerfully than many realize, this is largely due to associating our emotional response outside of self then battling the world around us to appease these feelings outside of self.

Emotion is a massive subject which is dear to us all, because all people are constantly feeling something, and this can be enhanced for the better, regardless of life circumstance more readily than many believe.

I simply ask you to try and understand this perspective, to try and hear the depth of where I am coming from. I believe this education is worth the effort.

After all there is nothing more important than **YOU**, which of course, includes us all!

Love Richard.

Part One

Painting a Picture

Introduction

There is nothing more important than that we **all** feel good, and the way we feel is completely within our own individual control, even if it does not appear to be so at the moment.

All we need is an understanding of how we create our own feelings, create our own state of being, and **apply** this knowledge in our daily life.

It is my intention to convince you that there is literally nothing more important than that you feel good, that feeling good is really, the only, legitimate life career choice. Everything else must come second to that, and that feeling good is achievable regardless of any circumstance. (Of course I am not suggesting that you will not have horrible feelings during some traumatic situation.)

It is my intention to introduce you to a better way of interpreting your emotions, backed up with practical skills so that you can move forward enhancing your own feeling space with time practice and experience. You must make it your **dominant intention** to feel good.

Because the way you feel is everything to you, everything in life is about how you feel, have you noticed?

Sadly, many people don't do anything until the emotional pain becomes too much and they can't stand it anymore, or others are living a hum drum existence, or have given up on life and simply believe this is the way life is, thus don't come to this work at all. Yet these people would benefit beyond description should they work towards embodying a gradually improving state of being from this boarder perspective.

I understand that we have all lived a life, been on our own journeys and are at different stages within life, we all have our own 'stuff' to deal with. We all have differing emotional set points regarding our life stories and all subjects within our stories such as, health, work, money, school, relationships, everything!

That said, regardless of your story, whatever the details are in your story, your journey, your life, this information will show you a way to develop ever increasing places of feeling better and better. Emotional set points, are not as set as the term implies. What you consider to be your natural and normal state of being which appears set, or what we term as conditions such as PTSD, depression, phobias, etc., are not set either. Especially once this work becomes second nature within you. In fact, once you naturalize it within yourself, you have the ability to overcome any issue because an issue is only an issue whilst it is dominating your emotional state. When you can sustainably hold a higher emotional state regardless of circumstance there is no longer an issue of any consequence!

The information offered here works, I know it works through personal experience, as well as seeing others get results with it.

I know the information offered here has the power to transform anyone willing to listen, study, and seek answers to questions generated, and most importantly do!

This book is crammed to the brim with powerful education and will have many heads spinning. Just relax and take your time to study the material here, this is not a race this is far more important than that; this is your life.

This book is an introduction to an education which specifically creates harmony, happiness and inner-peace within you, and once you become proficient at that you move even further into a vibrancy and zest for life; many people such as those who have given up on life possibly cannot imagine that at this stage. However, reach to imagine a **higher** state of being to your own choosing, because it is through your state of being that you **interpret** your life, and frankly **is your life.** If you feel flat you interpret your life as flat, if you feel tough you interpret your life as tough, if you feel vibrant you interpret your life as vibrant and so on. I believe in self-empowerment, I know each and every one of us can do this. I also know that it won't be easy for some, and for others they will take to it like ducks to water.

What you read here will make more sense to you in time, after you have actually used it and naturalized it within yourself thus gained experience and embodiment of a higher feeling state. At first applying the knowledge learned here takes a bit of getting used to just like learning any new skill, but in time it becomes second nature.

Some of what I say will annoy some of you, especially if you have traumas, issues and contradictory beliefs of some kind active within you, or if there is something hard going on in your life right now. What I say may trigger an angry response or piss you off. That's ok, In fact that's everything. Because it's in reactions like this **where the real work begins, where happiness is born**! Just relax and be patient with studying this book, be patient with yourself and absorb this knowledge at your own pace. Because when you get it, when it clicks you will find a freedom unsurpassed, truly.

Chapter One

So what is having your shit together?

What does it mean to have your shit together? What does it mean to you? Everybody who reads this will have their own perspective regarding what having your shit together means. Many people hold some version of society's status quo concept so aptly summed up in George Thorogood's song lyrics, *"Get a haircut and get a real job"*

This belief, this pattern of thought, is so powerfully held within many individuals and mass consciousness world over that it has become a 'truth' for many.

The massive pressure this limited and ridiculous concept of obtaining wealth, status, and things as being defined as successful, or having your shit together, is causing havoc in many individual's lives, and society as a whole.

You will see as you work through this book, that **these things are all wanted for the emotional response you unconsciously believe you will attain once you achieve or get these things.**

Of course there is nothing wrong with wanting these things, but associating a **feeling of self-worth or success** to these physical things on the other hand can be highly destructive for individuals first and foremost, and then our society. This is due to the feelings that are generated for better or for worse which are associated outside of-self relative to where you want to be in your life. Meaning we associate successful feelings outside of-self relative to our accomplishments or lack thereof.

Many people unfortunately gain what I call false self-worth in this way by associating their self-worth to the degree of success they think they have. Meaning, if you have some semblance of physical success you may feel good, or if you do not have some semblance of physical success you may feel not so good, especially when you compare where you are in life to where you would rather be. Even if you do gain physical success often there is still an inner void felt which can cause you all sorts of grief if you continue to battle outside circumstance attempting to fill this void. **These voids can only ever be filled from within by aligning mind with emotion.**

Many self-help education streams and books focus on gaining success or abundance in physical form and can thus continue to perpetuate this inaccurate need for physical success to therefore gain good feelings such as to feel worthy or successful. These books often talk about goal setting and taking action etc., they also often focus on self-motivation and numerous other tools and techniques to gain your particular physical version of success whatever that is to you. However, success in physical form is always wanted for the emotional feeling you believe you will gain in achieving your version of success. You do not require anything outside of self to feel worthy or to feel successful. You simply are worthy as you are right here and now regardless of any circumstance, but of course coming to this knowing, coming to this realization requires challenging and re-developing your current beliefs about what self-worth and success is, whilst simultaneously developing a happy, vibrant appreciative state of being regardless of your current circumstances. This is no easy feat, but the education taught throughout these pages gives you enough insight to work towards a higher happier self regardless of your circumstance, therefore you will truly be successful because true success is always within your state of being, within the way you feel.

For many others, having your shit together simply means *"I want to feel better now dammit"* especially those suffering with things like depression, PTSD, suicidal tendencies, anger, addictions, phobias, anxiety, grief, a need to forgive etc.

Or perhaps you may have your shit together from society's point of view, the job, the haircut, the house, the car, the life partner, the nice bank account and still be depressed, or any other condition just mentioned. Thus feel as though you don't have your shit together.

Holding one's own 'shit together' has therefore become quite a conundrum for many.

Just look at the volume of people on anti-depressants alone, let alone in therapy, rehab, AA, prison, suicide rates and so on.

Having your shit together is totally about how **'you feel'** moment to moment, because that's what life is, your **state of being**, your inner reactions. Life is not so much about having a job, a haircut, a house etc., although these are wonderful things, we have to go deeper. Why do I want these things in the first place?

The answer is because, **"Anything anybody does, they do because they believe they will feel better in the doing, having, or achieving of it"**

There is no exception to this quote anywhere in your experience and we will cover this more fully throughout the entirety of this book. Really think about this quote from Esther Hicks, ponder it over time, develop thoughts about it, challenge it for sure, but **keep looking to see** the fundamental truth in this statement in all situations. Especially those situations that do challenge it as it relates to you in **every** aspect of your experience, and thus everybody else's.

The entirety of your life, my life, everybody's lives is about how you/we feel, our state of being; period!

Emotional responsibility stops blame transference within society.

I believe a lack of emotional responsibility causes almost all people to inaccurately interpret their emotional response outside of self. This then translates into chasing our own tails around and around in life trying to feel better, thus the battling of circumstances and other people ensues. This in turn translates to how our societies evolve.

True social harmony can only begin with your personal emotional responsibility first, you need to take **full** responsibility for **all** your inner reactions if you want to enhance your own state of being, which means stopping all blame of others and circumstance for the way in which **you feel**, thus the battle outside of-self ceases which is where your circle of influence is most noticed, because you are society! Emotional responsibility is truly at the heart of self-empowerment, because you get to choose all thought and perspectives, which in turn creates all feeling spaces within.

This means taking responsibility for **every** emotional reaction you have regardless of any event that takes place in which you think caused your reaction. Without taking full emotional responsibility for your inner reactions you cannot ever hope to find true sustaining happiness! This means that when you are living or observing any situation that bugs you in some way, you must reach for a **lighter feeling** perspective within the subject at hand or get your attention off it. This conscious reaching or letting go must take place rather than just accepting any negative emotion as 'normal because of the situation,' which is blame transference outside of self, a lack of emotional responsibility. Reach higher, reach deeper, reach to understand your thought structure relative to your inner emotional responses within all life experience.

Firstly, my definition of emotion.

I need you to understand that I define the following terms interchangeably. Your emotions, your feelings, your state of being, your bodily responses, your reactions, your tone, your niggles meaning every nuance and impulse small or large that you feel are all part of the same thing. The way we feel is the way we feel, and we always feel it in our physical body no matter how we wish to label it. I am not distinguishing a difference between any of these labels they are all sides of the same coin. So when you hear me use any of these terms you know I am using them interchangeably.

An interpretation, of emotional responses you can use.

Due to a lack of emotional responsibility most people unfortunately and **inaccurately** believe that the way they feel is dependent on the behaviours of those around them, and the events and possessions within their life experience. Therefore, we tend to **unconsciously** believe that the way we feel is out of our control and blame other people's behaviour, or our life situations for the way we feel. For example, if things were better with my relationships, work, school, health, possessions, world events etc., I would feel better and if he/she/they had done, or not done, this or that, or if I owned this or that, then I would feel better.

This is interesting because what we are living or looking at in the moment **appears** to determine our feelings. If we are looking at good wanted things, nice behaviour etc., it is easy to feel good. Whereas if we are looking at what we **personally deem** to be bad behaviour, or an unwanted life situation or unwanted world event, then we naturally feel bad.

As a result of this **unmanaged** internal response, we have come to **inaccurately associate and attach** our feelings to everything outside of ourselves, and therefore falsely believe we have to control and dominate other people and every aspect of our life outwardly in order to feel better. Work, money, health and the biggest of all, relationships, the behaviour of others.

In actuality, it is our thoughts, our point of view, our awareness that **feels** off not what we are living or looking at.

This is the key to this education right here, the way you feel is in direct response to your active thoughts, your active beliefs, your point of view, your awareness on something, **nothing** else.

Your happiness, your state of being, your joy comes from what you choose to think about **and how** you think about it. Period!

Of course this is hard to hear at first, as almost all of us unconsciously believe we feel the way we feel because of something. For example: -

- I feel bad because that horrible person did something to me.
- I'll feel better when this problem is fixed.
- But I just need more money so I can….
- Yeah but this happened to me when I was a kid, you wouldn't understand.
- I will feel better when I get a partner.
- My partner needs to….
- I will feel better when I pay the mortgage off.
- I will feel better when I own that.
- I will feel better when they lock that person up.
- I will feel better when we eradicate all of those people that do that.
- I will feel better when I get rid of this problem in my life.
- But I am unwell.

This list of examples can be extended to include all human experience. Can you see how these examples are associating emotion outside of self hence blaming a situation for the way in which we feel? This is utterly disempowering to say the least.

Here's two everyday examples to show you how feelings have been associated outside of self yet are actually caused by your thought.

1. Have you ever had a problem in your life, thus in your mind, that is really in your face and you feel like shit? Then you go to work, or catch up with a friend, go to a movie, read a book, play a sport, go for a run, or you have done something else that has distracted you and then you notice that you're feeling better?

   That is because your focus has changed, your thoughts have shifted, your awareness is on something else. Yet the problem is still there waiting for you, but you **are** feeling better. This is not because of your friend, work, book, movie, physical exercise, or whatever it is you are doing. This is because your thought has shifted. Your awareness on the subject(s) that have been bugging you has been reduced or removed for the moment with the distraction that you're engaged in. Nothing else has changed the problem is still there. Meaning, the distraction you are engaged in has **naturally shifted your thoughts, your awareness.** Therefore, you are no longer actively thinking about your problem in these moments you are thinking something else, your awareness **is** somewhere else. Thus you feel better.

Please note, distractions do not require physical exercise to evoke a feeling shift as you can see in the small list just given, therefore telling you your emotive response has more to do with your mental focus than anything else, which is highly empowering especially for those that struggle physically to get around in life. We all have full power to direct the thoughts we think and can distract ourselves in a multitude of ways. All distraction regardless of the distraction is always mental distraction even in the midst of any physical activity because mental awareness is always present to some degree.

2. Imagine you go to a doctor and you get a very troubling diagnosis of some sort which sends you into a tail spin with fret, worry, concern, fear and panic perhaps.
   Then let's say in the days following you spend a lot of time fretting about it, perhaps worse you go into depression.

   Then for some reason you end up getting another opinion and this doctor totally refutes and proves the original diagnosis is utterly wrong, and actually you have something very minor and it isn't really a problem after all. Then you find yourself feeling relieved over the moon and excited for life again.

   This is a clear example of your thoughts, your beliefs, your points of view, and your awareness being on an unwanted illness causing your feelings, not the illness. Because it didn't actually exist to begin with, nothing actually changed except your thoughts.

   Even if the illness did exist you can still find a point of view that feels better or worse, it's up to you, and frankly there's nothing more medicinal than finding a feeling of hope and eagerness rather than fear or panic.

At any rate, I know this is hard to hear at first because it is so hard wired within us to change things around us to feel better. It is natural to blame what others have done to us, or what has happened to us, or is happening to us for our inner reactions and feelings. However, this is the key that you have been looking for. The freedom in this is huge once you get your head around it and embody it within yourself.

Take notice when you have experiences similar to these examples, because life experience will prove to you over time that it is all **you.** It is your thoughts within the subject matter that creates your feeling space good or bad. So **the true cause of your emotional response big or small, good or bad is between your own ears!** Again this is exciting because we ultimately have full control of how we direct our mind. So from here forward I am asking you to relate your feelings, your emotional reactions to your mental activity alone. Not to anything outside of yourself such as that bugger over there whom you may believe has pissed you off. This is a big ask when you first hear it, nevertheless **this is key to individual and social harmony.**

We have heard many times from many teachers, that happiness comes from within, well so does all other emotional responses. Anger comes from within, rage comes from within, guilt comes from within, feeling pissed off comes from within, hopelessness comes from within, depression comes from within, believing you no longer feel anything thus having no zest or passion comes from within. Every single emotional nuance and response you feel is caused and created by your chosen and activated thought, and is felt within you! Therefore, you can take full control of your life because life is largely about what you think thus feel.

Chapter Two

Life is an interconnection of three things, physical life, thought and emotion.

What the prior chapter shows us is, that **for all people** (no exceptions) our life is an interconnection between our thoughts, emotions and physical life experience, they are intrinsically tied together. This interconnectedness is where the confusion lies regarding individual and social inner-peace and happiness.

As you come to realize that what makes you happy isn't actually the things you're doing, having or achieving in your actual touch wood physical life experience, but rather emotion is evoked from where you allow your thoughts, your point of view and your awareness to go regarding your preferences (desires) within your physical life experience. This is really what is evoking your feeling space, good or bad. Although all three go together to make up your life, it is your thought alone that evokes your inner emotive experience. Coming to this full realization in **all** circumstances is emotional responsibility!

This is exciting because this means we are in full control of our own life when we realize that it is our thought alone, 'not our experiences' that creates our moment to moment state of being. Meaning, when we drop all outside of-self associations (blame) for any feeling we feel, whilst taking full responsibility for our own inner reactions, then we can deliberately work to feel better by consciously seeking thought that feels a little better than the last thought, gradually shifting your state of being higher. Then and only then do we have full control, this takes gentle steps in each of us to practice. This is pure self-empowerment, meaning we have the free will to direct our thoughts, direct our awareness, find a new point of view, find a thought, find a belief that feels better.

This is everything, your state of being is everything, your perception is everything, it just is. We have full power over our own thought nobody else ever does. Therefore, that gives us a freedom unsurpassed, truly it does. Learning to see the association of everything you feel relative to your **active** thoughts and awareness rather than anything outside of self is paramount for your own well-being. Without developing this awareness, you can feel out of control, lost and at the mercy of life. However, we are never at the mercy of life, it just appears that way to those whom haven't yet taken control of the way they direct their thought in relationship to how it feels. Most people who are upset within their life simply want their life to change so they can feel better. This is life's biggest trap; this is blame outside of self.

Emotion is your friend.

So if you choose to see and use your emotion your internal reactions, every nuance you feel small and large positive and negative as your friend helping to guide which way to direct your **active** thoughts and beliefs within any moment in time, you will gradually take control of your state of being thus life in an exceptionally profound way. Really think about this, try and see the depth of it if you cannot readily at the moment. This is truly what **'going within'** means, recognizing and associating your emotional responses to your own conscious and mental activity, thus directing your thought relative to which direction your emotion is building. Negative emotion is telling you to stop that particular train of thought (let go), shift what your awareness is on, or re-develop your thought, your belief in that area. Conversely positive emotion is telling you to continue thinking about that subject, enhance that point of view, look in this direction more as you are on the right track in that moment.

The bulk of us were born with 6 powerful senses, sight, scent, taste, touch, hearing and your **emotions,** your **inner reactions**. It is easy to see how the 5 senses we were taught at school guides us through the physical world. When things are too bright we shade our eyes or look away, or not bright enough we shed light somehow. When we taste things, we either like it and enjoy it, or shy away from it. When things smell good we tend to lean into it more, or move away when it smells bad. Obviously when things are too loud we move away we block our ears. We will also move closer to listen when things are softer, and of course the sense of touch. When we were small we learnt very quickly what the consequences were of being too close to the heater and what was to far back if it was chilly. Comfortable was somewhere in-between. It is easy to see how your physical senses are guiding you through the world. So it makes sense that your emotions are guidance too. **Put simply, like heat to skin emotion to thought.** Emotion guides our mental world just as our other senses guide the physical world. You wouldn't put your hand on a hot stove top until you burnt yourself causing an injury so why would you choose thought that hurts you?

So again, your joy, your passion, your zest, comes from what you choose to focus on thus think about. The way we feel individually in any moment, is subject only to the thoughts we choose to think and **how we think**, relative to the subjects we allow our awareness to focus on or dwell in. This is also relative to our **wants and desires** for life within any subject or circumstance we are thinking about or engaged in.

This means when you see something in life, or are aware of something, this activates your beliefs, thoughts and points of view about that subject relative to your personal preferences (desires) and you feel the **resonance or discord** of those **active** thoughts which is your emotion.

I know some of this can be tricky to get your head around when you first hear it, if this is so please continue reading, all will come clear as you ponder this information moving forward.

So to recap, as a species we have all mostly associated our feeling responses to what we are looking at, and for the most part have not yet realized the way we feel is the result of our own in the moment activated thoughts (which includes activated beliefs) regarding what we are looking at. We naturally although **inaccurately** believe what we are looking at has caused our emotional response. So then we tend to go about trying to change and control everything around us in order to feel better. However, true power is in aligning mind with emotion as afore mentioned rather than forcing outside change. Because often we cannot change situations hence if physical change is the only tool in your well-being tool box you will battle many circumstances in your life to no avail.

Of course some of us live in very atrocious conditions and it's all very well sitting here saying it's your thoughts that are causing the off feelings within you, but they are all the same. Consider that mental activity is instantly activated in observation of anything and if you are living any situation which is not to your liking, not to your preference, not to your desire then it is natural to feel bad when you are thinking about or looking at the opposite of your desire. However, it is still your mental activity that is creating your feeling space. Even if the situation is understandable or justifiable. Any justification needs to become irrelevant to you because there is outside of-self-blame within this. I know this sounds harsh but stick with me because this is where everybody's self-empowerment is born.

So for the most part thoughts go hand in hand with your **personal desires, your wants** for life. If you are currently living something that you do not want, regardless of the situation and to whatever degree of situation, from most horrible to not so horrible, it is the hardest thing in the world to get your attention off of. Yet you can shift your attention, or you can reach for a new thought, a new point of view within the life experience you are living. Your awareness your thoughts are most often on the subjects you are living and experiencing or interested in to some degree or another. Hence we can feel bad if living something not in harmony with our own wanting, our own preferences, our own desires. Negative emotion is evoked in these situations because **our beliefs about our situation is limiting our own desires in some way** therefore it is **limiting thought** regarding personal preference causing any and all upset not the situation itself as we naturally but inaccurately believe.

Every situation is reacted to in different degrees per individual, and we all have different tolerance levels regarding how much emotional pain we can personally take, or suppress regarding any human experience you can think of, big or small. (Suppression or tolerance is ultimately not that helpful if it's the main tool in your well-being tool box.)

Hard or not you can do it, you can feel better, you can take control of your life because life is largely about how you feel no matter what human experience you factor in here, given time the wherewithal and the desire to do so. It is not so much the life situation itself that is the issue but rather how you feel within your experiences which has more to do with what's going on between your ears than anything else. So, harmonizing yourself becomes a case of building a repertoire of **knowledge**, **tools and new thought** you can use to redevelop your thinking processes relative to how thought feels to you whilst moving forward in life. This means your ability to thoughtfully thus emotionally deal with more life situations as they occur develops for the better thus you cultivate a sustainable happiness beyond simply trying to dominate and control outside circumstances which we cannot do all of the time.

Sure sometimes we believe we simply have to find a way to change the physical conditions around us to fix problems, of course we do. It's only when you make a lifestyle out of this one habit we all tend to over use that it becomes a problem, which frankly it is for the bulk of us.

For example, I'm sure we all know of a control freak, someone who feels the need to control all situations in their life, perhaps you are one? This is simply natural behaviour due to inaccurately associating our emotional responses outwardly. Someone termed as a control freak tends to dominantly use this one tool to feel better. The tool of trying to change the details, the conditions of what they are living. Usually control freaks are unaware they are doing so for their own emotional gain. Often people like this may offer many justifications as to their reasoning to why they are doing what they are doing. Regardless of any justification the bottom line is, "Everything we do, we do because we believe we will feel better in the doing having or achieving of it."

As most of us are aware, it is not always possible to change things around us to feel better hence many of us are left hanging blaming outside circumstance for the way in which we feel. Hence trying to change physical conditions as our only option is literally chasing one's own tail, yet we are all doing this to some degree. In fact, we make a career out of it by physically trying to change our life's details in order to feel better. For example, acquiring this that or the other thing, or forcing others to behave etc., really is chasing an elusive ghost outside of self.

Obsessive compulsive disorder also falls into this category, but control freaks and OCD sufferers are just extreme examples of what we are **all** doing within all subjects in our lives to varying **degrees.**

So, if you are consciously and deliberately doing the internal work of aligning thought with emotion mostly, rather than the constant and incessant chasing outside of self, then gently and surely you begin to thrive inside.

If you attempt to only do this work in the midst of some big problem, or try only on the big issues and have not naturalized this dynamic and mindful directing of thought by how it feels, then that is like ignoring someone trying to give you good advice before something bad happens. (In this case, 'before something bad happens' is referring to out of control strongly negative emotional states.)

For example, imagine your emotions both positive and negative are good advice from a friend (which they are) and all negative emotions regardless of which label you give them are saying to you, 'Hey you have to sort that mental point of view out, or let go,' and you ignore it, and then they say again, 'Hey you have to sort that mental point of view out, or let go,' and you ignore it, and then they say again, 'Hey you have to sort that mental point of view out, or let go' and you ignore it. Then before long you find yourself feeling worse than ever, and you can't see how it happened! Your friend is your emotional responses always talking to you, negative emotion is nudging you to reach for a better feeling perspective, it always is. Therefore, if you have ignored all the little inner negative feeling impulses and have thus allowed your negative emotion to build to such a degree that it is now seemingly out of control and you are feeling terrible, depressed, anxious, fearful, frustrated, angry etc., etc., these strong feelings are simply your emotional friend now screaming at you to sort your mental points of view out, or bloody well let go!

You have completely done it to yourself, you have created your emotional state by not re-directing thought in the early stages relative to your smaller inner emotional niggles.

Henceforth, true empowerment comes from gently quietly following your emotional indicators, all day, every day on all subjects. Learn to lean away from thinking about things and situations that feel bad to you, or reach for better feeling perspectives within these subjects. Conversely lean into subjects thus thought processes that feel good to you, deliberately and consciously.

So by changing our thoughts/beliefs, by changing what our focus is on. By shifting where our awareness lies our feelings, our state of being shifts, and that is everything to you, thus us!

This practice gently develops new beliefs over time because as you consciously choose new thought by how it feels, rather than allowing thought to randomly wander, you will ultimately be changing your habitual patterns of thought, which is all a belief really is. This practice ultimately creates a sustainable inner harmony few experience without the application of this knowing.

Given this understanding, any example of any person's state of being, or tone hasn't just randomly happened due to life experience alone. Everybody's overall demeanour, attitude to life and all things has happened **gradually thought by thought** over an individual's lifetime in response to experience. This in turn creates belief after belief within us, understanding that **a belief is really only a thought we keep thinking, a repeating pattern of thought which we may then hold as our truth.**

This is essential to understand regarding the creation of beliefs or the perpetual kept aliveness of beliefs, please ponder and consider that, **a belief**

is only a thought you keep thinking, a repeating pattern of thought.
Reach to fully understand how this is so moving through life from here.

At any rate, due to the thoughts you have chosen to think, or ideas
you have been exposed to throughout your life which you then began
perpetuating as your own thought process, no two individuals have
exactly the same set of thought patterns or beliefs. This process of
habitual thought with no heed given to how thought feels is also why
people feel that certain issues in life are deeply ingrained, when really
issues are simply repeating patterns of thought, that is all. Yet thoughts
can be changed, and will be changed if you make it your dominant
intent to feel good consciously throughout **all** your daily activities
not just within your big issues. Remember your emotional friend is
reminding you each time you get too close to the hot stove top to pick
another thought before you burn yourself.

Of course life experiences and how we interpret our experience influences
our patterns of thought thus our beliefs, **until** you really start to direct
thought in this way.

So it becomes obvious that some beliefs/thoughts serve us as individuals
and some do not. It also becomes obvious that society's, cultures, religions,
and world view is also just collective belief (thoughts) that a group of
individuals have in **similar** form within themselves. Some of which serves
the society and some of which do not.

The good news here is that contradictory to popular ideas, you don't have
to go back in time and sort out all your beliefs. What you can do is move
forward from here, thought by thought gradually and gently using your
own feelings to guide your thinking. Thus creating and building new
beliefs that serve you better gradually over time. Which means you feel
better which is everything to you.

Your power is always in the now, through your own choice of thought now.

Your feelings really are the answer to all your problems.

Your feelings really are the answer to all your problems even though it may appear that they are the cause of all your problems. Please understand that feelings only appear to be the cause of our problems when they are large and uncomfortable thus we inaccurately consider them to be a problem or a condition, when really they are our consciousness steering wheel. Also we have mostly associated our emotion outside of-self which can sometimes result in a behaviourally negative action. Whereas if we utilise each emotional nuance for inner conscious change as I have suggested then we build an ever increasing stable state of being over time.

This isn't at all complicated, if other people around us had led by example by being this way (rather than the common critical authoritarian way) and had they simply said to us when we were small, 'Honey there is nothing more important than that you feel good and that's easy, in any life situation you always have the option of choosing a thought that feels a little better or a little worse. Honey always choose the thought that feels best to you.'

Then we would have easily and naturally developed thoughts and beliefs that would serve us much more effectively, meaning our state of being would more easily and naturally be one of loving self, vibrancy, confidence, passion etc., whilst also naturally having emotional responsibility. In other words, you become a well-rounded person naturally. Thus **sustaining** an ever expanding space of feeling connected, alive, free, passionate and zesty for life and so much more. The better it gets, the better it gets. There is nothing more important than that we take control of the way we feel as individuals and pass on this different type of thinking where we consciously utilise our emotional indicators, firstly for our own well-being and secondly because it stops blame transference in its tracks. By being this way our self we become a true teacher because a true teacher leads by example not simply words and demands. You cannot teach happy if you are not happy. This means when you embody this way of thinking and living thus finding a sustainably better disposition through being emotionally self-responsible you are naturally leading by example by default. Monkey see monkey do, our kids and others copy us unconsciously until they really start to examine themselves later in life, so let them copy an empowered thinking behaviour (which you have embodied) rather than the usual critical authoritarian thinking process which is utterly limiting.

Can you see that if we have a critical and authoritarian thinking process that this has developed due to a lack of emotional responsibility in the first place? An authoritarian demands others change to suit their own preference so as to appease an inner niggle of their own. This is disempowering for the authoritarian because they have no inner sustainability of their own and will often live out a life with a mediocre state of being which they may be blind to, whilst upsetting many around them. Authoritarian's are not emotionally responsible in any way whatsoever. However, you can change this way of being by taking full responsibility for the way in which you feel and direct thought by how it feels to you without trying to coerce outside circumstance, thus in time you thrive inside and a brilliant side effect is this rubs off on others in positive ways.

So mindful thinking, or mindfulness from my perspective, is realizing your negative emotion is telling you that your thought, your awareness, your point of view is off! Not another person's behaviour, or life situation you may be in, and therefore you **can** do something about it between your own ears! Conversely positive emotion is telling you to ponder this more, think about this more, engage in this more.

Again I know how hard this is to understand in some situations initially such as when someone **appears** to be pissing us off. Nevertheless, your reaction is your reaction caused and created by you and this only becomes truly clear through self-observation of the control you are gaining of your own feeling state over time in many life situations.

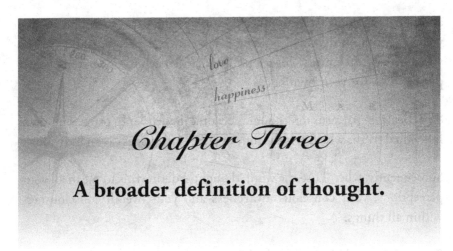

Chapter Three

A broader definition of thought.

As we move forward in this book let's develop our definition of the word thought to encapsulate the word consciousness.

Firstly, understand that a belief is only a repeated pattern of thought, a belief can be created by thoughtful consideration within the mind, or from your mental **interpretation** of life experiences. This means when you experience something, you then interpret the experience mentally in a way that fits your current beliefs, which in turn solidifies your belief often becoming your truth. This happens with or without conscious awareness yet it is all creating your overall consciousness. Sometimes your belief, your truth, is limited through missing some other information or perspective currently unknown to you, yet we may say our belief is true due to our own **interpretation of experience** or our own thoughtful ponderings. Which is often vastly different to somebody else's interpretation of the same experience or their own thoughtful ideas. Be careful in what you perceive as 'truths.' Reach to understand other perspectives, learn to see things more dynamically. Learn to walk a mile in another man's shoes. Therefore, develop understanding of others which will aid you in sustaining your own happiness.

Also, new experience can create new and different beliefs, this is worth some consideration especially when another person is explaining something to you from their own experience of something you have not yet experienced for yourself. For example, you may have set ideas and beliefs in contrast to another person's actual experience thus when you hear something that challenges your own experience and beliefs you may have an emotive reaction. Listen and reach to understand other perspectives for your own sake.

So repeating patterns of thought become beliefs and often our own individual truths which sets the tone of our consciousness as an individual.

Subsequently, when I use the word 'thought' I define this to mean all your perceptions, your conscious **awareness** and your overall consciousness within all things.

For example, when you are looking at something or your **awareness** is on something this is considered to be consciousness yet this is also thought, which sometimes evokes dialogue type thinking within the mind and sometimes does not. When you are consciously aware of something perhaps when watching television, you cannot necessarily always say that you are actually thinking in words or dialogue, yet you may be reacting emotionally to what you are observing, meaning any awareness on anything is thought. Ultimately the level of awareness you have on a subject (how much you think about it, or observe it) in turn evokes all your inner emotional reactions, relative to how your personal preferences (desires) interact with your belief structure.

If a belief limits a desire in any way you will feel it in the form of negative emotion. Conversely if a belief is freely allowing desire then you will feel positive emotion.

Also, consider that when you visualize something you are also thinking, you are consciously aware and pondering within your visualization, this too falls into my broader definition of the word thought.

To simplify, imagine standing outside naked with your eyes closed facing a fresh comfortable breeze and feeling with all 6 of your senses. Smelling the scents in the air, feeling the air rush around you, hearing the breeze blow around you, what are you tasting in your mouth, also what are you feeling emotionally are you self-conscious etc.? All this awareness whilst in this simple act of standing in a breeze. This awareness in all areas of your physical experience I consider to be consciously aware thought. It is thought, it is awareness, it is consciousness, it is mental activity. Notice that where you allow your mental activity to go within even a simple act as just outlined, is where **your emotion grows**. In other words, what you give your attention to expands in thought form first **and then** your emotion also expands in kind for better or for worse, emotion becomes more noticeable to you with more attention given to whatever subject.

Two types of thought.

Hear this, this is profound! **'There are only two types of thought, that which feels good and that which feels bad.'**

Positive thought is any thought which feels good, or better to you in any way than the last thought you had in the **moment** that you are thinking it, **regardless** of the content of your thinking. Negative thought is any thought that feels bad, or worse to you in any way than the last thought you had in the **moment** that you are thinking it, **regardless** of the content of your thinking.

The goal here is to gently, gradually learn to shift from negative **feeling** thinking to positive **feeling** thinking. This is the missing link within virtually all well-being education streams. That missing link is this awareness of the direct connection of individual thought to all inner emotional reactions! You thrive when you are in the flow of genuine connected positive thought, and it is a conscious choice in any now moment to pick better feeling thoughts now! I cannot reiterate enough how important it is that you as an individual feel good, and you have utter control over that, and the power of that control is reflected in **your state of being and perception** of your life experience, and that is everything to you!

Again most people unconsciously believe they have to change their personal situations to feel better, but this is life's biggest trap and often leads to a life time of chasing an elusive prey which always seems just out of reach, or fleeting at best.

Obviously if you are in an undesirable situation it naturally appears that you need the situation to change to feel better, and sometimes it would seem all too hard to feel better without the situation changing. However, like it or not, it really is your point of view and level of **awareness on** the situation that is holding you in your negative space. Meaning your constant attention to the situation and the way in which you are thinking about the situation, **not the situation itself** that causes the discontent. (Of course there are some people living in horrific situations where this statement comes across as cold empty words. Fair enough we can only do the best we can from wherever we stand.)

So sure change the situation as best you can, however you can, but also always continue to do the mental work of lining up your thoughts with those that feel better to you as best you can whilst using each life experience as an opportunity to consciously shift yourself, because you haven't really achieved much by only shifting your physical self and not your mental thus emotional self as well.

For example, you will notice if you have made a habit of shifting and changing your physical life situations to feel better, that not too much changes within you without you actually shifting your mental self as well. Because in time the new life experience you shifted too, is acclimatized too with your **current state of being caused by your habitual patterns of thought.** You may then find yourself discontented and not entirely happy in your new situation after all. Sure faces and places and situations may have changed, which often helps to evoke new patterns of thought through your new experience which can be for the better **depending** on how you think about things moving forward, or whether these things are closer to your personal preference. However, for the most part the same old people dramas will keep recurring, or whatever issue you were trying to mend will rear its head in some other form if you haven't consciously shifted your overall points of view, your thinking process into alignment with your emotional indicators in a sustainable way. In other words, you are still reactive to things happening outside of you, due to your belief structure and outside of-self associations. Genuine sustainable change can only be achieved through the work of aligning mind with emotion.

As a result of embodying this mental work thus the emotional shifts that ensues, you become what is often termed as heart centred, or coming from the heart so to speak. This is an accurate label, as is sustainable happiness, emotional literacy, spiritual growth, enlightenment, alignment, a well-rounded person and many other labels.

We have overindulged in negative thought.

Like it or not most individuals therefore all societies and cultures have overindulged in blaming outside circumstance for the way in which they feel. Meaning, people have not deliberately taken heed of their emotional connection to thought, but have instead associated their feelings outside of self and thus then battled everything around them in order to feel better, rather than consciously seeking for inner change as I am teaching. Therefore, we as a people have become used to it, acclimatized to it, thus consider it normal to battle circumstances which tends to produce more circumstance to battle and thus pain and suffering continues which is all due to this incessant emotional association outside of self. Therefore, as a people, as a species, as a global society who are continuing to inaccurately associate our feelings outwardly we have ended up with an awful lot of fearful, out of control feeling people, because when your inner emotional world is blamed outwardly you feel out of control and at the mercy of circumstance!

Take control of the way you feel consciously and you can never feel at the mercy of circumstance. Frankly many people are feeling very discontented within their lives, and with this rampant discontentment we get all sorts of horrible events taking place as each person is fighting against and blaming everything around them for the way in which they feel. This out of control feeling and behaviours can only take place when we haven't realized nor applied **the true power to life,** which is aligning your own mind with our own heart centre, which really means reaching for **better feeling** thoughts, beliefs and points of view!

When you develop **full** emotional responsibility yourself, meaning you are no longer blaming **anything** outside of yourself for the way in which you feel. Because you can clearly see how you are doing it to yourself in all life circumstance, it becomes obvious to you that all perpetuating problems within our societies always link back to this personal miss-association. Which is obviously perpetuated by mass consciousness belief structures, such as a country's overall culture, or world view, sometimes termed tribal mind. Consequently, the knee jerk outside of-self reactions as an individual to events around us (such as bopping somebody on the nose) are expanded within our broader society of human beings thus we consider it normal to fight and retaliate on a social level just as we do on an individual level. Hence it is easy for governments to manipulate the masses, because it is unconsciously considered normal to battle for outside change to feel better as an individual firstly, hence as a society also. This unconscious behaviour and belief that emotion is generated by outside circumstance is at the root of many if not all social issues, as we continue to battle each other incessantly.

For example, the disgusting foreign policies of some nations and draconian fear based laws created by people whom are also associating outside of self within the vastness of human interaction. From this broader perspective can you see that all negative social issues have their roots within limiting beliefs combined with outward emotional associations, which results in people trying to force their point of view on to others and the suppression of personal liberty's within all forms of governance thus authoritarian thinking processes are born of those that are not yet enlightened to this deeper understanding of self?

Before we fully develop emotional responsibility for ourselves as an individual, most of us only see the greed, the violence, the bad behaviour and the manipulation or propaganda of individuals, governments, regimes and organizations etc. We tend to only see the physical details of any life experience event or circumstance of which we get bogged down in the specifics. Then we tend to emotionally react to our point of view about what we are looking at, blaming the issue for our reaction, rather than realising it is our own limited thought that actually generated the emotion justifiable or not. We then discuss it, form more opinion about it, fight against it etc. We see the intelligence or lack thereof of people's actions, of which we then pigeonhole relative to our personal preference for life. All of this cluttered focus in specific details of each situation means we tend to miss seeing the true cause of these social struggles which is all peoples constant and never ceasing endeavour to feel better to feel free and happy, of which is associated and battled for outside of self for the most part, hence all people shit is born! This relates to all people in all situations from simple family interactions to the worlds massively complex geo political social issues. For example, the ignorant dictator or the draconian school teacher causing grief for many people or students, or the knee jerk reaction of a president bombing another country killing innocents from afar, or the disgusting military industrial complex mostly built on individual greed more than any real need for it, or low consciousness regimes and governments imposing limitation and restriction causing harm to the masses by suppressing liberty's in their own country and so on.

All of these issues are ultimately caused by the lack of realizing that any inner void (meaning any off feeling) can only ever truly be filled from within by redeveloping or dropping any limiting belief structures relative to your particular issue, situation or life circumstance, this is first and foremost an individual job. Hence global change is an intergenerational gradual change as people learn to connect to their natural love from within thus fill all voids. Understanding that a void is caused by limiting patterns of thought which does not allow for natural inner love to flow.

Yes of course the complexities of each (negative) situation in a geo political arena require practical solutions, however practical solutions usually require more mature minds involved in the process whom understand themselves to the degree I am teaching here, hence I see developing sustainable personal well-being and happiness **first** as the most powerful tool for sustainable social development.

Within all of this, all people want to live a good happy life from their own perspective, we all want to feel free and happy within our own life. This desire to feel good and free is constant in all of us no matter our state of consciousness or how happy or upset we think we are, everything is in degrees. There is an endless call within for more happiness, more connection, **more love**. Thus the constant chasing of one's own tail outside of self continues because we continue to associate our emotion outside of self, thus look for love in all the wrong places. Love can only ever come from within, from your consciousness allowing it into your experience. When we learn and naturalize this understanding and dynamic way of thinking as a way of being, then a natural progression of feeling better and better occurs. Really hear that, as a way of being. It's not as hard as it sounds. Directing thought by how it feels really does become second nature to you as you consciously link your feelings to thought, thus deliberately try and sort out your emotional responses and reactions by looking for a new thought, new point of view or belief rather than blaming this thing or that person outside of self.

So, as an individual who is endeavouring to find inner-peace, happiness or better themselves in any way and depending on where you are within your current mood and life situation, this work of self can seem an insurmountable task, especially if you have a lot going on within yourself and life right now.

However, those people who follow through and really do clean themselves up emotionally become the best at it and thrive inside in a way that is indescribably beautiful for them.

Then there are others in a reasonably good place through no conscious effort, and therefore cannot see the point in all of this, and yet they have missed a huge opportunity, which is missing out on the ultimate power of this knowledge through no attempt to think about it or apply. Often they are tolerating what negative emotion they do have and consider it normal to feel bad in this or that situation and therefore never really sort themselves out because again they are associating outside of self.

What you focus on expands, it expands in thought form within you getting bigger and bigger sometimes creating massively complex concepts, beliefs, and points of view. You know if this is helpful to you as an individual by the way you feel when the subject is active within your awareness, your mind or current life experience.

Most people judge their beliefs, their points of view, their concepts etc., on the intellectual component of these thoughts and say things like, *'But it's true, look at this thing, or those people, and everyone believes that, and surly everyone feels this way in that situation'* (they don't) and so on.

Nevertheless, in all of that you are actually causing a disconnect within yourself if those thoughts are feeling off to you. You really must learn to judge your thoughts not only by the intellect but **mostly by how they feel to you**, and mould fresh new ideas in your mind making peace with life subjects that concern or interest you gently, quietly thought by thought, day by day, experience by experience creating a new dynamic way of thinking!

Of course this can be extremely difficult to begin with, it can be very emotionally turbulent, so go easy with it, take your time be gentle on yourself and others as you endeavour to make inner changes.

Individual consciousness is expressed through your state of being not just the intellect of the mind this very much means your emotional state is part of your consciousness. Which of course it is, every thought/belief you carry has an emotional alignment or misalignment with self hence the fruit salad of your mind and emotional world is your consciousness that you are presenting to the world in the form of your state of being. Which in turn adds to society because you are an integral part of society.

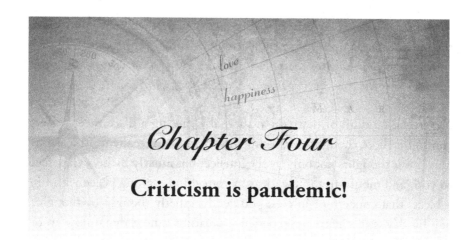

Chapter Four

Criticism is pandemic!

Society and those around us, have **unconsciously trained** us to look at all aspects of life and put everything into piles of right and wrong, good and bad, categorize and pigeonhole all things, and fight against unwanted concerns within our society.

Therefore, that's what we do, we **critically** judge everything around us, and within us, trying to discern and work out what is right and wrong, good or bad and then go about trying to change, dominate and control the physical conditions and behaviours of everything and everyone around us all in an effort to feel better! Everything we do, we do to feel better there is no escaping that!

Many people chase their tail for their entire life trying to sort everything out by attempting to discern the shades of grey within right and wrong ways to live from **their** perspective, then try and get everybody else to agree, abide and behave in a way that suits them whether individually or as a society. Socially this becomes the creation of rules and laws etc. Some of which serves the society some of which do not. This is truly searching for happiness outside of self, by dominating and controlling everything outside of ourselves yet again, both individually and thus socially.

Virtually everybody does this to some degree for example, how many times have you heard people say, *"How do you think that will **make me** feel?"* In other words, they think something **'makes'** them feel bad. Therefore, they need something outside of themselves to change to feel better. (Please understand I am not trying to make bad things sound ok, or good here. Nor am I pardoning bad behaviour especially harm crimes in any form. I am merely pointing out the emotional associations outside of self are rife everywhere, when really all emotion truly does come from within.)

So, our societies are geared this way, we inaccurately associate our inner response outwardly then criticize outwardly with habitual critical thought processes. Just turn on the TV, computer or radio, and there will be somebody **criticizing** something somewhere! We are geared this way largely due to this emotional association outside of self, which in turn creates limiting beliefs about all manner of things. Which in turn creates all fighting and bickering, to all degrees and complexities from small family units to larger social issues.

There have been many great teachers who have said we must drop our criticism if we want to move forward in a loving way. This means as an individual first, then as a result of many individuals our societies evolve into a more loving caring understanding and appreciative body of people. Meaning rather than pushing against another country you can truly appreciate the beautiful diversity of all peoples and cultures. Sure there are issues within all societies but again these are mostly due to these outside of-self associations which haven't been consciously worked past as an individual nor as a group of people. So be the change in your society!

So I say again to reiterate, when the bulk of society including ourselves, are constantly putting everything into piles of right and wrong, good and bad, categorizing and pigeon holing all interactions within the shades of grey in all aspects of our life experiences and then go about fighting against what we **personally deem** as these unwanted things in a blameful way we have subsequently been **trained** to **critically** judge. Consequently, criticism has become a habitual pattern of thought which is passed on unconsciously from generation to generation. When we are like this, when we stand in judgment of others and ourselves, criticism has become a part of our own individual behaviour, a part of who we are and we consider it normal not even realizing there is another way of being. In fact, very few even realize that they are doing it let alone that there is a different way of thinking thus being!

You must find this different way of being. All criticism is felt within you and utterly suppresses your own state of being first and foremost. Criticism always feels bad, of course to varying degrees and whether it is directed at yourself or others it still feels bad.

You must have noticed that one person's good is another person's bad, and it can drive you crazy trying to sort this out within yourself. There will always be shades of grey and people will always have different personal wants (preferences) to your own, hence the beautiful diversity of us all. It takes more than one to build a world you know!

You must become aware of all criticism of self and others and make a deliberate effort to simply cut it out, **STOP IT**, for your own sake.

For example, **any time you feel embarrassment you are being critical of yourself** and also usually worrying about what other people think. This means when you are observing a situation, or a TV show, or said and done something which is evoking a feeling of embarrassment you are being self-critical in some way towards yourself. In other words, the feeling of embarrassment is your emotional indicator that your thoughts about-self need tweaking, even when you think you are embarrassed for somebody else such as watching another person in an embarrassing situation. Where is the self-criticism within your thoughts and beliefs which is evoking the feeling of embarrassed? You must let criticism go.

Or any time you are critically judging another and pointing the finger, or fighting against something in some way, (justified or not) you are feeling critical within yourself.

You are certainly not holding a place of appreciation or love as all the great teachers have preached. (Dropping criticism does not mean you are ignoring or condoning bad behaviour, but rather coming from a place of understanding, of unconditional positive regard of our fellow man.)

When you criticize anything, you are feeling criticism, therefore suppressing your **own** state of being with **your** criticism. **Again, you are hurting yourself terribly whether self-criticism or criticism of others because it is you feeling the criticism.**

In this instance, you must seek to change your point of view, change your thoughts, and change your beliefs, which translates to dropping all your habitual critical thought regarding any subject you are critical of. Meaning when you notice any critical thought do your best to simply let it go, stop engaging in the thought process. This will begin to allow us that connection we all seek, **that other way of being** which is to **feel** appreciation, to feel love flow through us, to hold a space of appreciation within more subjects as best as we are able. You cannot feel critical and feel love at the same time. Love truly is the answer, and what we are all unconsciously seeking whether we are aware of it or not.

When someone really is connected to themselves (meaning holding a steady appreciative space more often and for longer periods), and their inner emotional reactions are now more positive **naturally** then they only ever have positive outer behaviours to share!

But don't forget that their preferences may still be different to yours, this does not make them bad or wrong and you right, just different, diversity is the spice of life.

Your negative reaction to others is your issue, your drama to sort out in your own self. Yet almost everybody tries to get others to change to suit their own sensibilities. Almost all of us do this to some degree, in personal relationships, at home, at work thus in society.

So the real work, the trick, is to personally find better feeling ways to look at and think about the unwanted behaviours that are bugging you, or stop thinking about it, or fighting against it turn the other cheek. Because it is in your attention to the subject and the way in which you think about it, meaning how you interpret it within your mind that is causing the disconnected feeling, not the person, situation or event as it appears.

If you do what almost everybody else does and fight against other people and situations to feel better under some self-righteous pretence, (this includes all activism) without realizing your emotional response is all **you**, then you haven't achieved anything of true value within your own individual state of being, even if you do win your fight.

In other words, 'If you haven't changed the way you feel **with conscious inner work**, you haven't changed anything of substance within your own self.'

This does not mean not being involved in a movement for change within activism, many things need changing to a more loving nature of course they do. However, that can only happen when the individuals you may be battling against become more loving themselves so battling them is futile because you yourself are not loving in your battling plus there will always be more disconnected people to replace them, so again personal well-being is truly the most sustainable thing we can do for ourselves as an individual then society as a whole. This means holding steady in your own skin in a truly connected way thus coming from a deeper place of understanding and appreciation for all things, including the horrible ones you may be fighting against within your activism! Can you do that when observing the truly horrible people? This is a big ask, a big question, but one to consider if you want true inner power. Because with this truly connected appreciative space (love) comes more effective practical solutions. Mostly we disempower ourselves by accepting a critical angry position as required and normal in X, Y, or Z situation therefore inaccurately consider anger as right and just. Solutions to problems cannot come from the same consciousness that created it. Be careful with associating your anger your criticism outside of-self there is massive limitation in this because you have limitation in your own thought form which is evoking the feeling in the first place justified or not. Therefore, you cannot find genuine sustainable solutions of a higher nature from any angry place.

Learn to critique.

Criticism and critique are distinctly different; you can have critique without criticism. Critique can be considered a desire for improvement and expansion whilst coming from a place of **feeling appreciation**. Whereas criticism is feeling critical, or pointing the finger, coming from a place of judgement and feeling critical in any form.

If you feel criticism, anger, resentment, revengeful, or jealousy outwardly projected at any one, or anything, this is like drinking poison and hoping the other person is going to get sick! Plus, actions taken from these low feeling states aren't necessarily beneficial.

Hence, there simply is nothing more important than that you feel good. That is everything to you as an individual and ultimately the world as a whole, because actions coming from a higher inspired place tend to be non-combative thus not perpetuate more negativity!

When you feel appreciative, instead of fighting against something, you are more often inspired to a powerful new awareness you otherwise couldn't see from your fighting against position.

Accordingly, powerful new solutions to problems that you may be interested in can come into your experience more readily, you become solution oriented with bright ideas.

Not to mention you're shining your own inner light and others will want a piece of it, they will aspire to it, gravitate to you.

Then you are teaching through the clarity of your being, leading by example, teaching people to take responsibility for their own internal world. Spreading the good will into your own community, just by being happy yourself.

But first you have to do the work, you cannot lead by example if you have not yet made this inner work second nature thus made positive change within yourself. You would be a preacher with no authenticity if you parrot words that are not embodied within you.

This work does not mean you will always be happy and vibrant, it means that you are more sustainably happy and vibrant because you begin to see how you create your own negative states, thus you learn to direct your mind in a more valuable and dynamic way therefore, those around you also benefit. It also does not mean you won't feel appalled at some horrible event; it simply means you no longer blame the outside event for your appalled reaction regardless of any circumstance! This feels counter intuitive at first I know, but the power in this understanding is huge. Let me elaborate a little, it is natural to feel appalled in observation of something which is in complete contrast to your own personal preference for life thus natural to want to change it, there is nothing wrong in that. However, please reach to understand the depth of what it truly means to be emotionally responsible, then in time as you truly begin to understand yourself you can at least begin to understand the horrible behaviours of others, thus making it easier for you to let go and make peace thus live a good happy life yourself. With this approach you potentially find more productive solutions rather than simply battling outwardly trying to force change. You have to make it your dominant intent to feel good for yourself first and foremost which then influences the world around you for the better.

Those of you that take this work by the horns and strive forward into your own personal harmony will become the shining lights in your own world of influence, and that is a very powerful, loving thing. To simply be happy in your own skin. On the plus side you will have powerful personal experience from shifting yourself, shifting your own state of being. You have the power to transform yourself, nobody else can do it for you because nobody can think for you. Nor can you force change in others, however we can do our best to lead by example.

Taking offence, is criticism.

Are you a person who is easily offended? **Taking offence is your 'critical' emotional reaction within yourself, which is outwardly projected onto someone or something else justified or not.** Taking offence means **you** had an emotional reaction **within yourself**, a niggle, a nuance an impulse and you usually unconsciously expect others to change so that you don't have to feel your own inner reaction, thus we often tell others to behave or we may look down our nose at them etc. Ponder this, look inward at yourself gently over time. Then use any critical, offended inner impulses for positive mental change within your own self, rather than blaming outwardly.

Expecting people to be excessively P.C or trying to be excessively P.C yourself is an outside of-self behaviour which on the surface appears to be a good thing where you are striving not to upset others, when really it is a band aid for a much bigger problem, which is a reactive and messy inner world of your own which is blamed outwardly that you need to clean up for yourself. As does any other person you may be trying to appease, they need to take responsibility for their inner reactions also. If you are running around telling everybody to behave and to be P.C and fighting others by trying to force them to behave and be P.C. from your perspective, then you are fighting an inner battle associated outside of self, not helping yourself nor those around you as you believe that you are. You are actually adding to the problem unwittingly because there is zero emotional responsibility within P.C behaviour! Of course use your discernment, there is a distinct difference between not caring about others and shooting off at the mouth, compared to being mindful not to upset someone further whom is suffering from some form of trauma or another, or someone whom does not yet understand this work to this degree, in other words common kindness and compassion for another's pain, goes without saying!

Let's take this further, do you get upset if you see or are within an unjust situation? Do world events upset you? Climate change issues perhaps. Do you react if someone says a racist or perhaps sexist comment, or if somebody swears? All negative internal reactions to any subject is **your problem created by you!** You **must** come to a place of being at peace within your mind regarding all subjects **you wish to give your attention to** if you are ever to find a sustainable happy place in your own skin. Then and only then more evolved solutions to issues can begin to develop within you and others on this path of self-improvement.

As previously mentioned it is natural to be upset (remembering every feeling is in degrees) when in observation of anything which is not in harmony with your personal preference for a life situation whatever that may be. Thus you must reach for inner improvement anyway, because if you don't you are trapped on an outside of-self emotional roller coaster seemingly at the mercy of the world around you, and this does not have to be so. This means more than just tolerating, for in tolerating you are really just putting up with, suppressing or ignoring your negative emotion and not really sorting **yourself** out. You have to get over yourself for your own sake! You have associated your response outside of self to varying degrees, we all have.

You must take full responsibility for all your inner emotional reactions regardless of circumstance, and strive to understand how you personally created them, thus learn to move into holding a deeper place of ever increasing **appreciation** for all of life. **Then in gentleness 'true power' is born! True solutions can be seen.** This will make more sense conceptually as we move through the book, ultimately becoming 'your knowing' once you have actually embodied a higher, appreciative state yourself.

Understand I am not condoning bad behaviour in any way, I am simply pointing out that your inner reaction is not caused by the bad behaviour, **it just appears that way.** Also **true** bad behaviour always comes from a low place in the first place where negative emotional reactions are outwardly projected in the form of harmful behaviours. This is due to powerless and limited belief structures within individuals whom then do whatever it is they do to appease their own created feelings. Even if they appear powerful given the standard interpretation of the word 'powerful.' For example, when someone is wielding physical power or violence over others this appears powerful because of exerted influence outside of self. When really this shows a weakness of somebody's inability to truly look at themselves for change from within.

So, the happier we as individuals feel from a sustainable and genuine appreciative place, the inspiration to behave in such ways dissipates and disappears. Genuine happiness coming from a place of full emotional responsibility for all your internal and external reactions is truly a cure all for all human interaction. Of course you can only do this for yourself then lead by example.

To sum up, the problem with being P.C. so as not to offend another by pandering to other people's sensibilities is, **they are not learning to utilize their own inner impulses in an empowered way!** Thus in effect we are hindering another person's ability to learn for themselves that happiness comes from within if we continue pandering to them, they also have to take full emotional responsibility for themselves thus are self-empowered also! Of course not withstanding common decency, kindness and compassion from an understanding place.

Evolve emotion, rather than control emotion.

Generally, people talk about controlling our emotions, controlling our behaviour, this is hard work and ultimately we still tend to react outwardly at others or inwardly at ourselves in some way relative to the inner emotion we are feeling thus struggling to control. Rather than trying to control our emotions, this education shows us how to **develop** and evolve our emotional reactions so that they **come naturally from a higher place.** (By creating new beliefs, new patterns of thought.) This is our ongoing lifetimes work as individuals. Although the word, 'work' implies effort and continued struggle, when really once the overall education offered throughout these pages becomes second nature to you, you cannot imagine not directing thought in this way because your overall state of being is constantly improving thus less and less effort to maintain, and that is everything to you, thus us all!

Sure we need to control ourselves, of course we do. However, what I am talking about evolves you beyond the need for self-control to a point where the negative reactions no longer exist within you in the same way as they did before. Therefore, there is no need to control oneself because you are not reacting negatively within yourself to begin with!

Usually when we have a negative or critical emotional response, we tend to then have a knee jerk behavioural or verbal reaction outside of ourselves in response to **our** inner emotional reaction, and that usually relates to our personal preferences within the situation, meaning what we would rather see happen within the situation. Not realizing our inner emotional reaction that we are reacting too outwardly, was created by our own self to begin with, not by the situation we are faced with as we all naturally but still inaccurately tend to believe.

This is natural and normal, but you can and must evolve to an understanding of how these reactions all came from you to begin with, thus evolve **yourself** to understand and hold deeper places of appreciation within **you** regardless of circumstance.

This work is not about, 'not reacting' it is about evolving your **emotional reactions** beyond what we often consider to be normal negative emotional reactions. Understanding ourselves and evolving ourselves to a higher state of being must come first for you as an individual, before we can ever truly begin to understand the work involved for others to overcome their pain.

For example, imagine understanding anger in such a way that you can see the **pain that anger really is** when another is in a fit of anger or rage. This means you are not upset yourself in your observation of another's anger, but rather you are naturally holding a steady appreciative space within yourself regardless of what's going on. You truly understand that each life experience anybody is living is an opportunity to grow from should they choose to, whether at the time or in reflection of the experience later in life. Here's an illustration of what I mean.

Imagine seeing an adult presumably the father, bending through the back door of a parked car screaming his head off verbally abusing a child in a most disgusting way. He is also punching the seat beside the child, he has really lost his cool and is totally out of control, people are starting to mill around and are unsure if he is hitting the child or seat of the car. He is quite a large rough looking fellow.

What is your emotional reaction if you see this behaviour? If you are upset by this behaviour in **any** way, and by upset I mean you could feel sick, you could feel anger towards him yourself, you could feel worry or concern for the child etc. How do you think it will go down when you confront him over this if that is your chosen course of action whilst **feeling like any of these examples just given?**

For example, perhaps a larger, fitter, stronger person may say that they would beat him up, they themselves coming from a place of self-righteous anger. Or perhaps somebody may approach him with genuine concern for the child whilst coming from a place of worry and concern trying to tell him not to be so angry or display such violence towards the child, good luck is all I can say. None of these approaches are usually of any intrinsic value, because again you have associated your negative emotion outside of self by attaching it to the situation thus you are coming from a limiting perspective whilst associating outside of self. Whether you like it or not you want him to stop abusing the child for your own benefit, so that you don't feel sick, angry, worry or concern or whatever negative feeling you feel. Even though you are believing you are desiring to help the child because you care, you are also desiring to feel better yourself, you are still wanting the situation to stop because of your own inner reactions!

In any situation like this where we care, we tend to want to fix the situation **'outside of self'** to feel better ourselves and we say and believe it is because we care. Whilst it may be true that you care, the deeper real reason you want to stop the situation is mostly because of the incessant desire to feel better ourselves, **to feel love flow through us.**

There is no escaping that everything we do, we do to feel better ourselves, there simply is no escaping that fact. The reason this feels flat out wrong to most people, or feels counter intuitive is because we have another misinterpretation of emotion going on within all of this, and that is, in the case of 'caring' we have associated our negative emotions of concern feelings, or worry feelings to that of caring.

Hear this, this is profound, **'caring has nothing to do with feelings of concern or feelings of worry.'** You can care without these feelings of worry or concern! Caring is caring, feeling is feeling. Caring does not require these negative feelings. You must drop this inaccurate association. Concern is not feeling love or allowing love to flow through you, concern is feeling concern. Worry is not feeling love; worry is feeling worry which isn't loving either. Therefore, there is room for improvement within your belief structure to allow for more love and appreciation in these moments.

Meaning, you can care whilst holding a place of appreciation of love and understanding!

I know this is hard to grasp at first because most of us naturally care for the welfare of the child coming from a place of worry or concern which we have unconsciously associated as a part of caring, we think worry or concern is caring.

Of course we will argue that he is a horrible person and should stop abusing the child, fair enough not many people like these sorts of horrible situations and I am not suggesting that you should learn to like these negative situations. What I am saying is you need to come to a place where you understand yourself so deeply that you can understand situations like this thus not be emotionally moved in such a negative way as before. Meaning you hold steady in your own skin first and foremost from a place of love and genuine understanding for other people's outbursts, thus when coming from a steady appreciative space caring has much more practical power. What I am also saying is anytime that you are worried or concerned, you actually want to feel better yourself whether you like it or not, which is associated outside of self, and that these feelings of concern and worry have been inaccurately associated to caring when in fact caring is a whole different thing. You can recognise these feelings of worry or concern as inner indicators for conscious change thus can work towards a place of **care whilst holding a genuine place of appreciation.** Please ponder this, try and imagine how you can care from a place of steady appreciation of love. You simply don't need worry or concern to care!

So let's play out a possible interaction that could occur if you choose to approach this situation of child abuse if you are a person whom understands your own inner world, have dropped your criticism of others and can see a deeper perspective. You have found a higher, deeper place of **natural appreciation within yourself for yourself, and for all people.** Therefore, you can see his pain, understand his anger and are not upset by his behaviour. Plus, you care for the group as a whole the father and the child. Therefore, you approach the situation holding a **non-critical,** natural and steady place of caring from a place of **appreciation**, because you **care** for all people **including** the angry man!

Person A. Hey bro what's going on?

Person B. Fuck off this is none of your fucking business!

Person A. Yea I know it's not, sorry bro, I just understand your anger is all, it sucks to be so fucked off, can I help?

Person B. No you fucken can't, fuck off before I kick your fucken head in.

Person A. Oh sorry, I really don't want to interfere, I just understand your pain bro, I know how much it sucks to be pissed off, is that your boy he looks like a good boy?

Person B. He's not a fucken good boy he just stole those shoes the little thief!

Person A. Bro that sucks, I understand truly I get ya, no one wants to love your boy more than you do. I can see that clearly given how pissed off you are, and it's certainly not my place to tell you how to discipline your boy, that's your business. But when you are angry like this are you loving your boy? I know you don't really want to hurt him you're just fucked off that he stole those shoes and you want better for him. Man I understand truly I do.

Person B. Yea your right I don't want to hurt him, but fuck man? His constant stealing is doing my fucken head in, what would you do?

Person A. Fuck bro It's tough I know, it's a shitty situation you're in, I dunno what I would do off hand I'd have to think about it, but I know I would want better for him like you do. Take a breath man, and I can give you some ideas to calm yourself down so as to help you think if you like? Perhaps now or at a later date if you want too?

Person B. I dunno bro, you're fucken weird aye man, but you're right I don't want to hurt him, he pisses me off is all! Ya know what I mean?

Person A. Yea I do, it's all good, I get ya, well you take care of yourself and have a good day ok, look after yourself bro. Take care now.

I know this is a quick and verbally violent example, however the point I am trying to make is if you are not upset in yourself in any way, therefore understand yourself deeply you will also understand another's loss of control and can help a situation like this in a more beneficial way if you choose too. Who knows how the angry person thinks about this unusual interaction afterwards, he may start to self-assess himself more in the future. Beating him up would not help him address himself in a truly positive way nor help the child either by seeing his father beaten up. If he was beaten up the father would likely just get angrier at himself, life and take it out on all those around him as he moves forward in life from here thus not a helpful outcome. Or in the case of the person simply wanting to tell him to stop abusing the child from a place of criticism, worry or concern, (even though they care, the feelings of concern or worry is causing the problem here) this too would likely be ignored as he moves through life because the whole of society is telling him how to behave one way or another, (this is societies lack in emotional responsibility) and nobody likes being told what to do. He's probably got his toes dug in on multiple subjects in his life where he is sick of being told what to do. Whereas after an unusual interaction like this where the good Samaritan was not criticizing him, nor telling him what to do but offering help whilst holding **genuine care and understanding** for both the angry person himself and the child, then there is a stronger likely hood the angry person may think a little differently moving forward, perhaps seeds had been sown of a truer deeper value.

Of course to be a good Samaritan with this level of steady eddy in such a potentially violent situation is no easy feat to create within oneself, but you can find that steady place in time, and dropping all criticism is part of the process whilst also understanding worry and concern are not caring but really emotional feelings that have been associated to caring.

Consequently, if love is the answer, therefore happiness and peace of mind, which I believe it is, can you see that an individual holding a place of appreciation possibly helped this situation a little better than any of the usual critical reactions? Where is there room for criticism in any form, under any conditions? Frankly there is not. So become self-aware, introspective, and stop it!

Can you see the immense problem criticism is within our society? Frankly I see criticism as a pandemic from many different angles, criticism suppresses an individual's personal well-being first and foremost which is usually projected outwardly to others around them causing themselves and others grief one way or another. Also If you hold a low state of being, which criticism does, in time your physical health is affected also! Criticism truly is a pandemic of mass proportions.

Knocking criticism on the head is quite simple conceptually, but takes time and a little work. It is a process of consciously recognizing the thoughts as they occur and doing everything in your power to think something else, anything else. Simply stop it, cut it out, for your own sake! There are only two types of thought and criticism is obviously a pattern of thought which always feels off.

Chapter Five

Humanity is created in the world of thought.

Political crap is personal individual crap multiplied, a miss interpretation of our emotional reactions outside of self, combined with limiting beliefs which in turn perpetuate the utter childishness and utter insanity of war and other dumb shit.

So, let's translate emotional reactions into a global scale. Can we all agree that we are all human, we all breathe, we all think therefore have beliefs, understanding that a belief is only a repeated pattern of thought?

We all have emotional responses which are created by our thoughts/beliefs in relationship to our life preferences. Yet our emotive responses are usually inaccurately associated outside of self.

The diversity of all people is largely created through differing thoughts, thus beliefs, which in turn creates cultures, religions, societies everything in the human experience. The awesomeness and beautiful diversity of humanity is firstly created in the world of thought. So the only thing that really differs between any of us is, 'our chosen patterns of thought thus beliefs.' We are more alike than many like to accept and there is no need for the constant crap that people engage in. Any one pointing their finger at another country, culture, race, religion, belief structure, sexual preference, or otherwise really needs to grow up. Frankly this goes without saying surely? Anyone who is still fully engaged in this type of limited behaviour requires compassion and understanding from us, offering gentle education where we can. Not more battling against, as was shown in the brief child abuse example just given.

Some will argue that our beliefs, cultures, religions and values are not chosen so much as passed on to us by the society we grew up in, and those of influence around us. Well, of course this is true to a degree, but your thoughts are still your thoughts, sure they have been influenced as you were growing up by whichever education system and social environment you engaged in etc., but I am sure you know a black sheep in a family, someone who thinks differently than the status quo? How did that happen? Free thinking that's how. Do you honestly think all your beliefs are serving you? Culturally, personally, spiritually, religiously, scientifically or otherwise? Many will automatically answer yes to that question, and yet have never actually, truly, deeply examined their beliefs, or themselves, or have any clue that their emotional responses and overall state of being is the result of their own self-inflicted patterns of thought.

We always do it to ourselves (our emotional reaction) regardless of absolutely any life experience you can think of.

Sure, we will naturally react in anger, fear, grief, etc., in any situation that is unwanted to us. That's fine natural and fair enough.

However, it isn't the reaction in the heat of the moment that counts, it's how you think about it afterwards that truly matters as this evolves our habitual patterns of thought and beliefs **thus our future reactions!**

Frankly we haven't been taught how to dynamically think, using our inner impulses, our emotional response as our guiding factor in choosing our thought, **to resolve and solve** our internal world. However, on a global scale more people than you might realise are beginning to figure this out. Many are realising emotion is self-generated and is what is meant by "going within." Which as an individual gives you full power **because if you take control of the way you feel you will profoundly take control of every aspect of your life**, and that is everything to you!

An example of people shit.

So Joe Blogs is a mess inside himself and is reacting to his inner shit (emotional turmoil) created by his limiting beliefs and preferences for life etc. Perhaps he had many freedoms suppressed in many different ways, or is simply taking that which he desires with no care of others and so on etc., etc. Therefore, does something horrible to person x. Person x then reacts in a negative way (understandably) and seeks revenge, or becomes suppressed, depressed, suffers PTSD or trauma in some form. Person x then believes they need justice and blame Joe Blogs for their woes and so the circle of shit continues. Joe Blogs did whatever he did from a position of trying to feel better regardless of any life situation you factor in here. Now person x is seeking justice all in an effort to feel better as well. Both have associated their feelings outside of self.

Around and around the mulberry bush we go!

An example of how it becomes far reaching.

I recently heard a politician reacting to a horrific crime saying things like, *"You have attacked us, you have made us feel angry, we will get you, all of our might will be bought to bear on the perpetrators"* etc., etc., blah, blah, blah. Oh my god what an amazingly disconnected limited pile of shit coming out of their mouth, and thus the cycle of shit therefore continues! **Leaders like this are emotionally illiterate like everybody else who is still reacting outside of self to their own inner reactions**.

Notice the politicians statement *"You have made us feel angry,"* did they? Hmmm actually **no they did not!** A lack of emotional responsibility causes the perpetuating problems here. Meaning the politician had an emotional reaction from a limited series of beliefs about life within themselves which caused the angry reaction in the first place, and then they react to that feeling with a revengeful, seeking justice emotional reaction, resulting in the usual knee jerk response outside of self which everybody understands as normal, understandable and justifiable. Thus public opinion and/or emotional manipulation on a mass scale is clearly visible to those whom have embodied this work. A lack in emotional responsibility is an individual weakness, thus social weakness normal or not. Therefore, strive for your own internal connection first thus we all benefit; **social harmony begins within you.** If you keep blaming society and its wider issues for your personal inner issues you are more often than not adding to the wider issue and/or your own personal problems with this outside of-self battling. This could be in physical form for example displays of aggression. Conversely undealt with grief may translate to an unsettled feeling which could create a flat suppressive demeanour thus little energy to really get on and live your life. Which now becomes a social problem because those around you are often affected by their own uncontrolled reactions to your mood! Meaning, you and those you interact with are society and all these issues stem from associating emotion outside of self.

The worse you feel (about any subject) the harder it becomes to think and act clearly everywhere else in your life.

From a wider social perspective such as geo political issues a lack of emotional responsibility hinders glaringly obvious practical solutions to many social issues which could easily be implemented were it not for this widespread lack in emotional responsibility thus unnecessary bickering and fighting continues!

In all fairness.

In all fairness I know this can be hard to get your head around at first. It may feel quite counter intuitive to you especially **before** you've embodied this teaching, in fact it can only make any real sense **after** you have a good handle on your own internal reactions, in other words cleaned yourself up. Moved yourself beyond old hurts and baggage and discover that you, and only you affect your state of being, through your own mental activity. Meaning the first step to truly understanding what I am saying is you need personal experience of actually shifting your own self by creating a happier, emotionally stable, self-responsible you. This work is experiential; words mean nothing until you embody a higher state of being consciously, thus can clearly see for yourself.

The first step towards more social harmony is taking full emotional responsibility for yourself as an individual, which in turn creates personal inner-peace, passion and a zest for life. This also means you stop all criticism or fighting against anything for any reason because you have made it your dominant intent to feel good, therefore any time you criticise or fight against anything there is an off-ness felt within you which you can consciously strive to shift for the better, before taking any action if any.

Remember the only legitimate life career choice is that you feel good, this is far reaching for all.

Also understand that the desire to fight anything is an outside of-self battle to gain some semblance of inner power (better feeling). Anytime we fight and bicker we are trying to appease an inner feeling from outside of self by fighting and battling outside circumstances, this is regardless of any justification.

Once you achieve personal harmony, **which you can fairly readily with this teaching,** you are therefore in a better position to raise children who naturally have this ability because they learned naturally from their parents. Thus, the cycle of individual pain which translates to social disharmony in some form or another reduces.

For example, you could be upset in some way thus you may bark at a friend or colleague simply because you were upset, which then upsets that relationship due to others not having emotional responsibility either, or a full scale social issue, there really is no separation here regardless of the complexities of detail within any subject.

The more people whom develop emotional responsibility the more social issues will slow down and become sustainably resolved as yourself, others and our children grow into a more self-responsible politician, husband, wife, neighbour, teacher, police officer, business owner and so forth, our society evolves. This is an intergenerational process with far reaching positive outcomes. Such as the implementation of practical solutions to all forms of social issues are more likely to occur with people whom aren't battling one another but rather communicating in a more mature format, taking full responsibility for individual inner reactions whilst striving to work together without agenda!

Not to mention you are much happier now! Living a more vibrant happy life of your own which is everything to you, whilst not adding to the cycle of pain as you once may have before. Breaking the link in the chain so to speak. An example of breaking the link in the chain could mean when you feel pissed off in a situation you don't transfer that pissed off feeling into an outside of-self behaviour or verbal comment that another person then reacts to outside of self also, hence the typical chain of misery we tend to engage in is stopped in its tracks. Be under no allusions as to how far reaching and powerful these breaks in the chain are.

Every aspect of life can be traced to how you think thus feel within any moment in time.

Life can be vibrant, alive, amazing and awesome, you can have this state of being more often and more readily than perhaps you realise, even if everyone around you is still being reactionary, not working their own shit out, or even remotely close to understanding what we are talking about here. They don't need to. Only you need to! Don't let other people's stuff rock your apple cart, because yet again this is outside of self.

In other words, learn to think differently thus ultimately in time react differently with more positive emotion even if other people are still reactionary around you.

This can be hard work to begin with, but it does get easier with practice and the personal gains far outweigh the effort. In other words, do this work for yourself first and foremost. I am simply trying to point your mind in the direction of a substantial reason why dumb shit continues to happen in the world. But don't worry about that, the more you worry about it and push against it the more you add to it. Sort your own shit out by finding your own inner connection, it's the most powerful thing you can do, truly it is.

If you have a desire to force another to sort their shit out because clearly they are doing dumb things from your perspective, justified or not, then you still haven't sorted **your** shit out. You cannot force anyone to work on themselves who is not yet asking to, or are even aware that they need to, any more than you can fuck for chastity, or fight for peace. Of course we can lead by example and offer kindness, compassion and education where we can and where appropriate. Such as displayed in part within the child abuse example earlier. Personal happiness with full emotional responsibility is utterly connected to social happiness always has been, always will be, for you are part of society.

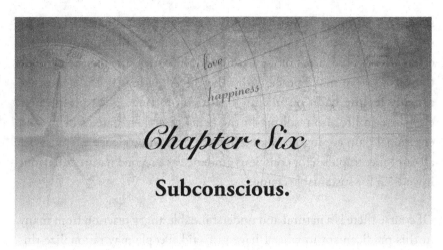

Chapter Six

Subconscious.

There are many people struggling with traumatic emotional reactions within themselves which seem and **appear** out of their control.

For example, people suffering from post-traumatic stress disorder complex or otherwise, and other things we label as a condition such as long standing states of depression. Many have struggled for years like this, at times it can permeate their entire life as it did for me before I learnt what I am sharing here. Many believe their condition is out of their control and think it is deeply ingrained in who they are, it isn't.

We simply keep blaming the emotional reaction on anything other than the true cause which is our habitual thinking patterns and beliefs. This is really the ultimate cause of the trauma, not so much the past experience that we are still **in reaction to** thus thinking about in regards to conditions like PTSD. I know this sounds like an over simplification for something that appears complex like PTSD, however when you direct the way you feel all day every day in **all regards** therefore shift your habitual patterns then in time you will see for yourself as your tone rises.

For example, someone has a horrible experience reacts to it, and continues to react to it as a result of not being able to truly drop it out of their awareness which means there is always some attention on it, some thought going on which keeps it alive and kicking within themselves thus causing emotional stress which can become their constant inner turmoil. In this type of situation reaching for a new **lighter feeling perspective** on the subject, or letting go hasn't happened to a degree that is required to fully shift the emotional reaction as yet. Any ongoing emotional pain like this often affect's other areas of life because in their pain moving through life they struggle to make peace with other life situations because they **are already feeling bad** thus making it difficult to find lighter perspectives elsewhere in life also resulting in the belief that their state of being and emotional pain are ingrained and hard to deal with. Hence we must use all our inner impulses for conscious guidance as a second nature behaviour if we wish for sustainable change.

Of course there is a natural and understandable angry reaction from many in this predicament to what I have just said. People may rationalize this anger with comments like, *my mind is too busy, the thoughts are out of my control, they keep coming incessantly there is nothing I can do about it, I've tried everything nothing works, you wouldn't understand, its subconscious, its biological etc.*

If this is you, please relax. I believe anyone can overcome anything should they want to, of course it's a personal journey and a process of time. With the application of education like that found in this book and more besides, such as with the use of a modality or therapy.

Frankly most people simply don't work within their thought/belief structure to the **degree** I am talking about, mostly because they are unaware of the immense personal power in directing one's own mind in relationship to their own emotional indicators as a moment by moment way of being.

Many believe that strong emotional reactions can be caused by subconscious beliefs, and or a series of memories or a single memory. What people perceive as inner subconscious pain, or painful memories is never subconscious, it is consciously evoked pain in the now. It is your current **awareness** your **thoughts** about an unwanted situation whether it is past, present or future. In other words, if you are thinking about an old memory from an old traumatic time, you are thinking about that memory **now!** Even though it may have just popped into your head apparently out of nowhere. Of course people are not always aware why they react so strongly or what they are reacting to. The awareness required to see this grows within you as you begin to look at how your own thoughts and emotional reactions interrelate. This takes time, a discerning mind and gentleness with yourself, just like becoming proficient at any skill.

So a negative emotional reaction to a memory, is an active awareness, an active thought **now**, therefore evoking and creating your emotional reaction **now**. Sometimes these reactions are big and all-consuming such as phobias and instantly evoked seemingly out of control feelings such as grief, jealousy, PTSD moments, or anger for example. Strong instantly evoked reactions like this are often due to a congestion of limiting beliefs which cause a suppression of freedom within-self resulting in all forms of negative emotional feelings. These types of reactions are caused by what I call congested understanding.

All feelings and emotions are current time, now in this moment because of what you are thinking about, **have your awareness on**, or are observing in the moment no matter if it's past, present or future.

You can think about things in the past that evoke good feeling reactions or bad, you get to choose. You can think about possible events in the future which evoke good feeling reactions or bad you get to choose.

You can choose a lot more of what you observe right now which evokes your feeling space good or bad, you choose.

For example, you can, make an effort to change what you engage in on social media, the radio, computer or TV.

This observation thing is interesting, because what you perceive to be your natural reactions to life situations, is a result of your belief structure and habitual patterns of thought, relative to your personal desires and wants for your life experiences, more than it has to do with what you are actually looking at. At any rate, when you are awake and feeling, it is always in current time, therefore **now**, and therefore conscious as you are feeling it.

This gives you unprecedented power you didn't realize you had. Honey you always have the option to pick a slightly better feeling thought, or a slightly worse feeling thought you choose, but honey, always pick the better feeling thought from your perspective.

The point I want you to hear and understand is this. All emotion is caused by current time thoughts and awareness on something, if that awareness is on a memory, then that awareness is still current time, not from the subconscious. Understanding this gives us an immense power over re-creating ourselves from the inside out as you will see moving forward.

Congested understanding.

Congested understanding is having a series of limiting beliefs, limiting patterns of thought, that cannot **freely process** an experience or new idea in thought form through the mind without some form of resistance due to these limiting thoughts or belief(s), thus you feel the discord.

Your current beliefs may not allow new experience, new ideas to build in your mind thus you may be struggling to deal with whatever is in your life and mind. Struggling to find flow, you may get confused, frustrated or angry etc.

An example of reacting to congestion created in the past where new ideas and beliefs have not been developed to deal with an old issue, or an inability to simply let go may be displayed with thoughts and statements such as, *"That shouldn't have happened to me for fuck sake."* Someone may say **still feeling pain** 35 years after the event because they still have not gotten beyond it with a new lighter fresher perspective or let it go, because the congestion in their mind (limited beliefs) cannot allow their thoughts to flow freely therefore painlessly.

Another example of a thought generated in reaction to present time congestion, *"Fuck I hate this shit"* says someone with anxiety, depression or any other current strong emotional state **now** because of their thought reactions to their **now** life experience.

This is not allowing their thoughts to flow freely and painlessly either. This is often referred to as subconscious reactions to life, but it is always conscious when the feeling is active therefore you can strive beyond it in the moment.

Of course this second example could also be somebody experiencing something in opposition to their own wanting thus annoying them in the moment, you have to discern the difference for yourself within self. In either case you still want to feel better and the reaching to feel better is what counts.

We all have complex patterns of beliefs and differing desires for life which are never perfectly identical to anyone else's hence a large reason for the beautiful uniqueness and diversity of all people, cultures and societies.

However, these complex patterns often cause **congested understanding** because no heed was given to how the thought felt in the first place, hence building congestion in your belief structure. Which in turn is not allowing the thoughts to flow freely through the mind thus creating more congestion over time.

Creating a natural flow system between the ears is of paramount importance for anyone's mental health, thus quality of life, which ultimately becomes your well rounded happy state of being.

Developing beliefs and patterns of thought **which allow for the processing of life events** to flow through the mind and out of the mind effortlessly, thus not holding on to any emotional pain is vital. A good indication if you have achieved this is being able to go to bed at night with an empty head!

Just ask a person with PTSD, depression, out of control anxiety, or anger etc., how it's going. It's a hell of a struggle that's how it's going. Their inner pain is hell on earth, quite literally for many in any sort of long held emotional traumas.

Learning to think dynamically utilizing the emotional connection to thought is ultimately going to build and create this flow system within you, it is a personal process because we all have different belief structures to work through and no one can think for you. Your patterns of thought are yours to deal with. Of course this often requires professional help, love and support to help you through so use it if needs be!

A congested understanding, analogy.

Imagine the mind as a very complex system of interlacing and interacting pipe work, try and picture zillions of pipes all interlaced together in what appears to be a bird's nest of complexity. This pipe work represents your belief structure, patterns of thought, your memories, and experience in all things, all your points of view, your preferences and desires, life skills etc.

Imagine that this pipe work is malleable, or dynamic in the sense that a whole series of pipes, (beliefs) can be re-organized, subject to developing thoughts and new experience. This is learning. The pipes are not set in stone.

Now if everything is running smoothly in your belief structure then the developing thoughts and mental reaction to experiences can flow through these pipes and modify these pipes as required with no problems at all, creating a feeling of vibrancy and passion etc. If you have little congestion you can easily feel your specific patterns of thought as you think them.

But if there are blockages in a series of pipes, (your beliefs), this hampers the moment by moment thought flow through the pipe work and you feel it relative to the degree of blockage.

In other words, a series of limiting beliefs (your pipe lay out) is not allowing the flow of new thought to continue in these areas, and you know it, because you feel it with your emotional nuances big or small. It is usually not that easy to feel specific thought patterns when there is still quite a lot of congestion in your understanding! However, gradually over time this clears as you make the effort to direct thought little by little by how it feels to you creating clarity of mind.

So rather than calling all these beliefs that are causing any congestion thus emotional turmoil subconscious, which makes them seem hard to find and figure out, simply acknowledge that when you feel any negative emotion at any point in time you have found a thought or aspect of belief which needs work because it is active in this moment thus causing the emotion. There is a blockage or the beginnings of a blockage forming. So reach to harmonise the mental activity as the feeling is evoked within you if you can. If this is too hard in the moment then rather than trying to figure it all out, right here, right now do everything in your power to feel better now by getting your mind off that subject. This will ultimately serve you better because it is your active thought evoking your feeling, and it is hard to think new positive feeling thought about a subject that currently has you down.

Often people will want to understand their blockage (which belief is causing the problem).

Trying to understand often adds more blockage and is not always helpful, sometimes it is, sometimes it isn't. It is possible to simply lay new pipes around the blockage without having to understand the blockage and allow the energy to simply flow therefore, feel better. Modalities are great for this laying of new pipes so to speak, this is really what all modalities are designed to do. Modalities often unlock congested understanding, which can appear magical as all sorts of emotional and physical transformations can take place. Modalities can never eliminate negative emotion and nor would you want to eliminate negative emotion, it is there for a dam good reason, **to guide your thought process**. We will cover more about modalities in part two.

Sometimes it is of value to find a new belief altogether meaning cut through the pipework and lay a new path of pipes, which often means a lot of mental gymnastics, finding better beliefs, and points of view that serve you better. Ultimately allowing flow (feeling good) has to be your dominant priority.

It takes a discerning mind time and experience to create a flow system between the ears in this way. But by consciously utilizing your emotional nuances, and reactions all day every day thought by thought on all the small things as a conscious way of being you will ultimately create a flow system as you sort yourself out bit by bit over time. However, sometimes the use of a modality releases congested understanding energy (emotional blockages) which in turn makes this mental work easier! At any rate, use everything in your power to feel better, working mostly with your inner world, rather than forcing outer change.

I want but have not got.

Many people cannot tell you what they are thinking about or what their awareness is on if they feel trapped in a strong negative emotional space such as depression. That is simply because they have not yet started the work of self-examination to the depth and degree I am teaching here, and that's natural and normal.

For example, you may be a deeply depressed teenager and not know why you are depressed you just are. Everyone may be saying to you, why are you depressed? You have everything you need, a loving family, a partner already, a neat allowance etc., yet you find yourself deeply depressed. Why is that?

Because all those examples people are throwing at you are outside of self. Life's conditions which others are perceiving as good things, and therefore cannot understand why you, the heavily depressed teenager is depressed. You the depressed teenager often can't figure out why you're depressed either usually because you too are looking outside of self for 'a reason.'

The reason is always a mental focus on the absence of something(s) personally wanted somewhere in your experience, this often has heavy criticism within the thinking process as well. Trying to figure this out can be a pickle in the early stages of self-examination. Simply put, your awareness is often focused in negatives rather than positives within your life preferences/desires. Therefore, nailing it on the head meaning trying to figure out the what and why thoughts and awareness's that are causing the depression is not necessarily the best approach for a depressed teenager, or anyone for that matter. Just endeavour to find something to think about that feels good to you, such as exploring different hobbies or ideas that interest you whilst also doing anything else that evokes a better feeling space. Some such ideas could be to play sport, go for a bike ride, walk, run or swim, using any distracting activity is often a better tactic for a depressed teen because activities naturally evoke different thinking processes which in turn shifts the depressive state because the minds focus has been diluted away from the thoughts causing the depressed state. Remember, what you think about creates your joy or lack thereof and anything that distracts you can be highly beneficial in shifting a low mood, so get out and live, move that body kid! However, do start the lifetimes process of learning to direct your thought process relative to how it feels, this is the most powerful thing you can ever do for yourself.

Of course there are many cases where there is an obvious mental focus in the absence of something personally wanted.

For example, here's a teen concern which is also a common enough concern for people in general.

"I want a partner, but I haven't got one, I've never had one, will I ever get one? Probably not because I am fat and ugly, but I want a partner, but I'll never get one."

A repeating cycle of this type of, **'I want but have not got,'** patterns of thought and awareness mixed with self-criticism is the cause of much negative emotion.

In this example, the mental activity is very obvious regarding the **focus and awareness in the absence** of a wanted life experience plus heavy self-criticism thus evoking the depression. The person focuses their awareness on the absence of a wanted desire which is causing the depression, not the missing wanted thing (partner). Learn to shift your **point of view** within any awareness that feels bad to something that feels better, or get your awareness **off it!**

In this example it is easy to see the mental activities focus in something missing. I want a partner but I don't have one. However, the teenager in the first example who doesn't specifically know why they are depressed will have multiple thoughts that are in opposition to areas of want in their life also.

Criticism always has aspects of, 'I want but have not got' within it, anytime you criticize anything you are looking at an unwanted aspect of some behaviour or event or circumstance in a judgmental way. This is really an awareness in an aspect of something that you personally don't want. It is the opposite of your preference, the opposite of your desire. Criticism always has an awareness in some aspect of that which you personally don't like. This means there is a behaviour, event or circumstance that you would prefer, but your awareness is in the absence of this wanted preference because you are focused or aware of what you don't want within any and all criticism, hence you feel bad you feel criticism. Again it is the mental activity's awareness of something missing or limited that is causing your negative emotion, (the critical feeling) not the situation event or behaviour!

This next example shows how instantly evoked anger is also really instantly evoked mental awareness in something missing, something I want but now have not got.

"Argh, I stubbed my toe, bloody hell that hurt dammit, grr now it's bleeding on my new carpet…grrr."

Let's say anger was evoked firstly in the stubbing of the toe for this individual, and a second wave of anger, because now they have blood to clean off their carpet as well.

So the wanted experience was not having a stubbed toe to begin with, but **instant awareness of a sore stubbed** toe was evoked. The second part of the wanted experience is, *"I have nice clean carpet, and I want a cup of tea before work, but now I have to clean the carpet instead of having a cup of tea."* Thus awareness is instantly on something other than what they wanted to do, and anger grows and/or is evoked in the awareness of having to do something other than what they wanted.

A simple enough easy to see life example, and many people obviously and naturally learn through experience to let go and relax within these experiences.

The point was to try and show you the mental activity thus awareness in the **absence of something wanted,** is what really evoked the instant negative emotion, the anger. Because again we've associated our emotion outside of self at the stubbed toe, and blood on the carpet when really it was the instantly evoked mental awareness in what we don't want, which was really the cause of the angry reaction. Can you see that anger is an intense focus in something you don't want to see, don't want happening or where you don't want to be, therefore utterly aware of and focused in what you don't want? Any time anyone loses their patience or is angry this is happening, their awareness is intensely focused in an unwanted experience (the angry man in the earlier example **didn't want** his son to steal shoes). Ask anyone who has lost their patience how easy it is to think say or do anything positive whilst in the heat of that type of experience, bloody hard is what it is (hence the angry man says fuck off). We have to figure our own way through life's frustrations and support all others as best we can in their journey through it. Also don't beat yourself up for losing your patience, just concede, *"Yep lost my patience again oh well, will try not to let things get at me so much next time."* Move on and try again, and again and again…

Another example of emotional misinterpretation regarding something, 'missing,' the song lyrics *"Only love can hurt like this"* written by Diane Warren and performed by Paloma Faith is a clear example of how we can misinterpret our emotion. Firstly, Love does not hurt, love feels great. The absence of feeling love flow through you on the other hand doesn't feel so great.

What I presume was meant by the song lyrics is a story of lost love.

For example, Joe Blogs falls in love with Jane Doe and is feeling love flow through himself like never before. When he is around Jane the feelings of love are evoked within him, when he thinks about Jane the feelings of love are evoked within him, he's on cloud nine, everything appears amazing (because he feels good). Then Jane decides she's off to greener pastures leaving Joe with a broken heart like he's never felt before. Joe then truly resonates when he turns the radio on and hears the lyrics blasting from the speakers, *"Only love can hurt like this…"* Well actually love doesn't hurt at all, love feels great. A broken heart hurts like hell though, **but that's not love, that's grief.** In this example, this grief, this heart ache, is caused by an intense focus in the absence of Jane. Joe has associated his feelings of love outside of himself towards Jane, (I need Jane so that I can feel this love.) No more Jane to evoke Joes love feelings, Jane has gone. So Joe is naturally, extremely aware of the missing Jane.

An intense feeling of grief, although natural under these circumstances is still caused through mental awareness of the missing Jane and can be perpetuated in the mind subject to Joes beliefs about such subjects and his previous experiences. Of course it is ok to feel grief, or any emotion for that matter, non-critical self-validation regarding all your emotional states is vital to personal well-being.

However, in some case's people can carry grief of lost loved ones their entire life, and many consider this normal, especially if we are talking about a death. But the fact remains Joe is causing his grief with his intense mental awareness in the lack of Jane. Again that's fine, that's fair enough under the circumstances. But is it still fine if Joe is still feeling this pain 3 year's down the track and has missed out on other life opportunities due to feeling bad? Of course not.

However, if Joe is striving to consciously find his own inner connection therefore taken responsibility for himself and has made a determination to thrive in life, to feel good, and discover emotional literacy, knowing he's doing it to himself (feeling bad) through his thoughts, his beliefs, his point of view. Then in time his thoughts thus beliefs will evolve as he deliberately, consciously does this work, therefore an intense pain like that will be much easier to handle should he be unfortunate to experience something similar again. In fact, it's unlikely anything will hurt as much again if he is directing his mind like I am teaching here. Of course we need varying life experiences to practice utilizing this mental/emotional behaviour, because nothing teaches like life experience. Also, how are you interpreting your emotion? Are you associating feelings outside of self? Do you think you must feel certain ways in certain situations? If so then you will be at the mercy of life happening around you. Again, all emotion comes from within and is always linked to thought/preference within any experience.

As a little side tag here, it is possible to find yourself feeling deep love flow through you whilst still single and pondering different thoughts which don't necessarily have anything to do with a partner, because love truly is a connection to self. Or you have found a way to simply allow this connection. To simply love, to simply appreciate, to simply be. Because love is obviously not a thought nor combination of thoughts, however thought either allows or disallows this connection we all seek.

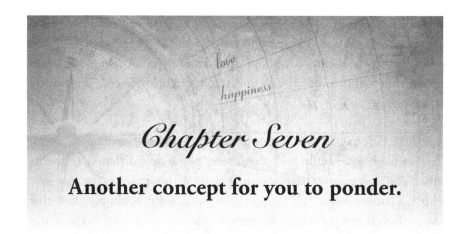

Chapter Seven

Another concept for you to ponder.

There are people whom believe emotion is nothing more than a series of biological, chemical and electrical reactions going on within the body, and we can manipulate that with drugs such as anti-depressants, and surgeries etc. So why bother doing this head work when we can simply take a drug to feel better?

Well, we all know the body is a miraculous work of biology, made of trillions of cells having trillions of interactions chemically and electrically constantly going on within.

We also know that we can influence the feeling space of our body with alcohol, recreational drugs, medication, diet, health supplements, and to some extent surgeries etc. With this knowledge, many have come to believe we are nothing more than a biological machine that can be tampered with biologically.

To a degree there's some value in that, just look at the amazing things medical science can do and how far it has evolved in the last 100 years or so.

Truly it is astonishing the depth of knowledge and help available on human health from a biological point of view. But do you truly know anyone, who is genuinely thriving and passionate within themselves, free and excited, clear and calm, who is using alcohol or drugs of any kind to try and induce this type of feeling space? Of course not.

Please do not misunderstand me I am not saying medicinal drugs, or surgeries are wrong. Medicinal drugs such as anti-depressants and anti-psychotics, are very definitely a powerful tool and aid on the way to sorting yourself out. They are just not the 'be all, and end all' as a more holistic view is required. People whom require these medications could consider this inner work as an empowered way to help themselves alongside medication if medication is required. Do everything in your power to feel better which most definitely includes modern medicines! Solely relying on drugs alone to feel better however is sort of like using a chainsaw to sort the problem out, when really you need the finesse of directing your own thought for sustainable long term results. **Learning how to think dynamically with discernment, understanding the link between your thoughts, and each emotional nuance you feel is your most powerful life skill to develop.** Of course when someone is suffering life debilitating depression for example, a chainsaw is often the first step required and highly recommended.

So obviously drugs of this nature need to be seen as a tool to aid in well-being, not the sole answer to well-being. Use everything available to feel better that fits your view of the world whilst also continuing the work of aligning mind with emotion to develop and enhance an ever evolving self-sustaining state of being.

What I am trying to point out in this section is, although the bodies reactions are felt through all the physical chemical and electrical reactions going on within the body, they cannot effectively be controlled solely with physical, chemical or electrical means. Nor would you truly want to because it is your inner emotional guidance relative to your thought that you are tampering with.

Another biological example of creating improvement within people's states of being is children with ADHD. Apart from drugs such as Ritalin, there have also been studies done that have concluded diet can aid in the behaviour of these children, awesome use these things for sure. Again as the child grows into adult hood, learning how to direct and use their own thought by how it feels to them to create their own state of being to their choosing is of far greater value to my way of thinking.

An old analogy springs to mind here, 'Give a man a fish and he'll eat for a day, teach a man to fish and he'll eat for a lifetime.'

So if it's not all biological as is the belief of many, what is it? **Everything is energy first and still is.** The body the air we breathe and everything we perceive as physical, is energy first and foremost just as consciousness is also energy. Consciousness, energy, frequency, thought, universe and everything we deem as physical is not separate other than in terms of frequency.

The thoughts you choose to think are energy first which then creates the biology of the **mind** and **body**, which in turn means you feel every nuance of emotion within you, which is obviously felt as what we perceive to be physical. You are more energy than you may realise. Physicality meaning all matter is really focused energy. (What one perceives as God, another perceives as science there is no separation here.)

In time you will see the thought to feeling interrelationship within yourself if you do the work of this book to the depth I am asking.

Clear mindedness in the sense of what I have been talking about this whole time, ultimately comes from using your body's responses, your emotions to direct and guide your mental activity toward less limiting thought, day by day, thought by thought ultimately resulting in a more vibrant, alive, clear minded you. Which is what we are all striving for really, just imagine how life would be if you were happier, more vibrant, more excited about your life, than where you currently stand.

Once you become proficient at this self-directed internal behaviour you'll wonder why you never did it before, and why it has been so hard to find this basic principal of human well-being.

In conclusion, it does not matter if you believe the body is simply a biological machine that can only change with biological tampering. Until of course, a belief like this hinders your own conscious effort to feel better by not even trying, or only giving a half-hearted effort in a limited way. If you are hung up on believing you cannot overcome an issue because it is biological, or for this reason or for that reason, then you will probably prove yourself right. **Seek a higher state of being and you shall find a higher state of being, however you choose to do so.** Also understand I believe in using all and every way to feel better as is appropriate to the individual such as a holistic approach which obviously and most definitely includes professional help, medications and doctors from every department as required, so please use these beautiful people if needs be. I say this because many people are unnecessarily turning away from professional help coming from all sorts of limiting perspectives. The pendulum has swung from seeing doctors as all-knowing to realising they are not all-knowing which has resulted in an exodus to some degree from using professional help. Doctors are beautiful people wishing to help, please find a balance in the swing of the pendulum if this has been you.

A brief energy connection, analogy.

I believe our emotional make up has far more influence on our health than many realize. Science and research has definitely started to notice that correlation. I believe Nikola Tesla when he said, "If you want to find the secrets of the universe, think in terms of energy, frequency and vibration."

Now through examining my own life experience I believe this also. I translate what he said to mean, everything is energy first, therefore physicality, our bodies, the earth and everything perceived as physical must be a dense form of focused energy which is subject to the perception of the observer (you). Hence we perceive physicality as physical because that is the frequency we are currently perceiving from. I also believe that since we are more energy than the physicality we perceive ourselves to be, we must get to direct our energy, our life force.

Thought or consciousness is energy first which converts to what we see physically as the biology within the mind and body as a whole. We get to direct our thought therefore influence our life force, and we can tell what we are doing with that energy in any given moment by the way in which we feel, which of course is seen as the biology of the body from a medical perspective, because that is what is being observed under the microscope so to speak. Meaning, the manifestation of thought effecting state of being is what we see scientifically and medically, as the neural flows, serotonin, dopamine, adrenalin and the trillions of other hormone, chemical, and electrical reactions going on within our physical bodies. Our life force is a finer yet unmeasured frequency of full consciousness affecting our body's by the way in which we direct thought which is firstly felt as emotion. Substantiating this statement would take some doing both scientifically and spiritually. However, what you **can do** is **prove to yourself** over time, that every emotional nuance you feel is in direct response to your mental activity with where you allow your awareness, your direction of thought to go. Of course not withstanding biological influences, which confuses this mind/emotion connection thus has caused the incorrect belief that emotion is solely biological.

My friend John once gave me an analogy regarding health, oxygen and the cells of the body.

He said, *"Imagine your cells are like the hot coals in a fire, when you shut down the damper, therefore the oxygen supply to the fire, the hot coals slow down, if you shut down the oxygen supply to your cells they also slow down, thus potentially cause health problems"*

So I would like to take that analogy further and relate your emotional state to the damper on the fire.

The better you feel the more life force you are allowing; the damper is open. The worse you feel the less you are allowing, the damper is closing. In other words, your thoughts, or what your attention is on allows, or disallows, your life force to flow or close. Thus the cells and entire physiology of your body are influenced, which can be seen as all the physical reactions that occur in the body in an emotionally high state compared with a low state. Hence your health is influenced if these states are held for long periods of time. This then means that medically a positive vibrant state is often a key difference between survivors and thrivers. Also this means biology isn't the cause of a depressive state, but rather the biological makeup is the result of negative mental momentum (energy momentum) causing the biology! I know this flies in the face of mainstream belief, and I am not about to try to substantiate that here beyond what I have already said, this is just a part of my current ever developing point of view which I find self-empowering and of use to me therefore possibly for others as well hence sharing it here.

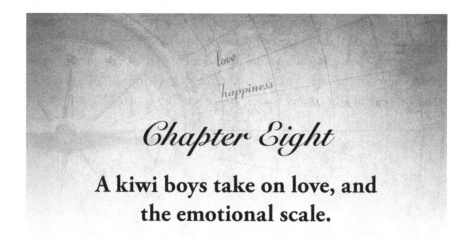

Chapter Eight

A kiwi boys take on love, and the emotional scale.

Get ready, take a seat, this will take a lot more pondering. Love is far more than a feeling. Nevertheless, let's just examine the feeling aspect in this book. The feeling of love goes beyond the limitation that many have, which is reserving it only for intimate partners and family members etc. **Love is ultimately our guiding light, it is drawing our consciousness forward hence that constant and incessant need to feel better in every life experience in the first place, love is calling us all!** Appreciation is really a better word that means the same thing and can be used more dynamically than the word love. Appreciation as a word has far less baggage attached to it for many people opposed to the word love.

Stop for a moment and try to remember or imagine a situation where you feel **natural appreciation,** perhaps walking on a beautiful trail, perhaps at the sea side or watching children play. Although it feels different to love for a partner, it is still love.

For example, notice how the love for a child feels different to the love of a partner, and yet it is still love, or how delightful you may feel in other situations, such as walking on that beautiful trail. In other words, expand your awareness to include the concept of 'appreciation,' because when you love something you are appreciating that something and vice versa. A feeling of appreciation is love. The frequency just feels different from subject to subject so we confuse ourselves to what love is.

Discovering life is about loving can take a while!

The conundrum of romantic love. So Ann is well into her adult hood, having fallen in love let's say twice in her life for the sake of this story. In each relationship although it started off ok it ended up deteriorating fairly quickly, she thought she loved each person at the time. She felt the yumminess of romantic love flowing through her in the beginning of each relationship. However, each guy had his issues he hadn't yet worked through, likewise, nor had Ann. So in each relationship Ann and her then partner were often triggering each other's issues and reacting fairly negatively towards each other, (outside of self). I like to call this lack of emotional responsibility 'people shit' it's at work, home, school, politics, its everywhere man! Anyway back to the story.

Before long Ann no longer felt she loved her partner and one way or another each relationship ended, leaving Ann confused, worried, and unsure about this whole love thing. Yet she believed deep down that fairy tale love exists even though she hasn't experienced it yet. So Ann incorrectly concludes that her problem was in not finding someone who loved her back as much as she believes should be the case in a romantic relationship.

Then along comes Bill. Her third long term relationship, well into her adult hood. Bill on the other hand is instantly smitten with Ann, it's pretty much love at first sight for Bill. Ann doesn't entirely feel the same, but she loves the attention and she does like Bill. In fact, he ticks every one of Ann's logical boxes of personal wants for a loving partner.

So Ann makes the logical yet flawed decision to marry Bill because he's everything she believes she has ever wanted. But at some point along the way in their marriage (you add a time frame here) Ann realizes it doesn't matter how much Bill loves her, (which he still does) She knows there's something missing… She simply does not love him back.

No matter how hard she tries she cannot evoke a natural feeling of love for Bill, and boy she tried. Again the relationship ends. Now through life experience, Ann has learned a fundamental truth about life and love.

'It's not about being loved; it is about loving.' Although Ann's friends did point this out to her before she married Bill, she now truly understands what it means. Nothing teaches like life experience.

What a conundrum romantic love can be for us mere mortals!

It is interesting to note that at the root of Ann's experiences (and Bill's) was the desire to feel love. We all have this desire within us, to feel better in all areas of life. To feel better is a path to love, because love feels best of all and is at the top of the experiential food chain drawing your consciousness forward within all life experience. This means, learning to **appreciate** each moment as it unfolds regardless of what is going on is also striving for sustainable happiness.

As all the great teachers have preached love is the answer. So let's explore that concept in a big and powerful way.

And you thought I was going to talk about romance!

If you deeply ponder this statement, "Anything anybody does they do because they believe they will feel better in the doing, having or achieving of it." As you move forward in life you will not find an exception to this at all anywhere, if you can look deeply enough within your own thought to emotional link relative to your personal preferences and desires.

Therefore, everybody is striving to feel good, and most are striving outside of self as we have discussed. It does not matter what person or situation you apply this statement to, regardless of the details, regardless of the truth, regardless of the justification, regardless of selfless acts, regardless of when you are doing things you dislike. (See the section titled, 'Where is there emotional gain in doing things I hate?' Starting on page 277 for deeper clarification.)

There is always an internal desire **to feel better**, whether individually or as a society. For example, regarding laws and war, or in any act to control others you are endeavouring to **rest easy** knowing you stopped those buggers over there from doing this, that or the other thing. This means, at the heart of all of that 'people shit' **is the desire to feel better,** to rest easy, to feel secure etc.

A lot of people baulk at this truth regarding our incessant outward projection of emotion, this is simply because they don't yet understand themselves to the degree I am teaching here, hence cannot understand others to this degree either. Often they are so hung up in the physicality, the details and strategic intelligence of whatever situation, or event that they are living or observing and want fixed or changed that they often flatly refuse to accept this truth, again this is understandable because you cannot understand the interactions of others until you understand yourself from this broader perspective.

But the fact remains, people want the physical life details changed so that they can feel better, they are reacting to their inner emotion outside of self! They are not emotionally self-responsible at all! This is the fundamental cause of all conflicts either individually in a simple bickering argument or a large complex social issue.

Whilst fear is still associated outside of self, therefore people are not self-responsible, fear will remain as the root cause of all laws and war, this is regardless of whether you are the perpetrator or defender.

I don't want to get into the depth of this concept to much more as it will deviate away from the essence of this book which is personal well-being first and foremost, yet there is no separation between personal and social well-being.

I just want to draw your attention to the fact that the more people who are emotionally responsible, the more this sort of fear based reactionary behaviours which translate into social issues slows down. Social harmony is more of a personal inside job than many realise. This lack of emotional responsibility is most definitely intrinsically connected to all whom are involved in the highly complex geo politics of the world and each country's individual governance. This also means that within all organisations involving people there is a limiting affect that is linked to emotional associations outside of self. Again I lovingly call this people shit. At any rate, what does all this have to do with love? **Everything**, because love, or appreciation which is the same thing, is at the top of the experiential food chain, and is drawing us all forward, hence the desire to feel better in the first place!

The emotional scale.

Below is the Abraham-Hicks emotional scale (Ask and It is Given by Esther and Jerry Hicks, October 2004; Hay House Publishing). It is a list **in emotional order of personal growth towards love.** It is core basic emotions we all have given in **'sequential' order of improved feeling.** Speaking in terms of raising your vibration you could understand the scale as moving upwards from coarser frequency (fear) to finer frequency (love). Therefore, the scale is a direct indicator of where you are within your personal development regarding each subject in life thus belief you carry. This simply means if you are holding more moments of natural appreciation (love) for longer periods then you are shifting your consciousness to a higher vibration. Feeling anything less than natural appreciation leaves room for improvement. Understanding your emotions in relationship to your thoughts means you know precisely where you are within each subject in your life by the way in which you feel when the subject is active within you. In finding this knowing please don't become critical of where you currently are, that just adds oil to the fire.

To understand others, you have to understand yourself. As you embody a higher state of being by consciously moving several set points higher up the emotional scale you will gain more clarity and understanding of yourself and others, through your own experience of shifting yourself. You will see how your thinking process is distinctly different when you are in differing moods. The worse you feel the harder to think positively, the better you feel the easier it is to think positively. Therefore, the actions you take are intrinsically connected to your moods thus overall thinking process. With this developing insight of self you gain some clarity as to why people do the things they do.

The scale is an extremely powerful education tool for anyone wanting to sort themselves out or to understand others. Every pattern of thought you have, every belief you hold, has an emotional attachment to it. Love is calling you from the top of the scale, it is calling you to evolve your thoughts, your beliefs to that of a higher, less limiting, appreciative nature. Hence the constant desire to feel better within all of us. When you get to know yourself better **by developing your own patterns of thought consciously** you will see the obvious improvement within yourself as you move up the scale in different areas of your mind, thus life.

This scale explains why violence happens, why people say violence feels good and all other reactionary behaviours. Coming to this knowing is experiential; it makes more sense as you embody a higher state yourself.

The Abraham-Hicks Emotional scale.

Joy/Knowledge/Empowerment/Freedom/Love/Appreciation
Passion
Enthusiasm/Eagerness/Happiness
Positive Expectation/Belief
Optimism
Hopefulness
Contentment
Boredom
Pessimism
Frustration/Irritation/Impatience
"Overwhelment"
Disappointment
Doubt
Worry
Blame
Discouragement
Anger
Revenge
Hatred/Rage
Jealousy
Insecurity/Guilt/Unworthiness
Fear/Grief/Despair/Powerlessness

As previously stated, anything anybody does, they do, because they believe they will feel better in the doing, having or achieving of it. Which really means love is drawing us up the scale, asking you to **evolve your thought structure** rather than change outside circumstance to feel better. Reaching mentally rather than outwardly in turn allows for more natural states of appreciation, of love to flow.

We all have an emotional range (set point) within each subject in our life. If that range is fairly low on the scale, then for the most part we will be aspiring to feel better, usually outside of-self one way or another, or we may have given up having decided this is the way it is.

Pick any subject in your life and take a look at the emotional scale, see where you mostly reside regarding that subject. You could be sitting on one strong emotion, but usually there is a range of emotions that you float through within any subject. This range varies subject to your overall mood and train of thought at the time.

Pick several subjects in your life and take your time to examine your feelings regarding those subjects by looking at the emotional scale.

Some ideas to get you started: -

- How do I feel about my Father/Mother?
- How do I feel about my childhood?
- How do I feel about my ex-partner?
- How do I feel about my Job?
- How do I feel about my bank account?

Please do not skip over this exercise, really take a look at yourself openly and honestly. You **must** become aware of your feelings, if you wish to enhance them. Frankly that is everything to you, even if you think you don't need to do this work. In fact, if you look at the scale honestly, you can safely assume that you have work to do if any subject is under hopefulness. Which will include virtually everyone on the planet, regarding several subjects at least, so take a look! The range you are floating in is your emotional set point on that subject.

The deliberate work of moving up the scale is a game of life worth pursuing. Of course it may not seem like a good game if you truly are a mess inside. In fact, it may cause you to put more critical pressure on yourself and make you feel overwhelmed. This is not my intention, go gently and quietly with yourself, take gentle steps, be kind to yourself, but take the steps.

It is not possible to list every nuance of emotion on the emotional scale, nor do we need to. It is not possible because everybody has differing interpretations of what emotion they are feeling relative to the words we use to describe them.

For example, I have a beautiful older friend who interpreted fear as love for many years! It amazes me how that can happen, but when you hear her story it becomes obvious. It would become quite cumbersome and inaccurate to use the scale if we tried to list all emotional words on it in sequential order, because of our individual interpretations. The important base feelings we can all relate to are listed in vibrational, thus scientific, thus psychological, thus spiritual order which is enough.

If we can accept that an appreciative loving feeling, or a joyous feeling, or a free feeling, or even passion is what our ideal target is within all life situations, then it becomes obvious to us when we are feeling anything less than that.

For example, if we are feeling arrogant, or are critically looking down our nose at someone, or think you are better, or superior, these thoughts all have a negative feeling basis within them and are not specifically named on the scale, and don't need to be. Obviously you are way down the scale because these feelings are far from appreciative or loving.

There is no need to try and figure out precisely where any particular feeling fits on the scale nor how to label it. You either feel good or bad or somewhere in between. If you are striving upwards thought by thought day by day you can learn to feel the difference regardless of whether you can place it, or label it.

If your state of being, your overall tone is hovering in the top five lines of the emotional scale, appreciation is more naturally felt in more moments in time without the mental effort that I **appear** to be talking about. It takes mental effort to train yourself up the scale **to begin with**, but as you get higher it simply is your natural place to be due to positive mental momentum.

Why violence can feel good!

In time, with the deliberate use of this work you will see the correlation between your thoughts creating your moods thus overall tone, actions, decisions and behaviours.

To really understand is experiential through your own conscious work up the scale, and that takes time, life experience and usually hindsight.

With this experience you will notice that there is a feeling of relief as you move up the scale on any subject, from anywhere on the scale. In other words, you feel better, you feel empowered, you feel in control!

When somebody moves up the scale from powerlessness to hatred, rage, revenge and anger they feel empowered which is why people say, *"But it felt good to take revenge or hit that person etc."* This can be understood by realising when an individual has limiting beliefs about their life which holds them within the bottom three lines of the emotional scale they will be constantly striving to feel better outside of self thus the feelings of rage, revenge and anger can feel extremely empowering within any angry, or violent outside of-self act because these acts are natural reactions to appease the lower feeling of powerlessness hence can evoke a feeling of empowered. It is an improvement in their feeling state slightly further up the scale from where their beliefs currently hold them. Usually they have unconsciously associated their need for control, and empowerment outside of self, as we all tend to do to some degree. In other words, in the physical action of taking **'perceived'** power back whether violently or otherwise, there is an appeasement of the base feelings of powerlessness, there was a slight shift up the scale within the act of violence whether with words intended to hurt or in any physical aggression. Hence this is why some people appear to feel happy within their violent or nasty behaviours, because they are battling their inner demons outside of self.

If you are in any place of fear or powerlessness, whether in your belief structure or during a current situation, it is common and normal to feel this empowerment, this relief when you move into any form of aggression from a place of disempowerment. Again everything emotional has usually been associated outside of self, therefore the perceived need to control outwardly in the form of aggressive behaviour.

For example, this could be as simple as having an argument where someone is trying to get one over you. Perhaps somebody has cleverly attacked you with words in a disempowering way. Then perhaps you move into anger or revenge from this put down powerless place, resulting in you fighting back, to get your power back so to speak. You will notice the sense of relief and empowerment; this can bring if you yourself are clever in your nasty word exchange. This happens in various degrees of one up man-ship all the time, trying to win arguments, debates or fights of any kind. Trying to be clever in this way is an outside of self-battle which you need to let go of for your own sake. This is a distinct lack of emotional responsibility. Virtually all of us have been involved in this sort of thing to some degree, not necessarily involving violent acts, but perhaps instances of school yard bickering or grizzling with friends, family and colleagues etc. This is really the same as someone in an act of rage fuelled violence just to a lesser degree, there is no separation here.

During any interaction like this there is an obvious up and down emotional flow going on inside you as you win or lose your argument or fight. Notice these smaller moments of inner reactiveness and strive beyond them consciously regardless of the degree, because you are suppressing your own state of being terribly if you accept this as normal. Take small steps bit by bit in many life experiences and see yourself shift to a more stable state.

A lot of people can relate as many of us have moved into anger or frustration from powerlessness at some point and can therefore relate to that feeling of self-empowerment or relief anger brings **when moving up the scale from**

powerlessness. Another relatable moment is the horrible feelings evoked when you are pushed down the scale into powerlessness when someone is lording it over you or giving you a hammering during your fight or argument.

Can you remember a time when anger felt good? Or remember any time you felt better in any way from any incident, not just in instances of anger. Take a look at the scale and see if you can relate it to your own thoughts, see how your thoughts have moved you up or down the scale emotionally thus reactionary within the incident or life situation, whatever your feelings were.

Please take the time to do this exercise on multiple occasions and ponder this information over time as you live your life, because self-awareness to this degree is a powerful part of finding your inner Zen, finding your happiness.

Look honestly at yourself, get to truly know yourself.

Reacting emotionally, to our own created emotions!

Imagine an offender who has lived a life of crime from a young age. This person will likely be floating between pessimism and powerlessness on most subjects in their mind, thus life experience. Therefore, they have a set tone or state of being which is not very pleasant, **although they will consider it normal and have acclimatized to it.**

In this example they have strong emotions evoked on a regular basis which are ignored, suppressed but still constantly acted on outwardly, yet are **created from his or her limiting and powerless beliefs**. Can you now see how individuals perpetuate a life of crime because they are just trying to feel better? Just like everyone else they associate the way they feel outside of themselves, therefore go about trying to physically change their conditions, and the behaviours of everyone and everything around them in order to feel better. This is so unconscious to most people; we don't even realize we are doing it.

This reactive behaviour to our own self-created emotion is why people often think it is their emotions that drive them and why people think their emotions control them. Hence we try to force control of our emotions when really we need to take control of our habitual patterns of thought which has allowed our feelings to **appear** out of control in the first place!

In other words, we think thoughts by simply looking at a life circumstance, and that then creates a positive or negative emotional state within which we created from our own belief structure in relationship to our own wanting.

Then we **react to the emotion itself**, try to fix it outside of self if it is negative, and therefore we chase our tails, and around and around the mulberry bush we go! Thus all people shit is born. I am sure you can see how we do this to ourselves in many life experiences.

Our emotions are really trying to draw our thoughts, our points of view, ideas and opinions up the scale, they are constantly calling us to expand our individual consciousness. This becomes obvious to you when you have done a year or two of this work within yourself, as I say understanding this work is experiential.

Of course it would be very hard trying to explain to an extremely tough, big powerful gang member, or violent criminal that he is feeling good or happy during his act of rage fuelled violence because he has come from a basis of limiting beliefs, which holds him in a position of feeling powerless in life, which in turn is why he feels good in his acts of violence.

Firstly, he won't accept that he was feeling powerless to begin with because of course like many in both gang culture **and society**, he may be walking around with an air of, *'I am the biggest, toughest, meanest there is, so don't mess with me!'* He or she could be carrying an air of staunchness or toughness, thus feeling empowered and tough therefore cannot see that these **false empowerment feelings** are an appeasement of base feelings of powerlessness evoked from their outside of self staunch behaviour.

Many people feel tough and mean, or aspire to feeling tough and mean, believing it is a strength but it **is not, it is total association outside of**

self. Perhaps they are very strong physically and have had many fights, thus experience has proven to them that they are tough (physically). Perhaps they believe they need to be mean to survive. Perhaps they are constantly on guard from possible attack, therefore deliberately walk around carrying an air of staunchness, an air of, *'I'm tough don't mess with me.'* This can feel empowering to the individual because it is better than the feelings of insecurity, unworthiness, fear or powerlessness which for the most part people like this are unconsciously striving beyond with this type of behaviour.

So of course if you told him his staunch, tough feelings he is aspiring too are based in trying to rise above his insecure emotional space caused by his limiting, fearful and powerless beliefs, he possibly couldn't fathom how that is so, because he thinks he feels empowered, thinks he is unafraid and thus feels strong and tough within his **false empowerment**. What a conundrum!

Can you see if someone is in such a state of mind, thus state of being, how hard it is to rise above it to one of a gentler more compassionate nature? Can you see how a belief as simple as aspiring to 'be tough' is really caused by a series of limiting powerless beliefs? Can you see the holding pattern these types of beliefs create within an individual's life? Holding themselves back from a truly vibrant life experience, ultimately causing themselves harm and potentially others harm as well as they may react outwardly. True freedom, true empowerment is inner connection to self, meaning love from within, holding and finding deeper levels of natural appreciation, always has been always will be.

Another violent example; here's a classic example used in movies all the time to evoke emotion from you, of moving from powerlessness to revenge.

The main actor John Smith has been captured, he is chained up, locked in a room of some sort. Here he is tormented by his captors who are up to no good. Then they kill his girlfriend in a most horrific way in front of him and leave him to rot in the room next to her dead body.

What emotions did that evoke in you watching the film? John is in a powerless situation and cannot do anything about the horrific act happening in front of him.

He then escapes somehow, as is usual in a film, and seeks bloody revenge on the perpetrators. Again what emotions does that evoke in you, the viewer, when he gets his revenge? It certainly feels better at this point to many people than when he was locked up seeing his girlfriend murdered. This feeling better is a slight movement up the scale from powerlessness, which has been forcefully achieved with action outside of self. Of course we all react differently relative to our personal states of being, many simply cannot watch these types of films at all because of the negative feelings it evokes within them. In that instance where a viewer cannot watch a film like that, they are obviously moving down the emotional scale, and choosing not to watch the film in the first place is an extremely wise decision. Obviously it is impossible to give an example of every nuance of feeling that all people may or may not feel in any situation, let alone watching a film like that. Use the example and look at the scale and try and see how **you** would react in watching a film like this.

Often there is a feeling evoked in some viewers of what I am calling **'False empowerment'** as the so called good guy, gets his so called revenge. People who feel this way may react in the cinema with, *"Hell yeah, he got the bastards"* etc. Sometimes you see people walking around after a film all pumped up in self-righteous false empowerment, or all amped up to go thrash their car after a film like, 'The fast and the furious.' I say false empowerment because although it feels better than powerlessness and it is moving up the scale, it has been associated outside of-self coming from a basis of powerless and limiting beliefs. Therefore, is not usually recognized as an emotional shift that needs to be maintained and strived beyond consciously rather than outwardly.

Whereas you will notice that there is empowerment at the top of the emotional scale, this is a whole different kettle of fish. Empowerment based in appreciation, love and joy is true empowerment, this also feels nothing like false empowerment, true empowerment based in appreciation is on a whole different vibrational spectrum where genuine care of self and others exists. Gentleness is the only genuine strength, are you strong enough to be gentle with yourself and others?

The only true way to understand this is to consciously move up the scale yourself and in time you will thrive inside in a way that only you can understand. Even if all your friends and family cannot see your internal change, you will, and you will have clearer insight to the world around you. It is not important that others see or acknowledge your inner change, nor perceive where you are coming from either, only you need to recognise it for yourself.

So love is the answer because we are all aspiring up the emotional scale and like it or not revenge and anger is closer to love than powerlessness, thus violence feels good to those acting in this way from a series of limiting beliefs.

Violence feeling good, is only ever fleeting for someone consciously moving up the scale, because although it feels better than powerless you cannot stay here long before that to begins to feel bad. You therefore need to consciously find emotional responsibility and continue moving up the scale to more happiness, harmony, love and appreciation. The only stable way to do this, is as an inside job of cleaning up your mental chatter, your habitual patterns of thought thus your beliefs in relationship to how they feel when they are **active** in your mind.

Can you see how life can become a cycle of pain for our gang member because he is trapped in a cycle of limiting beliefs, not knowing what else to do and is therefore trapped in false empowerment? Find this understanding of self and others and then with this understanding your own peace comes.

Conversely if you are overly sensitive to these types of situations portrayed in the movie example, you too have work to do in moving past these sensitive feelings to the true strength of appreciating all life regardless of circumstance, do everything in your power to move up the scale further, come to **understand** yourself even more than you currently do. I am not talking about desensitizing yourself nor condoning bad behaviour. There is a distinct difference between appreciative awareness, understanding and holding a clear space within yourself, compared to a desensitized person, or someone accepting horrible acts as normal in a desensitized type of way. There is massive power in holding an appreciative state.

Oh the self-important ones, what a trap they are in!

Self-importance in many differing forms is always quite off. It is usually unpleasant to observe in others and it isn't very pleasant for the individual either because as always they are unconsciously striving to appease a void from outside of self. Understand that a void is only a negative feeling of some kind.

Often self-important people display strong arrogance and they can be self-righteous in their arrogance as well, making it even more unpleasant not only for others observing them, but for the individuals themselves even though they are usually unaware of this.

This is no different to our gang member we discussed previously, the details of life experience may be vastly different, feeling good in violence and holding a staunch demeanour, opposed to a self-important person who may be feeling good in their self-righteous arrogance. However, even though the emotional turmoil and personal circumstances, beliefs and attitudes may be different per example they are both still fighting an inner emotional battle with the same old tool of trying to change their life 'circumstances' outside of self to feel better.

Many have limiting beliefs about careers, business and money believing these things make them successful and worthy. Therefore, when some people have attained these things they can be quite pompous and arrogant and strut around in their self-importance. These people have **associated their worthiness** outside of self and believe that they have attained life's success (to varying degrees of course), yet there is often a hollow feeling within, which is usually attempted to be filled from outside of-self with such things as pompous strutting and over inflated self-importance, thus people whom have associated self-worth to some form of physical success are often never fully contented, because the void within can only ever be filled with appreciation, not anything from outside of self. This obviously means, the feeling of self-importance and arrogance etc., is not feeling appreciation therefore the hollow feeling will continue until it is filled with an appreciation for life and themselves which is really the only way to fill any void felt.

The emotion of self-importance or arrogance is on a lower spectrum than love thus the hollow feeling to begin with.

Remember Ann? She discovered part of the equation by realizing in romantic love one must simply love. **The same goes for all aspects of life. One must simply love.**

If you are a pompous person then you have some work to do, because you are trapped in a life which may be amazing physically with all your neat stuff, house and dollars etc., but really the pompous strutting is trying to fill an inner void, therefore you are trapped in an inner pain. If this is you, please recognize this pain for what it really is because this work will give you what you have been looking for your entire life! Which is learning to hold an inner warmth of natural appreciation within more now moments.

On the other hand, if you are someone who is reacting to a pompous person, you see the ugly too much then you also have work to do. You are also trapped, needing the pompous person to change for you to feel better! You have to find a way to feel better regardless of anyone else therefore not needing anyone to change to keep you happy. Again break the link in the chain.

A bit more about self-superior states of being, that damn criticism!

Many people are self-important, self-superior, look down their nose types, or arrogant. This is simply criticism. Puffing themselves up with limiting beliefs of their own cleverness, status, sporting prowess, finance etc. This feeling often feels reasonably good to these types because they are unconsciously trying to fill that inner void with self-superiority, bought on from **competitive and limiting** beliefs about all manner of life situations. In other words, struggling up the emotional scale outside of self like everyone else. **Whether you are self-critical, or critical of others you are still feeling critical!** This isn't very pleasant for anyone, especially when you get a taste further up the scale! Dipping back to criticism of any sort feels terrible when you've been above it in your own being for a while.

If you are self-superior and arrogant etc., then this has an effect on **your** state of being, just like drinking poison and hoping the other person is going to get sick. This is because you are still feeling critical in some way.

You must move beyond this type of ignorance for your own sake.

Genuine appreciative feelings can replace these off behaviours and feelings, thus give you a taste of life and relationships that you have been seeking your whole life, which far exceeds your current experience!

So, when you catch yourself feeling and behaving this way; stop and take a look at yourself, do the work we have been discussing here and within part two coming up. There is nothing more important than that you feel good, from higher up the scale!

Seeking freedom.

Just briefly, can you also see in these examples and stories, how we are also seeking our individual freedom outside of self? When really, that too is an inside job, inner freedom simply is, once you move up the scale within your own state of being. Freedom has more to do with state of mind thus emotional literacy than the life liberties we think it relates to. Of course life's liberties are special, and to be treasured but the more you find your inner connection you feel free thus are actually free.

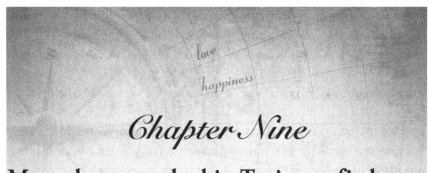

Chapter Nine

More about people shit. Trying to fix hurts.

How many times have you tried to fix a problem with a friend, co-worker or family member, or someone else because you believe they hurt you, or you hurt them? Often the problem only gets worse, or there is not entirely a satisfactory solution and you don't **feel** entirely right about it, or the more you try to fix it, the worse it gets.

This is because you did not hurt them! And they did not hurt you! We hurt ourselves each and every time!

Your reaction, every nuance of emotion you feel always comes from you.

As a result of our inaccurate societal and individual belief that our emotions are created by what we are looking at or dealing with, we can end up in a bit of a bind trying to fix personal grievances of any kind, due to the fact that we are often trying to take ownership of the other persons hurt and appease their feelings for them in some way. Or we are trying to get another to say sorry, or explain themselves to us, or whatever, in the belief that they hurt us.

- **You didn't hurt them; their reaction is their reaction.**
- **They didn't hurt you; your reaction is your reaction.**

The work of attaining sustainable happiness or unconditional love for that matter is in situations like this. Learning to develop your inner reactions to a higher place, by using every life situation as an opportunity to practice moving beyond these instantly evoked negative reactions takes practice and patience, and can be like suppression and self-control to begin with. However, as your overall tone moves higher in general and within more life subjects, your buttons become less and they get harder to press until there no longer is any buttons to push! Your reactions have evolved within you as you evolve your thought patterns thus there is no longer an internal battle of wills trying to suppress or control the negative reactions because they no longer exist in the same way. They have morphed into something else further up the scale! Therefore, emotional manipulation and drama becomes a thing of the past for you. Such as all bickering, condemning, blamefulness and fighting etc., simply disappears as your emotional reactiveness shifts into a more aware, understanding, accommodating, thoughtful, steady and stable state of being. All because you have made it your dominant intention to feel good through striving beyond all the negative inner niggles evoked throughout your life.

Don't make this understanding hard for yourself, I know how counter intuitive this can feel when you actually stop and take full ownership of your feelings in various life situations, relax, breathe, let go. Don't get impatient as you work within yourself expecting instant success. Knock all internal criticism on the head, gentle small steps, thought by thought build yourself from the inside out, gently over time within **the process of life.**

In the beginning stages taking full responsibility for your emotional responses often appears really hard to figure out in real terms, as I say tread lightly be patient, but strive upwards emotionally all the same with a relaxed gentle attitude towards your own growth.

For example, let's say someone close to you has done something really hurtful, their behaviour was disgusting to say the least and you feel hurt, upset, confused as to why they did what they did. This is a very unpleasant life experience, but it truly is where the work is. Sure they could have behaved better, or not done what they did, but remember, you are responsible for the way you react and feel, how much of their behaviour do you let influence you?

Understand, it's not so much your reaction in the heat of the moment that counts, but rather how quickly you can get beyond all the upset within you that is of real worth, because this affects all future reactions through shifting and maintaining a higher overall tone. Another's behaviour did not ever cause your inner emotional response. Therefore, once you take full emotional responsibility and remove all blame from all things, you can move forward striving to direct and maintain a steady space within yourself regardless of circumstance, thus you will find a freedom unsurpassed a genuine self-sustaining state of being and profoundly take control of your life. This far outweighs the effort. Seek!

Argumentative discussion is an emotional roller coaster.

When we are within an argumentative discussion of any kind, or when people are trying to be clever within their arguments and win the fight so to speak, or those that try to get one over you this is really an inner emotional battle associated outside of self as afore mentioned. Many people make a habit of this, even a lifestyle of it without even realising that they are doing it.

It can be utterly frustrating dealing with this kind of people shit, that is of course until you get on top of your own inner reactiveness, your own frustrations and then there is no issue!

We have all been in conversations where the whole conversation is off, it's feeling off therefore it is off! Yet either you, or they are fighting even harder to win, or you simply let them win because you can't be bothered with the crap.

What does, **'win'** mean anyway when you are lording it over someone, or think you are clever, or being horrible like this? Winning simply means you are struggling up the emotional scale from some place of powerlessness seeking appeasement of your own feelings of disempowerment by winning the verbal battle outside of-self, which is really a lack in self-esteem.

Behaviour like this never works to achieve sustainable happiness even if you are the best at it, and are feeling superior to all those you may perceive are under you. It is a false empowerment and is nowhere near appreciation, thus is reeking of outside of-self appeasement, a lack in emotional responsibility. You have work to do for sure if this is where you are at, cut it out **for your own sake!**

On the other hand, it is really hard not to react in an emotionally negative way if you are on the receiving end of this crap. Hence angry reactions, bopping someone on the nose, or engaging in the arguing whilst feeling an emotional roller coaster is fairly common when faced with these situations **'before' you have developed emotional responsibility that is!** When you are coming from a higher state of being where you are naturally holding a stable sure footed self-esteem regardless of what's going on, then there is no need to win an argument outside of self to feel good, because you already are in a steady place.

Emotional responsibility thus a higher self-esteem to this degree is attained through practice by redirecting your patterns of thought relative to your emotional indicators in many life experiences. In time you simply no longer engage in these types of behaviours or arguments, or you can often redirect the argument to one of a quality discussion with no agenda, thus the discussion is no longer an argument but one of upliftment. Or you simply walk away because it isn't worth throwing your pearls to those whom are not really wishing to understand your perspective.

However, emotional manipulation occurs in many forms not just within arguments. This is constantly happening within relationships of every kind, between people who are not yet emotionally responsible. This type of behaviour is very destructive for all involved because it perpetuates the belief that emotion is caused by outside of-self circumstance, thus is disempowering.

For example, some people may use their anger to coerce others. In these situations, the people are angry, or act angry to manipulate others to do something for them. People who use anger like this are really saying, *"I hold no responsibility for my anger, therefore you have to change so that I am no longer angry towards you."* Thus they expect you to change to keep them happy, they are trapped by associating their anger outside of self, blaming the other person for their anger. This could be as simple as the parent or school teacher who acts in a way which says and means, *"you need to change your behaviour so that you no longer upset me."* This is far too common within society thus perpetuating and learning a lack in emotional responsibility starts at a very young age, as it is copied behaviour from those whom are still associating their emotion outside of self! Some may also use their sexuality, or tears to manipulate (both sexes do this) and I am sure you can think of many other examples. Emotional manipulation of others is only possible whilst we are still associating and blaming our inner reactions outside of self, and have not yet gotten a handle on our own state of being. Therefore, emotional manipulation can only occur when people don't understand that their reaction, is their reaction caused and created by themselves and only themselves regardless of whatever is going on!

If you try to emotionally manipulate others in **any** situation you very much have work to do within yourself, to find emotional literacy a higher self-esteem where you no longer need to manipulate others so that you feel secure! Conversely if you are on the receiving end of this type of behaviour it is very hard not to feel disempowered, hurt or annoyed until you have a stable inner harmony, thus higher self-esteem yourself where you no longer react negatively to other people's words and actions.

So, within all bickering and arguing, whether you are the attacker, or the attacked one, your reactions are your reactions coming from within yourself.

Evolve your emotional responses over time within many differing life experiences, by practicing to reach for better feeling perspectives when an emotional niggle or nuance is felt within you, or simply let go of any off feeling niggle or nuance you may feel, then your reactions ultimately dissipate and morph higher up the scale as your perspectives shift thus becoming a non-issue for you. Your self-esteem will have moved up another notch so to speak. You are steady and secure within your own skin no longer reacting negatively as much as before if at all. What freedom! What a breath of fresh air, what relief!

So again, argumentative or manipulative discussions and debates, are an emotional roller coaster thus **a power struggle within yourself, not a power struggle over the other person as it is perceived to be.** In other words, each individual is trying to feel better.

Endeavouring to win fights of this type is always a power struggle within yourself to attain the feeling of false empowerment. The better feeling felt within the so called winner is often misinterpreted as power over another, especially if the other whimpers away with emotional disempowerment struggling to deal with their own inner reactions from the attack they just received!

The strongly manipulative or opinionated person is often trying to coerce or force change within another, by using their intelligence thus think they are clever which evokes their false empowerment feelings. Also this false empowerment feeling can be evoked within those who lord their physical strength over others. In either case, all of this is done by the attacker in an effort to feel better themselves, in their own striving for false empowerment, which is often perceived as power or control, when really it displays emotional weakness.

Generally speaking, a person being coerced whom hasn't yet developed a stable inner calm will either try to fight an inner feeling of disempowerment by arguing back or simply gives in because its less emotional work than arguing, yet feel disempowered among many other reactions. Until such time as you disengage from these types of interactions and simply let go of the battle you will be chasing an elusive ghost outside of self. Both people are really powerless in this example although the one who appears to win the interaction thinks they have the power and may think they are clever. When in reality this is a false empowerment of no real worth because they had to force outside conditions to change to feel better, rather than realizing that that's their inner job by finding a higher happiness, a higher self-esteem from within. Meaning love is drawing your consciousness higher should you learn to link your thought to emotion in this way.

In any relationship of reasonable length, if one person gets their way often in this manipulative manner, then the other usually ends up resenting them. All this takes place because of this outside off-self struggle to feel better, with both parties lacking emotional responsibility.

Some people become very good at this manipulation as a learned skill it can be very well articulated. Good communicators whom are still playing this inner emotionally illiterate game can appear relaxed and confident when conversing because they are relaxed in their skill and intelligence of winning such battles, however this is a huge trap for this type of individual, there is nothing of true intrinsic value in it to anyone until you are reaching for, or coming from a place of compassion, understanding and awareness, from a place of genuine care, genuine appreciation and love, then there is no struggle and is of much higher value because it is non-combative with practical solutions for all involved.

Often after an argumentative discussion we can go into a tirade of mental dialogue of how we could have won the battle, or we are critical of the other person or ourselves. Can you see in all of that mental dialogue you are struggling to feel better? You can and must change this inner mental behaviour from he said, she said, I said etc., to consciously dropping the dialogue altogether because there is nothing more important than that you feel good. Rather than re-living the argument over and over again trying to find clever words to attack the other person next time, which then only holds you in a not so good feeling place by continuing this pattern of thought, reach inside yourself to simply feel better anyway without the dialogue battle between your own ears. Look into your mind and endeavour to find a higher, lighter perspective within your beliefs, wants, and thoughts of this interaction or simply let it go! Learn to see any situation you find yourself in that isn't to your liking as an opportunity for you to fine tune your mind emotion connection.

The need to be right. Oh cleverness what a trap you can be.

There's also another aspect of false empowerment held within some people which is often overlooked, which is an incessant need to be clever, to be right or better. This is very often tied into worrying about what other people think, and often go's hand in hand with beliefs and desires about status and success etc. You can be intelligent and clever, coming from a place of care and appreciation, or you can be intelligent and clever coming from a place of arrogance for example. Which person do you think is more sustainably happy within these two examples?

Many people have this incessant need to be clever, better or right as an undercurrent in their being, a constantly comparative need to be clever, or better than others. Again this is a needy outside of-self clawing up the scale which is really a lack in self-esteem. Which results in un-sustained feelings of false empowerment relative to feeling clever, better, or 'I'm right.' If this is you, you need to move past this false need and find a higher self-esteem which does not require any comparisons to others, where you hold a **non-critical, appreciative and steady self-belief.** Conversely, a person could have a critical awareness of self, thinking they are not clever, perhaps they think they are dumb, these critical thoughts can eat away inside a person's mind knocking the zest out of them until they learn to nip these thoughts in the bud that is. Any striving for cleverness, to be right or better has never been about cleverness, it has always been about the incessant calling to move your consciousness up the scale thus developing less limiting beliefs coming from a genuine place of appreciation. Which means any outside of-self striving to be better or clever was an attempt to fill an inner void created by limiting belief structures about life, self and others. We have again associated our worthiness outside of self to an aspect we are critically judging, or comparing, in this case referring to our cleverness, better-ness or lack thereof.

Simply appreciate yourself as you are right now, however you are, clever or not so clever is irrelevant, to delight in yourself regarding any topic that pleases you, to simply appreciate yourself, life and others. Let go of any need for comparisons, condemnation or criticism and simply appreciate, if you don't you will struggle to find a genuine sustaining vibrant happiness which is everything to you.

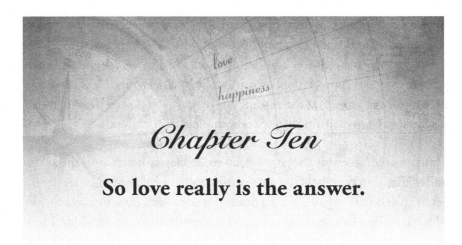

Chapter Ten

So love really is the answer.

Love really is drawing us up the scale because, "Anything anybody does, they do, because they believe they will feel better in the doing, having or achieving of it."

Therefore, the incessant desire to feel better within all of us, means love is attempting to **draw our consciousness forward up the scale towards love itself** within all life subjects should we listen. Thus love is endeavouring to fill our inner voids within all subjects pertinent to you. In fact, a void felt within any individual within any subject is simply a negative emotion held rather than a feeling of appreciation, hence the desire to fill the void within is unfortunately searched for outside of self in most cases. However, if we realize the negative emotion is calling us to develop our individual consciousness in that particular subject, as we consciously work to lift our emotional set points on all things, everything changes within you and your life.

It is only our emotional association outside of self, coupled with limiting beliefs that cause people to do horrible things to one another. Thus we point the finger and say they are bad. Perhaps they are, perhaps they aren't.

Understanding of others and compassion naturally grows within you as you understand yourself more fully in **your** conscious endeavour to move up the scale.

Regardless of where anyone is on the scale, there is always a feeling of relief, you feel better, as you move up the scale, hence violence can feel good to some. The trick is maintaining that new place up the scale, and that can only come gradually, thought by thought, day by day gently and quietly, by doing the work yourself within each life experience.

Love really is the answer because: -

It's really hard to think, say and do good feeling things when you are feeling bad. When you are low on the scale.

And conversely when you are in a more stable, sure footed, good feeling place and therefore more loving and higher up the scale, it's really hard to think, say or do things that feel bad.

Therefore, the higher up the scale you are in a sustainable way the better your life becomes because you are moving closer to a more harmonized state of being, which means your interactions are likely to be positive with your fellow man which is transference to the greater society. Therefore, love really is the answer!

When you start working with and taking notice of your emotional responses and have deliberately shifted some emotional set points higher up the scale this really starts to make sense.

Most of us have reserved that deep appreciation feeling (love) only for our lovers, family and children and don't realize that you can simply appreciate life! Appreciating the small things is truly equalling the statement, love is the answer.

All the crazy, dumb, stupid, insane things done by individuals and ridiculous warring governments can be traced back to limiting beliefs within individuals which is creating the fear of others behaviour **within themselves,** thus unconsciously striving to move up the scale by killing that bugger over there. Truly an under evolved consciousness.

A responsible mind knows he has caused all his inner emotional pain regardless of the situation, again I know this is hard to accept at first.

As the Dali Lama often says, *"War is obsolete you know."*

War is obsolete to an emotionally responsible mind! Because an emotionally responsible mind knows his anger, his hatred, and his revenge comes from within, thus realizes fighting others is a futile effort of less than zero value. It poisons you first and foremost (by suppressing your state of being), then your ignorant actions poison the world around you.

Nelson Mandela understood this as well, in fact many people do even if they cannot explain it like I'm attempting throughout this book.

Nelson Mandela has said,

"No one is born hating another person because of the colour of his skin, or his background, or his religion. People must learn to hate, and if they can learn to hate, they can be taught to love, for love comes more naturally to the human heart than its opposite." (Quoted from www. nelsonmandelamuseum.org.za)

And now you know why love comes more naturally to us, because it is at the top of the emotional food chain, the top of the scale and everyone is being drawn that way with their **natural under current, our driving force to feel better, to feel love flow through us.** It is a driving force sucking our consciousness higher should we choose to listen. We also now know that the emotional confusion within life comes because of this incessant emotional association outside of self, which in turn creates blame and that damn man made need for justice.

The conundrum of justice!

This section is a big section with regards to understanding emotional responsibility. It is big in the sense that it may challenge your belief structures around law and governance. It may be hard to understand possibly causing some confusion, please bear with me. My intention within this book is to paint a broad picture of personal and social well-being and how to attain it, within all areas of life.

Law and governance is a big part of our lives, it influences a large part of how we view the world around us. Law often struggles to deal with our overall lack of emotional responsibility by having no understanding of this within the creation of laws, because the law makers are like everyone else, associating the way they feel outwardly. Meaning, laws often shift blame for the way we feel on to the perpetrators of perceived crimes committed, like it or not this is an outside of-self limitation disempowering you! Because your inner emotional reactions are always your reactions created by you and felt by you, always! Again I know how hard this is to accept especially within subjects such as law and order, crime and governance. Conceptual understanding is one thing, **knowing** though personal experience of your own movement up the scale is another and this takes time.

Happiness comes from our mental ability to focus within our own personal preferences, it is easy to feel good when your preferences are met, in the case of crime where your preferences are not met it is natural to think your reactions are out of your control. In regards to creating law and governance, trying to pander to different preferences gets messy because we all have different preferences…

The need for justice is often another misinterpretation of emotion outside of self. Justice requires the domination and control of people's behaviour, or revenge such as a prison sentence, all in an effort to feel better yourself! Please don't misunderstand, of course we need to keep our community's safe from those whom are harming others, of course we do. However, there is a line that is often crossed within the justice system which is dishing out punishment to people whom we have inaccurately associated our upset onto. Everything we do, we do to feel better there is no escaping that fact. Therefore, the internal need from within for justice or to punish others, is to feel better ourselves, this obviously stems from an angry place, a powerless place, hurt, or revengeful place which we have associated outwardly, then we go about trying to get justice which is outside of self, all in an effort to feel better. This is a result of our overall unmanaged emotional responses in **all areas of life,** not just events such as **perceived** crimes. Any movement up the scale, from anywhere on the scale we begin to feel better. Hence we gain some false empowerment feelings by incarcerating a criminal because we are moving up the scale from some place of powerlessness, through exerting power outwardly. **Please try to understand it is your limitation in thought and belief, that is really holding you in a powerless state.** This is really what I want you to understand in this section, because you have full control over your mind thus state of being and there is nothing more important than that you feel good from higher up the scale in more life circumstance, this is our work as sentient caring beings.

Sure the inner reactions that cause us to seek justice are natural and understandable reactions, especially if you are on the receiving end of some sort of crime. Again it is not the crime that caused your feelings! Hard to accept I know. Understand that emotional responsibility does not mean that you won't have a negative reaction to such events, it also does not mean you condone crime or you are a goody two shoes letting people get away with crime. It means you can see the patterns of thought within **yourself** that causes **your** pain, **your** reactions, thus you have no choice but to take full responsibility for your own inner reactions. Emotional responsibility ultimately means you understand yourself so deeply through doing this work of self, that you can clearly see the disconnection within others who are still unfortunately reacting to life outside of self. You have a greater awareness of the **pain** of others due to their limiting beliefs they hold, because of **your own awareness** of self.

A criminals limiting thoughts in turn creates their low space which is where the crime was usually inspired from in the first place, this includes those that are heinous in nature, in fact, especially those who are heinous in nature. Anyone truly in touch with themselves are never inspired to hurt others, or offend in any real sense regardless of any law that may or may not exist, these people don't need laws to 'behave themselves,' they are not inspired to harmful crime in the first place. Of course there are infinite grey areas in all human interaction thus differing types and levels of crime, and we can all only do the best we can, which truly is the majority of us. The majority of people are good reasonable people not interested in criminal acts, because we are seeking higher naturally albeit usually unconsciously and outside of self.

For the most part law and governance is 100 percent man made to try and force others to conform to the perspective of the law makers which **'if'** fair and reasonable there isn't much of a problem with it, however this is not always the case. Please don't misunderstand me of course our justice systems are doing the best they can as a body of people to help us all to live happy secure lives. However, the way you feel is always your responsibility to maintain regardless of any injustices, or any circumstance.

Remember the politician earlier in this book promising to bring all of our might to bear on the perpetrators? That is a **pure revenge** statement, or justice statement that we can all relate to.

The need for justice is always driven by the incessant desire to feel better, to move up the scale ourselves. In the case of crime, we have associated our response to the perpetrators and we believe we need the outside conditions to change to feel better, we believe we need to see justice done. Of course the fear of more crimes committed is a fair enough reason with regards to keeping our communities safe as we need a form of dealing with those who are dangerous and disconnected.

Understandably many people will struggle to accept that to 'feel better' is a big part of how laws are created, especially if you have been on the receiving end of some horrible crime yourself of which you are still in reaction to. That's also fair enough, emotional responsibility in **all** regards is a big process to embody through each life experience that comes our way. As I've said before a lot of this won't make any real sense until you yourself have moved up the emotional scale and have dealt with your own emotional traumatic reactions to events in your life, therefore holding a noticeably steadier space within yourself as a direct result of doing this work.

So our incessant need for law and justice, stems from our **limiting belief** that we must control, and dominate the behaviours of others just in case they come into my life and hurt me. Again this is based in fear, understandably of course.

All laws are designed for people control, because of the **fear** of other people's possible behaviour, which of course is an effort to keep our communities safe, and operating fairly. So not only are we reacting in **fear** with our creation of laws, we are creating deterrents in the form of punishments to deter criminals from committing crime with **fear** based means. Really think about this, we react in fear, thus create a law and a punishment per situation to attempt to deter others with fear based means. I find this interesting. Since when has forcing people to, 'behave or else' ever worked sustainably at home or socially? It hasn't. We know how ineffective prison is in reforming people. Surely it is obvious that punishment **is not** a reforming tool, it is a deterrent based in fear alone, which means it's a Band-Aid that is all! Education and helping our fellow man to move up the emotional scale to a solid place of happiness, security thus self-esteem within himself, **therefore he is not inspired to harmful acts in the first place** is of far greater value to my way of thinking, surely! Of course no easy feat.

So where do we draw the line as a society? Well, that question has been mystifying the minds of lawmakers pretty much forever and sadly to many authoritarian thinking processes are involved in governance and law making!

Aside from law and punishments being used in an endeavour to keep our communities safe, almost everybody believes they have the right to tell another person how to behave to suit themselves and nobody wants another to tell them what to do, this obviously can become an issue in many forms of human interaction let alone within law courts, crime and punishment. Perhaps trying to draw a line is limited? Whereas emotional responsibility education on a mass intergenerational scale is a much more sustainable approach given the long term benefits and probably cheaper too.

As a result of being overly reactive outside of self we have developed the critical habit of placing every behaviour into pigeon holes, categorizing all aspects of right and wrong, (from our own individual perspective) then attempt to force people to comply to our point of view, or else they will be fined or punished etc. Just look at your own local by-laws many of which are not necessary serving only a few whom were loud enough to create some law to suit their own sensibilities or draconian point of view.

For example, some people often buy into this domination and control in response to some draconian law stopping people from doing something fun in their own district or country by saying, *"Oh well, they ruined it for us all."* Well, actually the ignorance of a blanket ban, forcing the behaviour of all the citizens is really what is ruining it for all! So again there is limitation in drawing lines! Especially as in many cases there are practical solutions which are often reasonably achievable to implement.

Can you see that the bulk of law is still only using that one tool to feel better regardless of any law written? The need to change conditions, force conditions (behaviours of others) to feel better? To **feel** safe, to **feel** secure, to **feel** as though you got your justice (revenge) etc. There will be many people baulking to that statement, flatly refusing to accept this whole section of writing actually. Understand I am not saying law is inherently wrong just pointing out how a lack in emotional responsibility permeates every area of society. Again this is experiential, and the only way to truly understand is through more conscious development of self, where your own inner reactions come more naturally from somewhere higher up the scale rather than what appears to be natural reactions from lower down the scale. Anything we do, we do to feel better in the doing having or achieving of it. There is no escaping the inherent truth and depth of that statement.

Of course law is a marvellous thing and very much required in our societies. It certainly helps us sort out our disputes, business behaviour, ignorance etc. Here's an everyday example followed by an emotional scale description as to what may have been going on within an aspect of the example.

Imagine two business's sharing a leased property, a large corporate service station at the front of the property, and a small locally owned LPG delivery franchise at the back of the property. The big corporate owner of the service station is planning to pull down and rebuild the service station and says to the LPG franchise owner that they will not allow them access to their business premises for up to 14 weeks over their busiest time of year. They say to the LPG franchise that they can truck in their LPG from another town and load it on to their delivery vehicles each day, essentially forcing undue financial costs. Another temporary yard would be required, more staff, double handling, cartage etc. Just an utterly ignorant no thought given arrogance, trying to push the small guy around attitude. Thank god for the law which doesn't allow this sort of unfair ignorance to happen and access was given. The examples of horrible behaviours in life of which laws are written to aid and help us are endless, again law in essence is a needed and a good thing, until the law itself is encroaching on **freedoms**, or has become an unfair bad guy itself which we know it has in many cases!

Bringing this back to personal well-being where do you think the individual in the corporate office of the service station was operating from? If you look at the emotional scale you will struggle to pick a place on the scale specifically, especially without knowing the individual extremely well yourself, perhaps not even then. But do you think this person was coming from a place of joy, appreciation or even genuine happiness? Of course not, ignorance and arrogance is much closer or perhaps pressure and stress form an external party thus they are in fear themselves. There is endless, **'reasons'** as to why someone may be low on the scale, you cannot list them all in any example. At any rate it is very hard to think, say, or do anything positive when you are low on the scale, and a mind that hasn't harmonized their inner world could only ever behave this way. The person in the corporate office probably wouldn't accept that they are feeling bad, because we acclimatize to our state of being thus consider it normal, wherever we are on the scale, but are they coming from a place of contentment and happiness in their overall demeanour? Of course not, therefore they are down the emotional scale somewhere, certainly not thriving internally to the degree I am attempting to teach here.

Even if they are clever, with degrees and great business acumen, they haven't got their shit together in what I consider to be any real sense! The person in the corporate office, wants happiness and contentment just like everyone else, but is unconsciously chasing an elusive ghost outside of self. Possibly also carrying a limited belief that says they have to behave in a certain way to gain success within the business world, who knows really where the individual was operating form and what beliefs he really holds, but it is blatantly obvious it was from low on the scale.

What would motivate that kind of person to do the level of inner work that I am suggesting here?

So of course law is a required part of our society. But the level of evolution in consciousness that I'm talking about which reduces our belief that we need rules in the first place is achievable for many, many more people thus our society will evolve for the better, it is evolving!

That said there is a massive amount of unnecessary governance and law in our modern societies.

Therefore, self-sustaining happiness within the masses, rather than the fear of punishment is a fairly good solution to pretty much all of life's problems.

Chapter Eleven

What's the point, I have a good life already?

Very few come to this work without the motivation of great pain first, whatever that pain may be, depression, anxiety, fear, suicidal feelings or perhaps frustration and confusion because life just isn't going as planned. Of course plenty do come to this work without pain as a motivator. Perhaps from what you may call a calling, or someone asking deeper questions about life. Someone intrigued in concepts such as spiritual growth. So for those who don't have pain as a motivator or a calling, and are not interested in concepts such as spiritual growth, and whom are already living a good life from their perspective, why would they want to do the mental emotional work to the degree that I am suggesting? Because your state of being is everything to you, truly the essence of life is found within holding deeper states of **appreciation** without the need for circumstance to evoke it from you.

Many have acquired some degree of the 'status quo concept of success,' thus can be living a pretty good life. It is easy to feel good when things are going your way, and you believe you are successful because you have these things so why bother with this head work you may say? Who cares about my state of being, I've got all I want, I'm happy, I don't need to do anything, all is well in my world what's the point? The point is you spend your entire life with yourself and most people never truly get to discover themselves, in fact very few people really know themselves! You could liken getting to know yourself in terms of the old star trek line *"Space the final frontier."*

Getting to know yourself to the depth I am indicating is an endless journey and **creation** of self, the more you examine and direct your thoughts and beliefs relative to your emotional indicators, whilst engaging in life, the more fascinating and inspired life you will lead. Thus, the deeper and richer your life becomes though this work far more so than any other factors combined. You are more fascinating than you realize. Look at yourself and challenge your thoughts and beliefs from a place of interest and curiosity, look at yourself with a gentle attitude not a critical attitude. The more you consciously direct your thoughts and beliefs the more you create yourself from the inside out, you could liken yourself to an intricate oil painting constantly adding to and changing subtle and not so subtle aspects, in an endless creation of self.

Also if you consider yourself to be reasonably successful and happy that's only a **mere glimmer** of the depth of clarity, appreciation and inner wonder you can feel on a more consistent basis through doing this work. Plus, there is always something in an individual's life they would like improvement in, which is always for the emotional response they believe they will gain in that improvement, so reach inwardly.

This is the true essence of life experience; to thrive with vibrancy, clarity and deep joy in more and more moments in time, **without** the need for life's conditions (such as what is often perceived as success), to evoke these feelings from you.

On the other hand, many are simply existing in the hum drum of work, eat, sleep, do something on the weekend. Yet they too can have the state of being I just described if they so desire without needing the 'stuff,' or 'success' to get there. Many people are not even aware that it is possible to have a vibrant life, because of the incessant association outside of-self coupled with limiting concepts of what success is. Many have made their minds up, *'that this is the way life is,'* therefore they may tolerate a mediocre state of being because they no longer believe they will attain their wanted life experience. Hence people often take a critical point of view when they talk about having led a mediocre life, thus may have resigned themselves to a given up on life attitude. **It has never been about a mediocre life; it** has always been about a mediocre state of being. **You can begin your conscious journey of self-discovery at any stage in life.**

A profound truth.

Hopefully by now you can see the profound truth, that **if you take control of the way you feel you will profoundly take control of your entire life experience** (by having a vibrant state of being), and thrive far beyond chasing an elusive prey outside of self!

This means engaging in all aspects of life just like you were before, work, school, relationships, hobbies and so on, but from a whole different and vibrant perspective. A self-responsible awareness **whether you are happy or not.**

For example, when you're grumpy at work, let's say because you don't really want to be there, a responsible mind realizes that you feel that way because you are mentally focused on the missing aspect of what you truly want (whatever that is to you). **A responsible mind is aware that they themselves are really the cause of their grumpy mood** by focusing on where they don't want to be, in this case at work. If these thoughts are left unchecked they perpetuate and seem out of control, then you become grumpier, snap at people and react in situations all because you're upset. A responsible mind knows that you allowed yourself to become upset because you didn't nip the train of thought in the bud earlier! A responsible mind knows that the grumps were created by the mental focus on an unwanted subject, and therefore endeavours to change their perspective or subject of thought within their mind.

People can torture themselves like this for years, thus live a miserable life blaming their job for their woes. A self-responsible mind can solve this problem, although you still may not like your job you can make peace with it, which has to be your dominant priority. Happiness is after all, the only legitimate life career choice.

An old proverb says, 'Before enlightenment, chopping wood, carrying water. After enlightenment chopping wood, carrying water.'

Let's modernize that to, 'Before happiness work, eat sleep, pay the bills. After happiness work, eat, sleep, pay the bills.'

The problem of wanting demystified.

Everything in life is about how you personally **want** to live your life.

Many people can't stand the concept of wanting. They may possibly see wanting as needy or selfish because they see people doing what people do which is chasing an elusive prey outside of themselves in order to feel better, which sometimes causes all sorts of grief for themselves and others in a multitude of ways. For example, the grass is always greener concept has been caused by our emotional association outside of self and in extreme cases to the ugly extent of greed, again everything is in degrees.

Many therefore believe wanting is inherently bad. However, can you see that everything is about your personal preferences, your wants? Within every aspect of every subject there is your personal preferences. How much sugar do **'you want'** in your tea dear?

People who think wanting is bad are often observing the ones they think are greedy or selfish perhaps they see others striving to get stuff and battling themselves and the world around them. Perhaps they themselves have been trying to get stuff to fill a void, and have finally come to realize that acquiring things, and status etc., does not fill their inner void, thus conclude wanting is bad. Many compare those with great wealth, with those with little and critically point their finger at the wealthy ones, saying things like why do they want so much.

In our interpretation of our experience of life, many associate, 'wanting' with their personal problems. This is simply because they have their awareness on missing wants in their life, and thus feel bad, hence may come to the incorrect conclusion that wanting is bad.

Let's say you believe wanting is bad because of what you perceive to be selfish and greedy behaviour, therefore when you look at these behaviours in others you feel negative emotions relative to your ideas and criticisms of their behaviours etc. You **want** people to behave differently so that the world will be a better place from your perspective. Can you see, that you still **want** the world to be the way you **want** it, therefore, you are still **wanting**!

Rather than seeing wanting as bad, consider that we all **want** to feel good and have a happy life and many are trapped chasing their tail outside of self, that's all, nothing more.

Wanting is not inherently bad, it is natural to want a happy life that is relative to your own personal wants and preferences, and there is nothing wrong in that!

You cannot escape your personal preferences as this is intrinsically connected to your happiness, you must harmonize yourself and make peace with all subjects if you **want** a happy vibrant state of being, therefore life. And you do **want** a happy vibrant state of being don't you?

Many believe happiness is different per individual because we all have differing personal preferences (wanting) within our life experiences. Happiness does not come from different things per individual. Happiness comes from your mental ability to focus on your personal preferences and life situations in a way that feels harmonious to you, therefore happiness is the work of aligning mind with emotion which is the same for us all.

Wanting is as natural as the air we breathe, and without it there would be no expansion within yourself or society. Wanting to feel better, wanting to be a better person, wanting to love, wanting to do a good job, wanting to understand a subject, wanting to learn, wanting to enjoy others company, wanting to be happy etc.

Mental Dialogue.

Frankly inner-peace, happiness, passion and zest simply boils down to your ability to **direct** the dialogue in your head, the stories you tell in your mind with conscious association to the way you feel whilst thinking your thoughts.

If you are constantly reaching to feel some degree of appreciation with mental focus within as many situations as you can, in time this allows us to naturally feel alive, passionate and zesty for life again. Our stories, the constant dialogue in our mind are intrinsically connected to our personal desires, our wants within every life experience. Our mental untamed dialogue, combined with the confusion created by the natural but flawed belief that we need to shift our physical conditions to feel better, has caused many to chase an elusive ghost for the best part of their life. Thus ending up unhappy, unsatisfied, depressed, flat and stuck in limiting beliefs such as; this is just the way life is, no one else is happy, or everyone would feel like this if it happened to them etc.

Of course some of us really are in such crappy situations that to hear someone say the way you feel is all in your head usually doesn't go down to well. We can only do the best we can from wherever we are.

What I am saying is, in time you will **train** yourself to a better feeling place with this work, and yes definitely do change situations to feel better if you need to and if you can. But please constantly do the inner work of directing your thought and awareness subject to the way it feels to you as your most dominant practice. Even if your thought changes are small, in time they add up.

Changing the physical situation alone (you control freak you) is never enough if you want genuine sustainable happiness.

This work may sound like an unnatural forcing of feelings to some. It is hard work to begin with, shifting and changing our internal dialogue is a challenge, it just is. There is an old saying that says, **'If you keep doing the same old thing you will keep getting the same old result,'** this is totally appropriate here. Do something different means **think something different**. Easier said than done, but you can do it.

So not only can we nip in the bud our existing thoughts with the tools we are yet to discuss in part two, and with the use of therapies and modalities etc., we can also start to build new ideas, new mental dialogue and stories. The tricky bit is, what do I now think? For example, making peace with death is a big subject with as many different beliefs about it as there are people on the planet. So, it is not a case of who has the right belief, but rather of making peace with the subject (any subject) in a way that is **appropriate to you**, and **allowing others** to make peace in their own way.

Many find peace in their religion or spiritual beliefs, others with a powerful near death experience, some believe once you're dead you're dead and that's it and have found a peace in that. Some have personal experience of an esoteric nature and thus have made peace with death with experiences and beliefs in this regard.

The point is, this is a personal self-discovery and self-harmonizing of **your own** thoughts and beliefs over time, and directing your mind by how it feels to you will get you there, whatever your chosen beliefs are. Of course many beliefs will simply morph, change or be dropped entirely as you reach to harmonise mind with emotion.

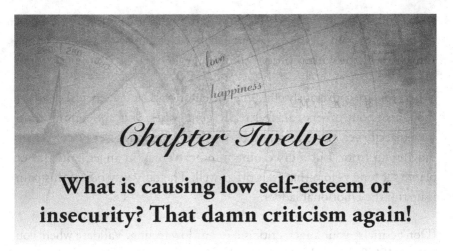

Chapter Twelve

What is causing low self-esteem or insecurity? That damn criticism again!

It's mostly that bloody inner critical voice. In other words, letting unchecked thoughts, your mental dialogue, grow out of hand in a negative critical way and become your dominant mental activity.

More often than not people grow out of their self-esteem issues as **life experience** naturally develops a self-awareness which in turn naturally helps change patterns of critical thought. In other words, experience often causes a natural reassessing of-self through thought and awareness resulting in self-esteem and confidence.

For example, perhaps someone gets a really nice partner, even though they have been telling themselves for years it will never happen because of some negative self-belief or internal dialogue. Thus the experience of gaining a nice partner adds to their self-belief. Belief in one self, or the lack of belief, comes from the way you **mentally interpret** your life experience.

Life experience can often build self-awareness. Thus self-awareness allows for self-esteem more readily subject to the way you **interpret** your experience within your mental chatter moving forward.

If an individual begins to direct their inner dialogue by how it feels, self-esteem naturally grows because all critical thoughts of self and others have a courser frequency which ultimately feels off as you climb the emotional scale. Thus you move past these limiting thoughts as you learn to drop or adapt them within all life experience that evokes a nuance, twinge, cringe emotional niggle within you.

When you are consciously climbing the emotional ladder, critical or angry thoughts about others can feel really good when you are coming from someplace lower, that's great, it's better than whatever lower place you are moving up from. But a discerning mind can't stay in anger, criticism or blame for long before that feels off as well. The only way out of this pain is up, up the emotional ladder.

(Don't criticise your anger, criticism or any low feeling. Validate where you are and if it feels good at the time, that is progress up in that moment and that is good work.)

You have no choice but to learn to use your emotions thus learn how to think with the dynamic direction given by your emotion. Think more if it feels good, think less or reach for a lighter perspective if it feels bad! Always reaching to feel good because you have made it your dominant intention too. Please consider that criticism is often synonymous with blame, and blame is not emotionally responsible ever!

More about life experience, and self-esteem.

Adventure therapy has been a powerful tool for young and old alike for a long time now. For those that may be new to the term, adventure therapy is exactly that, an adventure into the wilderness for a period of time often involving hiking trips, canoe or kayaking, rafting, high rope obstacle courses, team building exercises etc.

If a person with low self-esteem and limited experience in these types of activities partakes in an adventure therapy program, the net result is very often more self-awareness. This is **felt** as confidence, thus a natural growth in self-esteem occurs.

New Zealand had a government funded program operating for many years called the Conservation Corp. This was, as far as I am aware, for the express purpose of growing self-esteem in young people through life experience and community engagement. Although over time and with a lack of wisdom, far too much emphasis was put on the academic education component which resulted in an erosion of the adventure and work experience aspects within these programs. Thus in turn, the programs lost their oomph and now they no longer exist here.

What do I mean by lack of wisdom in this instance? You can be the most talented individual academically but if you are a mess inside yourself, academic ability may help to some degree but doesn't really mean a lot until you find your inner confidence. Sure academics such as reading, comprehension and math etc., is considered foundation skills that make life easier, but it is nowhere near as useful as self-belief and genuine confidence. Obviously confidence and academia equals a well-rounded individual. The people on these courses had often failed in the schooling system, and now they were forced back to academia outside of school within these courses. Frankly there are many other courses for academia outside the school system so why erode the physicality aspect within these courses which is so very important also? The net result; people didn't gain self-esteem due to a reduction in the activity based components by putting them back in a learning environment that was not conducive to growing self-esteem thus poor course outcomes, (people didn't get jobs). From a government funding perspective this is often required to continue these programs. Sure there were other reasons, many programs simply weren't run very effectively, usually not enough staff and or resources. Plus, there was often no real understanding of what was required of new tutors in regards to building confidence in students through activity and community engagement, thus things tended to fall apart in some cases. The point I'm building up to is there are many differing courses, programs and schemes all over the world trying to solve all sorts of social issues with varying results. All with differing points of view as to what is an outcome?

It must be clear by now that a strong part of my point of view is; the more well-rounded an individual is, the more relaxed, happy and secure in their own skin and with full **emotional responsibility,** the better our societies will evolve. More self-esteem in its own right has to be considered a good outcome although this is not easy to measure, or quantify into what would be considered social money well spent.

Another issue that we had within these types of courses was that only those that were struggling within the academia aspect of education were targeted for participation. If you did ok academically at school these courses simply weren't available to you. How many so-called "normal people" are well rounded and secure in their own skin do you think with high self-esteem and genuine emotional responsibility? Hence from my perspective these courses would do well to be re-established with broader intake criteria and a deeper understanding of this entire body of work built into the structure of each course programme.

Imagine the benefit of the education I am offering here if it were to be combined with these types of courses! Emotional responsibility would certainly reduce the bulk of people shit in the world inter-generationally. Of course the teachers that have naturalized it within themselves are going to be the only authentic teachers on the subject!

The best teachers are **parents** who have embodied a higher state of being themselves, thus children develop this mental, emotional ability naturally.

Perhaps added to school curriculums within all age groups would enhance and speed up social harmony! If math, science and English are compulsory subjects in schools perhaps emotional responsibility should be to?

Hmmm, what was that about giving someone a fishing rod?

One of my jobs.

One of my jobs was working with youth offenders. It is a brilliant organization of which I truly believe in. Of course it was government funded, and as usual to receive funding you must get some sort of result. So obviously in this instance, results meant a reduction in criminal offending by the youngsters from a government point of view.

Previous to joining the programme, these kids had either been locked up in juvenile detention centres, or were about to be sent to juvenile detention and were given the option of participating on a program such as the one I worked at rather than going to juvenile detention. From my point of view, if the young people felt better about themselves when they finished the program then we had achieved a great result for the young person, regardless of whether or not their offending was reduced. Which in the case of this organization there usually was great results in the form of a reduction in offending. I believe a strong reason for this reduction was due to the growth within their self-esteem, they had moved up the scale slightly due to the structure of the programme and culture of the staff working there. If you are surrounded by turkeys it's hard to fly like an eagle, these kids were surrounded by eagles they had to flap to keep up! Therefore, when the young people left the programme the **inspiration** to do dumb things was not as strong as pre-program entry due to their natural growth in self-esteem. Of course a natural growing up period helped, as they were still only 15-18 year olds as well as there being an extremely strong follow up support system in place when they went home.

Remember, if you are in a shit feeling place, (through a lack in self-esteem for example) it's really hard to think, say or do good feeling things, period!

There was a component of adventure therapy in this organization and also a work experience component. All of which boosted their life experience thus self-esteem, but a key ingredient that many miss which this organization excelled in, was a deliberate lack of discipline! Did you hear that? I said a **deliberate lack in discipline** with youth offenders! Many cannot fathom this concept. Discipline reeks of forced control of another for **you** to feel better! **Since when did forcing 'behaviour change' ever create sustainable behaviour change? Never!** The youth offender is the one that needs to feel better, and is therefore not inspired to do dumb things in the first place. This organization also had a great staff supervision system to help staff deal with their own personal issues evoked from trying to understand and cope with the bad behaviours and limited mind sets of these youngsters.

What replaced discipline was relationship building, the term 'love bombing' was used and heard a lot here.

The first month was spent in the bush hiking, canoeing, fishing, hunting, a solo experience etc., as staff our job was to relax and have a good time with these kids tell jokes, tell stories, share, bond and just be. Thus when the adventure therapy component of the program finished and we moved into the residential component, which consisted of living together in a shared home, engaging in work experience through the week and activities over the weekends, the usual trouble started where the youngsters bicker and fight etc.

Instead of a harsh telling off or discipline of some sort, there were more often than not father figure type discussions, this was possible because of the relationships that had already been built during the adventure therapy component of the program.

This type of fatherly discussion could have unfolded in a way such as the following, *"Bro you're being an egg man, cut it out ya wally."* These comments coming from a harsh authoritarian do as I say perspective never work. However, these same comments do work when offered from a place of genuine care and respect thus are well received by the young person due to the foundations of trust and genuine friendships that had already been built during the adventure therapy faze. Thus the young person started to think a little, rather than just react.

In other words, positive regard was always given as best as humanly possible regardless of the negative behaviour and who the person was. Therefore, their self-esteem was not eroded as harshly through heavy criticism of their behaviour, which is all discipline really is. Discipline is more of a hindrance to their growth than anything else. Discipline never builds self-esteem or evokes inner change. This was regardless of the bully or the one being bullied, the bully needs this understanding the most as he is always low on the emotional scale and needs love bombing (understanding) as much, if not more than the other guy.

A lack of self-esteem really is caused by the individual.

Any lack of self-esteem really is caused by critical mental chatter directed at one self. Stop it! Cut it out! You are doing it to yourself!

Remember what was covered in the section earlier about criticism; we have been trained this way with the constant criticism going on around us. Even if you are living in the most critical of families, you can start to cut it out in your own mind.

Of course redirecting your mental chatter takes some getting used to and takes practice, but seriously hear me when I say this, emotionally directed mental chatter is where your true power is born!

As far as self-criticism is concerned the best thing you can do for yourself is relax, smile take a breath and change the subject in your mind. Get your mind off your body image issues for example, body image is one of the most commonly talked about self-esteem issues. You should have seen the young offenders trying to build their bodies! The more you talk about it and fret about it, the worse it gets within you! You must make it your dominant intent to feel good which means, learning how to think differently. Find a way to think about something else! All self-esteem-issues are critical thought of self, regardless of what issue you are blaming it on! Trying to change your body image by physically changing yourself is working from the outside in! Sure do that, go to the gym, or hairdresser, or whatever it is you want to do, but make your inner work the dominant work, learn to accept yourself just as you are and appreciate your life's journey!

The confusion of loving yourself.

Often, people will say you must love yourself first before any good will come. Remember Ann? She discovered that really it is about loving, not so much about being loved. Truly ponder this, we want to feel love flow through us more than actually being loved, 10 million people can love you, can be head over heels for you, and it means nothing if you cannot feel love yourself! It is you that wants to feel love flow through you!

How can one love oneself or anything else for that matter? The answer is by allowing yourself to feel good no matter what, which is the only way to love anyway. You can only love when you allow yourself to, as you consciously reach too by climbing the emotional scale within every life subject pertinent to you. This is achieved through a process of time by consciously lifting, shifting and adapting your **limiting and critical** patterns of thought, which in turn allows love to flow through you.

Of course a singular thought is not love or any thought so to speak, it is a case of gradually shifting your overall tone up the scale in more and more areas of your life. Life experiences gives you the opportunity to do this, each experience is a chance to hone your mental skills into alignment with better feeling perspectives toward love. If we think about ourselves or others and feelings of criticism are evoked, then we are obviously feeling criticism not love. To love one self, one must work to drop all criticisms of self and all others.

You must come to understand that when you are in a good feeling place regardless of why you feel good you are moving closer to loving yourself because you are moving up the scale. Loving oneself simply means feeling love flow through you regardless of what evoked the feeling within you, better still without any circumstance to evoke it! If you feel love for whatever reason you are love in that moment therefore loving self, even if you are associating that love outside of self at something! Truly ponder this, life is about loving more than anything else.

Of course feelings of false empowerment and slight un-sustained shifts up the scale from a place of powerlessness which are created from outside of-self-assertions need to be discerned and moved past in a sustainable (mental) way as you figure through each life issue that you are dealing with. You have to make it your most dominate intent to feel good and discern and figure your own way up the scale as best as you are able. This is not a case of learning to love bad behaviour, this is a case of feeling appreciative and not allowing bad behaviour to pull you into angry, critical responses, ideally because you have developed a broader more dynamic point of view. Loving self simply means feeling love, feeling appreciation regardless of circumstance, which is thus then unconditional. Simply love.

Who needs respect?

When working with youth offenders there was often discussion regarding respect amongst the staff. Some of these kids often showed little care and respect for very much at all. The manager quite rightly said, *"How can they respect you, if they cannot respect themselves?"*

Genuine respect can only come from a place of love and appreciation not fear as many believe.

Some examples of respect from fear could be, fearfully interacting with somebody who has some sort of control over you, perhaps intimidation, or presumed status, an arrogant employer perhaps, the president of the bike gang you're a member of, or bad parenting practices. Perhaps the person in this place of power believe they are getting respect. When in actuality interacting with fear is not respect, it is forced behaviour through fear. Authoritarians who demand respect are again forcing conditions outside of self, this is not respect. Interacting whilst feeling fear is often interpreted as respect. This is false respect.

An example of respect from appreciation on the other hand, is simply appreciation. You appreciate this person, you feel appreciative. Thus respect is a non-issue, appreciation just is.

So loving one-self and genuine respect is the same thing, when you appreciate something you respect that something.

Part Two

How to Sustain Happiness

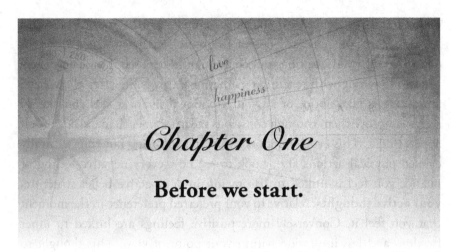

Chapter One

Before we start.

This section will have a little repetition. I believe the education itself is vital to individual wellbeing and repetition helps us to conceptually understand therefore making it easier to embody.

The main intention of this book is an introduction to the concept of using all your emotional responses as a way to consciously mould your thought process within each life experience to one that serves you better, meaning you create a more dynamic way of thinking as you move through life from here. This in turn creates a sustained, stable and gradually increasing state of being with a constant striving to look for, recognize and hold more states of appreciation. Appreciate appreciating. Rather than associating outwardly then reacting outwardly to your inner emotional reactions in a knee jerk kind of way, which is far too prevalent in most of us and is usually detrimental to yourself and those around you.

In other words, when observing a situation there is a thought, an awareness, a belief or opinion evoked that includes your personal preferences regarding the subject(s) at hand. This thought then creates an emotional reaction which you feel as a nuance or twinge within you which is most often inaccurately associated outside of self which you may then react to outwardly to appease the inner reaction, this can all appear to happen instantaneously. We then incorrectly label the outside circumstance as 'the reason' for our emotional response and possible physical actions, when really 'the reason' is always generated by you with your own thought, opinion and preferences. Of course there may not be a physical outward reaction, but you may still be reacting emotionally in a negative self-defeating way by associating your emotion outside of self. Please note there is nothing wrong with reacting to situations, this is life after all. What I am saying is take notice of all your emotional nuances and consciously seek to improve them through conscious means, rather than outside of-self appeasement. This evolves not only your state of being but your naturally evoked physical actions also. Look to see how every negative feeling or nuance you feel is linked to **limitation** in your active belief structure, **your active thoughts**, relative to your preferred preference in the moment that you feel it. Conversely more positive feelings are linked to inner freedom and less limitation within your point of view. This thought to emotional link is something you can prove to yourself over time as you get to know yourself better through self-observation. Observe how all your inner reactions are created by you even if you cannot readily see it to begin with. Like in the case of depression, we know we are depressed but may not as yet identified the mental patterns causing the depression.

This depth of self-awareness can take a year or two of work in cleaning yourself up mentally thus emotionally. Building a deeper introspective awareness of-self showing you how you do indeed create all emotion therefore finding the depth and **freedom** that emotional responsibility ultimately brings.

Without the emotional link to thought you couldn't possibly know there is something to sort out within your mind. There will be situations that really challenge this, you will be feeling bad and not know why for example, but check where your awareness really is, what is your awareness really on whilst other dialogues are bouncing around in your mind? Also consider that negative feeling momentum has a factor in keeping you in a negatively creating head space, in other words it is really hard to think positively when already feeling bad.

Another situation which may challenge you to see your own thought to emotional link is when someone, or something has really pissed you off, hence you cannot fathom how you have created your emotional reaction through 'thought,' and 'opinion' when faced with challenging situations, but you have nonetheless! Only in time with experience looking at your emotional response in relationship to your beliefs and personal preferences in many life situations will you come to this full realization and thus finally take full control of your life.

The more emotionally literate you become, the easier it gets to see within yourself. Consequently, the emotionally illiterate people are often blind to their own self-created problems, blaming and fighting everything around them in order to find some form of inner stability from outside of self, this never works out to well. We have all done this, or do this to some degree, because everything we do we do to feel better.

This work is as hard or as easy as we make it. This is not a race to fix all your immediate problems, this is far more important than that, this is how you truly create quality of life, because life is largely about how we feel moment to moment. Problems are only problems whilst they evoke negative emotion within you. If you are feeling good for whatever reason, then in that moment there isn't a problem! The trick to making this work easy rather than hard is **gentleness.**

Gentleness with yourself and others, go quietly, tread easily, use a discerning mind rather than a critical mind.

A critical mind is a harsh mind. Whereas a non-critical mind is a gentle mind, a truly powerful mind, **true strength is in gentleness**. Develop an appreciative mind.

You will come to realize in time with your newly developing self-awareness just how much control you have over your emotional state, **and gentleness with yourself is a key ingredient in this process.** Ultimately you have full control, although this is often hard to see in the first few years of this work because we are so used to living on an uncontrolled emotional roller coaster simply reacting to life outside of self, or worse in varying states of depression, anger, anxiety, fear etc.

It's natural and normal to have reactions and outbursts, inwardly and outwardly and that's ok, please gently relax and let it pass. I am not suggesting your reactions are bad, I am suggesting your emotional reactions will evolve to something from further up the emotional scale with this work. It's not so much what you do with your reaction in the heat of the moment that counts, it's how you think about it afterwards that is of true value. What the dialogue and awareness in your head is creating emotionally that's where the real work is. Your mental dialogue, the constant chatter, relative to personal preference within life is the creator of your overall tone your state of being, period! The information offered is to help smooth out the emotional roller coaster many are experiencing. This is a concept with tools and techniques you can empower yourself with over time. **This takes gentleness, patience and practice before it becomes second nature to you.**

As previously mentioned, the old saying goes 'If you keep doing the same thing you keep getting the same results.'

So by learning to follow your own inner emotional indicators, by nipping in the bud negative feeling thought patterns before negative feeling mental momentum can grow, and by deliberately learning to think new thoughts that evoke positive feeling momentum within your mental chatter **is doing** something different! However, many people are living on an emotional roller coaster, some with extreme highs and extreme lows. Some vulnerable people may be suffering from any number of mental health issues and can slump into strong states of depression, mental breakdowns, or worse suicidal thoughts or tendencies, hence may be in very vulnerable states and require support on their journey. Most countries have a health system set up for the purpose of psychological support so please use it if needs be. Don't ever discredit help from other sources because you are using a book such as this, all modalities, therapy's, medication and well-being education streams have their merit, do everything in your power to feel better.

Consciously choose.

This work does not mean that you are not meant to feel bad in traumatic situations. It also does not mean you will be happy all of the time either.

Simply get used to following your emotional indicators to help you consciously mould, direct and choose your thought patterns. This means leaning away from, or making peace with subjects that feel off to you, and following your bliss and linger within better feelings longer with deliberate mental intent. This in time, smooth's out the roller coaster creating a sustained steady state of being which means you are more equipped during times of hardship. In fact, times of hardship simply are not as hard anymore once you have truly embodied this dynamic way of thinking thus being! Ultimately you thrive inside in a way that is unique and special unto you. I cannot reiterate enough the power in using your 6th sense (your emotions) in the same way as your sense of touch. Meaning, you wouldn't put your hand on something hot until it causes you an injury, you wouldn't endeavour to tolerate the pain, you would shift away. Consequently, do not learn to tolerate too much emotional pain either, but rather learn to recognize it for what it is, guidance to mould your thought structure within that moment in time.

What you believe about feelings is another point to consider when beginning this work. For example, if you believe you must be angry at this or that, or sad at this or that, then you will be in a pickle within this work because that is 100 percent associating your feelings outside of self. Of course allow yourself to feel however you feel. I am never telling you your anger is wrong, or your sadness is wrong or any emotion for that matter, what you associate it to on the other hand is very often incorrect if you are blaming any outside circumstance whatsoever. I know this is a hard pill to swallow in many situations to begin with. Developing full emotional responsibility takes time and a discerning mind. Reach for a broader perspective whilst striving to move up the scale with a gentle relaxed mental approach as you move through life. You cannot do this effectively if you are associating outside of self in any way. So please don't misunderstand me, every situation is unique and personal unto you and allowing yourself to feel the way you feel is part of the process. Every emotion is natural to your mental interpretation within your life, relative to your personal preferences for your life. Sustainable happiness is achieved gradually over time as you deliberately direct and mould your thought patterns using the emotional link to thought.

Remember life is an interconnection of thought, emotion and physical life experience itself; it's our associations within this that get skewed off at times.

Validation.

Many like to talk about their feelings being validated, either by others or validated by themselves. **The only validation required is that you are not critical of the way you feel.**

The way you feel is the way you feel, and that is ok! You are allowed to feel the way you feel in whatever situation you may be in. Simply acknowledge it, and recognize it for what it is. Which is an emotional indication for conscious change that's all, no need to make a big deal out of it. We all feel and we are all in the same boat of life, so once you get your self-validation in order simply endeavour to move on to a better feeling place from **your perspective** as soon as possible. Of course some things are harder than others and require more understanding. Grief for example is a process that can obviously take time to work through, subject to the degree of pain felt and how the individual continues to think and believe about their particular circumstance. In other words, an individual's experience or lack thereof of in directing thought by how it feels obviously has a huge influence over recovery times. So be gentle, kindness towards yourself and others is a simple basic in my mind, and goes without saying.

A bit about dips back.

Your tone or the way you feel mostly is sort of like an overall balance of all the emotional set points you have on all subjects, caused and created by your **active** thought structure, your **active** beliefs. This is your moment by moment state of being. In other words, where your mind mostly resides thus you feel, this is your tone. Of which we often acclimatize to and consider normal wherever we are on the emotional scale. Of course you can be intensely aware of a limitation in even a singular subject and carry a space of depression for years, and in that negative feeling space it is difficult to find a positive outlook in other subjects thus we can unwittingly perpetuate negative feeling mental momentum in multiple subjects.

Thus when you **first begin** to evoke better feeling states through learning how to redirect your mental activity by how it feels, you can often find yourself feeling better than you have felt in a long time, you have shifted your tone up the scale which is great, good work. But if you then dip down again the emotional pain can feel worse than ever! This is because you are doing good work, you managed to shift your overall tone higher than where it has been for a while, if ever. Thus if you dip back you can feel worse than ever! That damn roller coaster! If you think in terms of vibration you have moved into a better feeling finer vibration nearer love, but then collapsed back into a courser vibration, this difference is now more noticeable thus felt with a higher level of emotional pain. Many instantly think they've failed or that this work is too hard, or it doesn't work.

Ironically the opposite is true, you are in the beginning stages of changing your overall tone, as is evident by now feeling worse than ever. After having moved higher for a period, the dip back feels awful! This really is a bi-polar moment, where you were feeling great, and now feeling not so great! The reason for this is because a lot of your belief structures, your habitual patterns of thought have not yet **adjusted** sufficiently to support a more sustainable state of being. No biggie, simply continue to introspectively feel and adjust your thought patterns sooner rather than later hence stop the dip back from even happening. That's all no need to make a big critical deal out of feeling bad, or any actions taken when in this negative feeling state. Breathe, relax, let go, distract yourself, move on.

In fact, there is no end to this work, you can continue enhancing your state of being endlessly the better it gets the better it gets as you work to understand yourself and this teaching. At any rate, don't let any emotional pain become a big deal for you, learn to appreciate all your feelings good and bad, including and especially if you are in a strong negative feeling state of any kind, negative emotion is not a bad thing! It just appears that way when you are feeling bad for any length of time. Relax, breathe, let go and gently strive forward thought by thought, moment by moment, day by day.

When you have let negative momentum build a bit too much within your mental chatter, or allowed your awareness to grow within a subject that is not serving you, which can happen pretty quickly in subjects you already have strong opinions about that you have not yet adjusted, this is no biggie, this is the work. Recognizing **the smallest subtleties of inner niggles,** not just the big emotional indicators, and then doing everything in your power to consciously feel better in the moment is the work. This means when a negative niggle is evoked you then nip it in the bud by redirecting your train of thought, or reach for a lighter perspective thus do not create a bigger emotional indicator which we then label as bad or a condition. Remembering that strong negative emotion is your friend yelling at you, this is a good friend. This mental introspective behaviour takes practice to get the hang of to become second nature, so please don't be hard on yourself. Learn to drop all criticism of yourself as part of this work. Learning to recognize the smallest subtleties of criticism and negative impulses within oneself builds powerful self-awareness, thus your ability to shift thought patterns in their early stages which is true self-empowerment.

Before we begin the 'how to' part of the book, I wish to bring your attention to the possibility of 'dips backwards' in your feeling space, because if you are a vulnerable person with long standing mental health issues of any sort such as depression, despair or suicidal tendencies, then a dip back can feel utterly insurmountable. If this happens to you then please get professional face-to-face help if required. Do everything you can to get back on an even keel. Please, please understand you haven't failed, you are actually succeeding, and ironically the feeling worse than ever feeling is actually evidence of that!

Realize this horrible feeling moment will pass. This would be a good time for distraction or meditation etc., which we will discuss shortly. Understand that I consider what appears to be out of control emotional states such as depression, high anxiety, anger, grief, fear etc., as only stronger emotional indicators which have grown large due to not working with the smaller emotional niggles earlier which are all asking you for conscious change.

Many people feel like their life is falling apart due to the stronger emotional indicators such as the few just mentioned this is why it is so important to maintain a discerning mind and a gentle approach to this work and yourself. Rather than considering these emotional states as a condition, look at them as your golden inner friend trying to help you out.

Frankly very few people have realized their emotional reactions are their personal inner guidance regarding their self-talk and mental awareness. Even fewer are actually making the effort to sort themselves out with this knowledge, let alone to the degree that I am talking about throughout. So if you trip over at any point on this journey going forward and feel really bad and also find that you are criticizing yourself, stop it! Cut it out! You will notice that negative critical voice only makes you feel worse. That damn self-criticism again! This really is a new skill we are learning to apply.

How many people do you know who consciously use their emotions to guide their thoughts deliberately? Bugger all if any probably. Even after reading a book like this you still have to actually do it, embody it, conceptual understanding is valueless without application. So just like a small child who is learning a new skill we tend to encourage them to try, try again. We too are small children in this work. This concept is asking for a 180 degree turn in the way you interpret your emotional response to life circumstance, to look within rather than out as we have all associated our feelings outside of self. **This is a big ask** hence this work can seem counter intuitive to begin with, it can turn you around inside in many ways especially in situations that are pertinent to you. Relax, breathe, and try, try again gently and quietly.

Direct points to ponder.

Up until this point I haven't been direct in the basic information that I wish to share regarding sustainable happiness. I have complicated things in my desire to paint a broad picture of how emotions felt during human interaction has been misinterpreted outside of self, which is an integral part of **ALL** society's issues. A lack in emotional responsibility is always linked to negative, biased and ignorant types of behaviour regardless of any complexity of circumstance. Anything we consider as an 'issue' within human interactions can be traced backwards to what individuals prefer, think/ believe thus feel, then associate within any situation. Of which action and reaction comes. Problems become an issue or get bigger because we fight and bicker amongst ourselves **with no heed given to taking responsibility for our own created inner reactions**, meaning any battle is really an **inside** roller coaster of emotion relative to what we would prefer to see happen, attain or experience within the situation at hand. Any negative feeling can always be traced back to limitation within **your own beliefs relative to your preferences** involved within the subject at hand. Regardless of whether your opinion is justified or understandable from the point of view of many. Emotional responsibility is vast to understand in depth, and as I have said before a constant and deliberate embodiment of a higher state of being gives the only **true understanding** of this level of inner responsibility. In fact, until there is definitive movement up the scale within oneself there is only conceptual understanding. When you embody a higher state of being with this overall education, you will be able to make peace with other people's behaviour through understanding yourself more fully by seeing how you do indeed create each nuance and twinge feeling within yourself in all situations. Therefore, you will develop a deeper compassion and understanding of yourself and others. This continual development of understanding yourself translates as an awareness of how we all create our inner world, for better or for worse. An awareness grows within you that we are all in the same boat, trying to get a handle on our own life which is usually messed up with outside of-self associations thus chasing our tails all over the place for outside appeasement. We all want to live a happy free life from our own perspective. Quality of life has more to do with what's going on between your own ears than any other factor, therefore, I am trying to build a broad basis of human interaction and how that relates to you whilst adding fundamental basics of happiness that apply to us all. This can be exemplified as: -

- There are only two types of thought; that which feels good and that which feels bad, and you get to choose. So choose the better feeling thought and climb that scale!
- Nothing outside of yourself causes your emotional response, truly!

- Therefore, the way you feel comes from what you chose to focus on, period!
- Focus means any awareness on any subject either in real life, or memories, and imaginings which equals your now thoughts.
- Emotion, feelings, bodily responses are all sides of the same coin and are always evoked via your now in the moment mental activity by what your awareness is on relative to personal preference (desire).
- Thoughts and beliefs are the same thing; a belief is only a repeated pattern of thought.
- Issues may seem ingrained and deep because it is constantly kept alive with your patterns of **now** thought.
- If you can change your patterns of thought, you can solve all your inner demons. An inner demon is only ever a pattern of thought and you can choose new thoughts.
- Congested understanding is a series of limiting beliefs which struggles to allow free flow of thought thus causes strong emotional responses.
- Congested understanding is our individual issues. Which can confuse our interpretation of our thought to emotional link. This usually makes us emotionally reactive and possibly physically reactive. Also leading us to inaccurately believe things are ingrained, or subconscious.
- This entire body of work is about **training** our individual disposition higher up the scale, firstly for yourself, which then ultimately translates to the betterment for all.
- All negative emotion regardless of which label you give it has an awareness in the absence, or limitation of something personally wanted. Every aspect of your personal experience has within it your tastes, and your preferences, from the big life experiences right down to the subtleties of every experience in your life. Any time your awareness builds in an area where something is missing from a limited point of view there is a proportionate negative emotional reaction.
- You can be thinking thoughts with mental dialogues but your awareness is really on something else. Remember awareness is also thought! Where awareness lies is the greatest mental

momentum which is predominantly evoking your now emotion. As you think more thoughts about something else perhaps by giving your attention to another subject, your awareness shifts, as does your emotion as the new momentum of thought changes what your awareness is on. (This is a huge understanding, ponder it.)

Chapter Two

The use of modalities.

Of course the work of the mind, of getting to know oneself, is an ongoing evolution within all of us within each life experience, and frankly can appear all too hard if you are just beginning to sort yourself out to the degree I am teaching here. Therefore, the first practical tool I am going to talk about before we get into the 'real work' is the use of modalities. With the use of a specific therapy type, or modality as I like to call them, we can often overcome many inner emotional ills without doing as much mental gymnastics. Congested understanding is often the cause of these ills both emotional and often physical. A good example of this congestion is when you have strong inner twinges of feeling which you think you cannot deal with mentally; this is where modalities are often used to alleviate such issues. Congested understanding is caused by limiting patterns of thought, your beliefs, where no heed was given to the way the thought felt in the first place thus builds a belief system which struggles with life and new ideas. By consciously shifting these patterns by following your emotional indicators as we have discussed always bears fruition but often takes time because of the confusion and overwhelming inner mess an individual may feel. Therefore, finding a modality that works for you to unlock this congestion by laying new pipes so to speak is often of high value, and a quality first step.

Frankly the work of the mind can appear impossible to some people because of this confusion, this congestion, it is not impossible; it sometimes just takes a bit of effort to get started. Trust that you can do it, trust that you have the answers within you. It is natural for some people to struggle to figure out where to start because they cannot see the trees for the forest so to speak. Their inner emotional world can be overwhelming and many have spent years hiding from their issues, suppressing them and so on, thus creating and adding to the congestion.

Some examples of what I consider to be a modality.

The list of what I consider to be a modality is exhaustive; there is no point in trying to list them all. I have however compiled a list to give examples, which some may argue are not necessarily a modality, or therapy because of the beliefs around how each modality works. But please consider **everything** that exists is a complex set of harmonic vibration of which we are all a part, thus what modality works for you has more to do with your vibrational offering than it does any perceived mechanics of how a modality may or may not work. At any rate, I am sure it goes without saying that any particular modality does not work for all people, and sometimes no modality works for you at all, in which case you have no choice but to do the real work of aligning mind with emotion anyway! Also many people are blending modalities, everything evolves.

- E.F.T emotional freedom technique.
- N.L.P neuro linguistic programming.
- Acupuncture.
- Hypnotherapy.
- All massage techniques.
- Bowen therapy.
- Body talk.
- Acupressure.
- Reflexology.
- All forms of spiritual healing such as Reiki and onstage healings at all churches and spiritual groups.
- Tai-chi.
- Kinesiology.
- Aroma therapy.

- Sound healing such as intuitive song.
- Yoga.

Many therapists will start off asking you if you have any memories that still upset you, or any recurring issues in your life such as angry outbursts, or are you constantly sad and upset for no apparent reason, or aches and pains and health issues etc. Questioning of this nature helps determine the best approach for their particular modality and if you answer yes to any of these questions, it is a good indication you have congested understanding within yourself meaning thought forms (beliefs) that are not serving you.

Talking therapies such as neuro linguistic programming (N.L.P) can be highly beneficial and fast at unlocking congested understanding, usually called a breakthrough in N.L.P, there are brilliant therapists all around the world probably one in your town. On the other hand, some types of talking therapies can add more blockages as some counsellors unwittingly do, hence some types of therapy can take years with limited results for some, this is simply due to this lack in understanding of the emotional connection to thought. **In any talking therapy the patients themselves must understand to reach for a lighter perspective, a new point of view, which is a new lighter thought!** Until you do find that lighter perspective which means you feel better, you obviously haven't achieved anything of lasting value.

On the other hand, often talking is too hard or not the best idea for some people so a good **first** step for those suffering could be a Reiki session, Body talk process, Bowen therapy Acupuncture, E.F.T, distraction or meditation for example. (Distraction and meditation is conscious head work not a modality, more about that soon.)

Whichever modality works for you, if any, is irrelevant, seek relief and you shall find it one way or another.

Modalities in and of themselves have been life changing for millions of people all over the world in all countries and cultures. **They can be simply magical.** Often eliminating problems such as phobias, irrational fears, anxieties and PTSD. They can often take the sting out of memories that bug you, or help with many other issues. Again all of these issues and many more are indicative of congested understanding somewhere within yourself.

When an individual has been suffering through a problem such as these, they often believe that if they can get over their particular problem all will be well. Most certainly life becomes much better when you overcome an issue such as these, but please understand, **'this is only the beginning!'**

The work of redirecting your mind and changing the dialogue in your mind to enhance your state of being is everything to you! **Obviously it is an individual journey which only you can undertake because no one else can think for you.** When you are suffering a debilitating problem like the few just mentioned, it may **appear** impossible to stop or change your mental chatter. This is simply due to the strong mental momentum already in play and not yet having any experience in directing the mind to the degree I am teaching here. In which case a modality can be of massive value to help clean up your inner world as it allows a flow system within your emotional state, making it easier for you to think more clearly and therefore you can engage in the real work of learning how to direct your thought more dynamically and consciously.

Unfortunately, after experiencing a powerful result from a modality many people do not follow through with the real work of the mind, they may be unaware of the possibility of continual enhancement, perhaps they simply see the therapy as their saviour, which in fairness often it is! Imagine suffering debilitating PTSD or a phobia of some sort, any issue which doesn't allow you to engage in life as you would like, and then just like that it's gone through the use of a modality! Of course you would think the modality is the best thing since sliced bread. Frankly some of them are damn right amazing and better than sliced bread! But whatever our issue was we did it to ourselves by creating all sorts of limiting patterns of belief because we took no heed of how the thought felt in the first place. Often because we were too busy blaming the 'outside reason' for feeling bad. For example, we often stay 'in reaction' to a traumatic experience that happened to us because we have associated our feelings **at** the circumstance, thus we perpetuate the 'reaction' as we think more about it moving forward in life. Of course this is because we were unaware that we can change our emotional response to such things thus the problem can build with more negative mental momentum.

Another way an issue can start to develop is by taking on other people's limiting points of view and beliefs as we were growing up, also with no heed to how that felt to us either. We hadn't been taught to choose thought with any emotional link because our parents and those around us were also unaware. So in time these issues grow inside us with the attention they get, the air time between the ears. The more your awareness is on an issue without looking for a lighter perspective, the more negative mental momentum grows into an emotional reaction which we often perceive as a debilitating condition. Often becoming congested understanding in your belief structure. Therefore, manifesting as an issue of some sort. Many people don't want to hear this; they still want to blame the outside reason and make comments like *'You wouldn't understand'* and *'Did it happen to you?'* Of course we've all had our journeys, some of them horrific, some not so bad, some not even bad at all! And yet we can **all** struggle.

Due to our outside associations many believe something must have happened to cause our inner demons, this is not the case, the particular life experience someone has led is irrelevant. **It is our mental journeys that makes us or breaks us relative to our emotional link to thought. Not the experiences we have lived or not lived**. This means it is our mental journey that counts, regardless of experience.

I know this can turn you around inside when your beliefs about life and emotion may say otherwise. As I've said before, when you get your head around all of this and do the work yourself, you will find the inner freedom you are looking for! Of course everyone has different degrees of resilience within their life experiences and emotional world. Yet within this education I am suggesting that you **do not** build resilience, strength, or tolerate negative emotion. Rather I am suggesting you move higher up the emotional scale using each nuance or twinge you feel as an indicator for inner conscious change.

Where is strength and resilience required when you feel good? It isn't! So learn to feel good! Being strong and resilient to negative emotion is not seeking conscious change, which is what your negative emotion is really asking you to do. Which means with time and practice as you move forward day by day, thought by thought, doing your best to nip off feeling thoughts in the bud and deliberately thinking in areas that feel better to you, that interest you in **ALL** areas of your life big and small, what once appeared ingrained in your psyche begins to gradually dissipate bit by bit. This ongoing work has to become second nature, a way of being, a way of thinking if you genuinely want control of your life.

E.F.T Emotional freedom technique. A lifesaver for thousands!

Emotional Freedom Technique (E.F.T) was created by Gary Craig, please visit his website www.emofree.com where he gives away all the information you need on the subject!

I love E.F.T because it is a technique that is yours and once you learn it you have it. Thus you have a self-empowerment tool you can use on yourself at any time without the need to go to a practitioner! It is exceptionally easy to learn and only takes an hour or so on Gary's website to get started, and once learned it only takes moments to apply. If E.F.T works for you, this in and of itself can be life changing. You can allow plenty of flow in your mind and emotional space with the use of it.

I personally discovered E.F.T while I was still riding the emotional roller coaster. I had been crying myself to sleep on and off for a couple of weeks and was fed up with it so I phoned my dear friends, a couple whom have worked together helping people in many ways for years, and asked if they knew of something else I could try (I hadn't discovered the emotional link to thought at this point.) Elizabeth emailed me a copy of Gary's "E.F.T the manual" I got to the sequence section in short order and applied the technique straight away and I felt a lead jacket lift off my shoulders, what a relief! No more tears that night either, problem solved just like that! I am sure hundreds of people reading this book will have similar results as well. Put down this book and teach yourself

E.F.T via that beautiful man Gary Craig's website and see you back here soon! It's worth it so go give it a go.

At any rate I was absolutely astounded with the inner shift that had occurred within me so I absorbed the rest of the manual with much enthusiasm and applied, applied, and applied E.F.T **introspectively on every little emotional nuance I felt**.

I wrote a list as was suggested of all memories that I held within me that still had any form of negative sting to them and tapped them all away. The inner freedom I felt after several weeks of E.F.T is indescribable. Net result; I was more me, more calm, more free, more relaxed and ready to take on the world! I had released a lot of congested understanding, thus could think more clearly, and more importantly began to **recognize my thought to emotional connection.**

What is E.F.T?

The Nuts and bolts of E.F.T is mentally focusing on an area you want improvement in, and tapping gently with two fingers approximately 7 times on various parts of your body, and also some eye movements and humming etc. It's actually quite unusual but by golly it is effective! The points on the body that you are tapping are considered to be your meridian energy lines, the same as in acupuncture and other pressure point type therapies.

Except no needles and it is self-applied! Brilliant!

Some E.F.T stories.

Listed below are some success stories of people using E.F.T

- I talked with an older lady in her 70's about a feeling of claustrophobia she had. To help her with this, we decided to try E.F.T. Well, boy oh boy did it work, the side effects were amazing, in approximately two or three sequences (about 10 mins) she had an amazing physical shift beyond the feeling of claustrophobia alone. She said It felt like energy flowing out of the back of her neck which had been sore since childhood, she said she felt like bungee cords were letting go in her spine and she straightened up from the hunched position she sat in. Afterwards we went for a walk on the beach without the need of her walking frame, which previously she had required even for short walks, and she's hardly used it since then! (3 years ago) She also had other symptoms alleviated such as long-term sore feet, as well as her sore neck, and she could sleep at night now which hadn't been the case in a long time. All of these benefits from applying E.F.T to a feeling of claustrophobia!

- A young man had extreme anxiety to the point that if his mother asked him to go to the supermarket on a simple errand he could barely do it. He said he felt like he may vomit at any moment whilst out and sometimes actually did vomit with inner anxiousness. He was essentially working at home for his parents as he really was quite incapacitated in many ways, and he hated it. He thought he was going mad! Forty-five minutes of E.F.T and the entire problem was gone, just like that!

- A young lady said to me that she felt unwanted and unloved and had felt this way her entire life. She said she had been to countless counselling sessions and therapists but to no avail. She began by telling me her story thinking she needed to tell it, as was normal for all other therapists she had been too. The thing with E.F.T is if you are teaching it, most often the person you are teaching does not always have to share their issue or their painful details, which is something that I personally love. They can apply the technique in the privacy of their mind.

She said that the feeling of being unloved and unwanted felt like a 7 all day every day on a scale of 0 to 10 where zero means you have no issue what so ever and 10 being unbearable. This feeling this inner trauma had permeated every area of her life as you could appreciate. As a result of this unloved feeling she was also a compulsive liar in general conversation about all sorts of things, it appeared to be part of her make-up and looked like a self-defence mechanism some develop to try and 'fit in' etc. At any rate we applied the E.F.T sequence two times to this feeling and boy oh boy as an observer the only way I can describe her **visible inner shift** was to watch a flower blossom before your very eyes! It was that special. She sat there glowing. Interestingly she couldn't string a sentence together for a good 10 minutes or so. She would try to speak, screw her face up and say, "*I can't say that I'm lying.*" That happened several times over the next few minutes as far as I am aware this was a permanent change in her behaviour. The feeling of being unloved and unwanted had simply gone it was vaporized permanently. (I spoke to her 5 years later and the unloved feeling had never been back!)

- I have used E.F.T to reduce and or eliminate the phobia of heights in at least 25 people whilst I was hiking guiding. And several other cases of a fear of flying!

- A fear of birds was a strong issue for one woman I sat next to on a 50 min flight across the country. She said the cost of the flight was worth getting rid of that phobia as it had hindered many areas of her life.

- A boy on the youth offender program said to me he was always angry and wanted the anger gone. He told me he had two specific memories that he was angry about most of the time which he kept private (I love E.F.T), we applied E.F.T to both memories and eliminated the anger within those two memories in moments. He said that it was trippy and awesome that it was gone. He was still an angry type of kid but his overall anger had substantially reduced in that one brief session, as was also noted by the other staff in observation of him.

I was able to have quite a few brief E.F.T sessions with these boys which really helped them on their journeys, a lot of their issues were hurts from the way they had been treated manifesting as anger issues of some sort, among other things. I believe the benefits of E.F.T are worth incorporating into these types of organizations as no harm can be done!

- A lady was suffering from many PTSD moments from her past, her stories were horrific. We had 100 percent success. An amazing hour and a half well spent! No more PTSD!

- I watched an E.F.T training video of Gary Craig using E.F.T with soldiers suffering from debilitating PTSD who had been hospitalized, they could no longer function effectively in society. One soldier was telling his story fully crying as he had done so for about 20 years, it was an horrific story. Within 15 minutes Gary had eliminated this soldiers PTSD! This soldier's sense of relief was palpable even on screen.

E.F.T is downright amazing and it is worth your time and effort to learn. In my experience it has worked for at least 90 percent of the people I've taught, which is a huge success rate for any modality! Take the time and make the effort to learn E.F.T if needs be!

Those of you that have experience in the alternative therapy world will notice that these few stories I've shared could have been helped and overcome by many other modality types. That's the point! Use any modality you personally like, find one that works for you! I love E.F.T especially as it is a true self-empowerment tool and is free to learn via Gary's website. Ironically some people steer clear of 'free stuff' thinking its inferior, in regards to E.F.T you would be making a terrible mistake.

Regardless of which modality you use (if any) they all have what I call a use by date.

They are not ever going to replace your thoughtful and conscious creation of your own state of being, all they do is help you unblock, or unlock congested understanding energy, the inner yuck and havoc within your emotional world caused by your habitual patterns of resistant thought. Therefore, allowing you easier opportunity to move forward, thought by fresh new thought.

For me E.F.T freed me up so I could really feel each thought pattern more readily. Not straight away mind you, it took introspection with a hell of a lot of practice within all aspects of my life experience. I am still learning now of course; this education is constantly evolving within me along with a gradually increasing positive state of being. Just as it will be within you should you engage in the work. A quote I once heard is relevant here: -

"Ageing is an extraordinary process where you become the person you always should have been"

Well that is certainly true for those that are seeking to enlighten themselves and figure a way forward. **Holding an unconditional space of appreciation (love) and happiness is enlightenment in its purest form.** I am certainly more myself and happier than at any other time in my life at age 42. I also know I will be more myself and happier at 52 because of my awareness and continual development of my thought to emotion connection. I intend to be the happiest 100-year-old you would care to meet as life moves on.

Many die having lived a mediocre state of being. It is **never** too late to move forward within your emotional world!

I have had a series of positive shifts through seeking to understand within life, yet I have seen a massive acceleration within myself beyond all other concepts that I have explored, with this realization of directing one's own mind with the understanding that emotion is in direct response to mental activity. Without your emotions you truly would be floating in the wind. Emotion really is your steering mechanism. Emotion is your rudder, so steer your ship!

Everything we do we do to feel better there is no escaping that inherent fact therefore, your state of being, your emotion, the way you feel is everything to you, it just is!

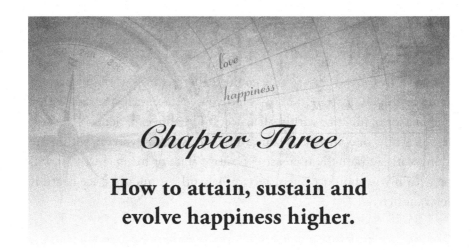

Chapter Three

How to attain, sustain and evolve happiness higher.

Introspection or being mindful of how you feel is the first **skill** to develop. Becoming introspective or mindful of your emotional reactions, which some call bodily reactions, is the singular most powerful thing that you can do for yourself. Right down to the smallest nuance or twinge of reaction within you **because you cannot clean up what you are not aware of**. In other words, developing a self-awareness of your emotional reactions right down to the **smallest subtleties** and then using that awareness as your indicator for either mental change if off feeling or more mental focus if good feeling. Very few people have used their emotional responses to consciously direct thought, most have ignored it, suppressed it, and interpret it outwardly. After a lifetime of this ignoring and suppressing etc., we often create a mess inside ourselves which often seems impossible to clean up. We may feel depressed, flat, unhappy, or just generally shitty inside. Perhaps have little inner-peace, or no direction wondering what our life path is meant to be, and how do I find my path anyway?

When you direct your thinking with your own natural inner guidance, your emotional guidance everything changes for the better. This is a path, a journey that is personal to each of us and takes time and practice **and a discerning mind.**

So the first skill to develop is introspection, a self-awareness of your feelings, become mindful of what's going on within you. Notice the subtle nuances, the tensions in your face, scalp and body, the cringe feelings, the inner anxiousness in all manner of situations, the embarrassment, the worrying what others think, the criticism in all its forms, also notice the warm moments, the happy moments, the appreciative moment's notice it all! But notice it with a gentle curiosity of self, please do not pressure yourself with it. This is not a case of getting technical with labelling each and every nuance of emotion. Just developing an awareness of how do I feel now? Good or bad, in which case I can follow that guidance to either a better feeling place if I feel bad, or enhance and bask in an already good feeling place more. Learn to appreciate feeling good. Learn to appreciate negative emotion because it is telling you to shift your perspectives. Noticing all small nuances of feeling flowing through you good and bad then doing something to constantly enhance your feeling space regardless of how good or bad you feel is key. Because making it your deliberate intent to feel good by consciously creating your state of being your entire life changes for the better and you wonder why everyone isn't doing it, because it becomes so bloody obvious!

For example, when you are in conversation with someone you can notice the reactions going on inside yourself and reach to feel better inwardly, rather than manipulate outwardly within your conversation as is a usual outer reaction to our inner reactions, which is where people shit would normally be born. This inner reaching to feel better rather than outside coercing of others has immense power in developing sustainable happiness. It is the work.

So most people react to their inner reactions, or ignore their reactions perhaps thinking they are normal in this or that situation, sadly not realizing this is where their true inner power is born. So the more you think good feeling thoughts a natural good feeling demeanour becomes a part of you, and everything shifts within you.

Sometimes people will argue that regardless of thinking positive thoughts they still feel bad. This is simply someone who has negative feeling momentum with awareness in areas of life that is causing the upset. Even though they are trying to think better thoughts their awareness is focused in limitation within a subject or subjects. For example, you may be aware of something you need to get done within an aspect of your life, this awareness is strong and you may be feeling overwhelmed or the pressure of it within you. Even though you may be trying to think positive thoughts about the situation, or something else altogether you have a stronger awareness on your issue than the current attempt to move that negative feeling with more thinking. In other words, your emotion is evoked from the momentum of what your **awareness is really on**. This may feel like it's in the background, but awareness is thought! In cases such as this, meditation and or distraction to get your awareness off the issue would likely be a good approach before engaging in any mental gymnastics of trying to think lighter thought.

Your inner world can appear to be a nightmare to begin with.

Although noticing your inner emotional world is key, it can also appear a nightmare and insurmountable to begin with for some people. It can certainly be a case of not being able to see the trees for the forest. In other words, where do you begin? Perhaps you know precisely what the problem is and it seems like it's here to stay. This is often the case for people with a debilitating condition, those whom were severely abused in some way or suffer from war trauma, or perhaps because you cannot see a way to change your life situation and the situation appears to be the cause of your negative state.

Often there is a belief that people can never fully get over there issues or feel better in certain situations. I have even heard some therapists say that you can never fully get over some things. This is in direct correlation to some therapists having seen patients not overcome their issues, and hence come to this incorrect conclusion. If you choose to look for those similar to yourself who **have** overcome their issues then you **will** find them and therefore, giving you hope and inspiration to figure away through for yourself.

Of course it's a personal journey and can take some time, but remember this is more important than a race! Everyone is capable of overcoming any inner emotional issue given the desire and the wherewithal to do so. Your pain is always self-generated, I know we don't like to accept this at first, but seriously this is where your true power lies, you ultimately have full control. Consider how limiting the belief becomes when someone says you cannot get over something, if you believe them then the chances are they will be right because you stop reaching, if you reach at all!

The all-encompassing box.

By now it must be obvious that the most powerful understanding of all: - **Is the knowledge, awareness and willingness to consciously choose your thought by how it feels to you!**

'LIKE HEAT TO SKIN, EMOTION TO THOUGHT'

This knowledge and the willingness to consciously use it by directing your own thought process in direct response to your feeling space, really is a positive step for all people world over. The all-encompassing box you could say for creating personal well-being first and foremost. This ultimately aids in social well-being as our understanding and subsequent embodiment of a higher state of being shows us that we totally create our own individual feeling state regardless of any and all circumstance. Thus a wider group of people evolves with the conscious realization that **their** feelings are evoked by **their** thoughts alone thus developing full personal responsibility.

Thoughts include your opinions and awareness on any subject, and thought includes all your actions because action is always in relationship to your thoughts/beliefs and preferences (values) for life. Observe over time that any negative feeling you feel is caused by some aspect of limitation within your personal belief structure **regarding your personal preference** within the life experience you are currently living, thinking about or observing. Therefore, you can do something about it consciously. Meaning you take full responsibility for the way you feel whilst making the effort to **direct** your thinking, making adjustments relative to **your inner impulses**, always reaching higher, gently, quietly thought by thought, day by day within each life experience. This process creates a natural path to higher degrees of self-appreciation, self-esteem, self-empowerment, passion, zest and **the deliciousness of truly appreciating your life.**

Two real life examples of doing the work go as follows-

- When you become introspective enough you will notice self-criticism more readily and nip those thoughts in the bud early on before they grow out of hand, thus dropping a substantial inner emotional battle.
- Embarrassment doesn't feel good and that's a strong self-critical opinion of yourself within a life experience situation. Thus in doing this work you would reach beyond the feeling rather than tolerating it and thinking it normal, ultimately developing a higher self-esteem in time.

Accordingly, this is an individual journey a process for each of us and it is within life experiences that we really get to hone this skill. This is your life, gentleness and patience with yourself and all others is paramount. Go easily, tread lightly with a gentle attitude for inner enhancement whilst consciously reaching higher. Understanding that genuine and naturally held appreciation is linked with higher consciousness, reach!

Analogy 1 - Snowballs.

To truly take control of our feeling space we need to discern what tools to use when we are in differing degrees of mood thus what tools are most effective at the time. The degree of attention on subjects which causes momentum in thought is directly proportionate to your mood. These analogies help us to understand thought relative to degree both positive and negative.

Thoughts are like snowballs rolling down steep hills, they grow and build momentum with the more attention we give them and with that attention sometimes it seems impossible to get our mind off the thought pattern we have activated. (We activate thought by giving it attention.) Thoughts sometimes **appear** to have a mind of their own. It can seem like the thoughts themselves are drawing you into strong mental rampages either positive or negative in feeling, we all have this; we are all constantly telling all sorts of different stories in our head and having imaginary dialogues, thinking about particular subjects and so on. The more attention you give any subject the bigger it grows in your mind. The thought builds momentum growing larger just as a snowball does rolling down a hill.

Your thought patterns grow in complexity and size with more attention given to them, which in turn grows the feeling attached to the pattern positive or negative. Your 'attention' is the slope that adds the momentum to your thoughts. The degree you care about a subject relative to your personal preferences and relative to any limitation in your beliefs about your preference is the determining factor as to whether your thoughts are positive feeling or negative feeling.

The more attention thus thinking you give any subject the greater the mental thus emotional momentum hence the harder it is to get your mind off it.

Of course when you are living any experience the momentum and direction of your thought is often intrinsically connected to the actuality of what you are experiencing. This means we need to consciously develop for ourselves different tools to use within different life experiences and for different degrees of mental thus emotional momentum.

You could liken every subject you engage in or think about to a snowball in your mind. Some have very strong downhill momentum (positive or negative), and some do not. As just described this is subject to the airtime a subject gets between your ears. You could visualize piles of snowball's representing your thoughts, beliefs, skills, issues and life passions. Some of these snowballs will be large, some barely a hand full, and that's simply due to the time you've spent engaging in and thinking about those subjects. This is also where learned skill is born. Some will be great feeling snowballs; things you like to do in life with all sorts of lovely feelings attached. Some won't have much in the way of emotion attached at all, and then of course there are the mean old grumpy snowballs with strong negative momentum.

Guess what? Grumpy snowballs can melt and happy snowballs can grow!

Grumpy snowballs melt through **lack of attention** which means the thought dissipates as it is not being activated as much. Hence the old expression 'time is a healer,' but really it is not time that is the healer, it is life's distractions which helps us shift the level of **attention** given to a subject between the ears. The thought then dissipates, the snowball melts. Making peace with a subject naturally over time in the case of, 'time is a healer' is similar to what happens when you consciously reach for lighter perspectives within an issue. In other words, by redeveloping your beliefs and points of view within an issue by seeking higher lighter relief is more of a direct approach, rather than simply ignoring an issue or accepting it as normal to feel this way in X, Y or Z circumstance, (which is associating outside of self), thus it usually takes time and life distractions for the attention on the subject to dissipate, thus resolve itself.

So stop thinking by getting your awareness off a subject, or change the thinking, both are relevant and powerful tools to understand which we will cover more fully shortly. At any rate we are always doing this, one minute we are thinking about something, then the next we are thinking about something else our mind shifts all over the place and is the cause of the emotional roller coaster many of us are on. However, it's when we consciously direct our mind relative to the feelings evoked that we gain control of our state of being.

For example, some people struggle to recover from the death of a loved one, or make peace with death at all, which of course is natural and understandable. Sometimes their mental activity, their awareness is drawn and focused in the absence of their loved one. (Meaning their awareness is on an unwanted experience that they care about, their preference is not met.) Plus, what do they believe about the subject of death? How much limitation about life and death is in an individual's belief structure? Is this part of the problem? Perhaps they need a lighter less limiting perspective about death?

This awareness in something missing, limiting or lacking regardless of what the subject is, not just in the case of death can stay active in somebody's mind for a life-time, hence the emotional struggle which isn't so good. Of course in time most people recover to varying degrees, hence, 'time is a healer.' On top of this, **many people believe they must feel bad;** therefore, think something is wrong if they feel ok within the subject at hand, thus can perpetuate their emotional struggle. Any belief that presumes you must feel a certain way in X, Y or Z situation is 100 percent associating the way you feel outside of self and will never do you any favours within your life. **You must make it your dominant intent to find mental thus emotional resolution within yourself regardless of what life throws at you.**

I know this can feel and appear counter intuitive and harsh, especially if you are raw and ragged in a recent hurt as horrible as losing your child or loved one for instance. Please, please try and grasp what I am saying here because when you get it, when it clicks, you will find a freedom of-self unsurpassed.

You certainly wouldn't go up to somebody at a funeral, or near after, and thrust a psychological concept like this in their face.

So apart from the deliberate and conscious reaching and seeking for new and different ideas beliefs and concepts within your thoughts to feel better, or melting grumpy snowballs through deliberate lack of attention, (not suppression), new beliefs, new thoughts, new points of view are also created through new experience. Thus potentially allowing for a freer flowing system between your ears, which is our goal for a free flowing appreciative life experience.

For example, someone may be suffering the loss of a loved one and has not yet made peace with death. Let's say this person has had no personal experience with esoteric experiences or belief structures outside of life on earth, therefore perhaps believes that once you're dead that's it, end of story. Perhaps they are very scared about dying. Let's say they are well into adulthood and have set ideas about this and are really struggling with a death from 5 years earlier of someone they loved dearly. Then seemingly by accident they have an experience with a medium or clairvoyant of some sort which they had never had or heard of before. This clairvoyant tells them many things about this dead person and themselves that they shouldn't rightly know and couldn't know in a black and white perception of the world. This gives them solid enough experience that there actually is something else beyond death and they now have questions about this subject thus seek out new knowledge about it and more experience like it. Or perhaps they personally have a clairvoyant or clairaudient experience themselves for the first time which was so vivid, so clear, they simply now know all is well. Thus they are able to move on emotionally from their hurt. **Their thought, their belief about death is changing becoming lighter through their interpretation of new experience**. The new experience has generated new points of view and questions therefore their snowball, their ideas and beliefs change shape.

Of course new experience can create new thought for better or for worse subject to what you do with it in your mind, how you interpret the experience. In any case your belief changes, grows, and depending on what you do between your ears **potentially** moves you up the emotional scale!

So obviously with deliberate seeking of thoughts that feel better, and especially once this mental behaviour is second nature to you, the time it takes to heal from any situation is enhanced 100 fold!

Remember every experience is an opportunity to reach higher.

Analogy 2 - The car and handbrake.

The second analogy goes like this, imagine a car at the top of a hill where the car is representing a pattern of thought, you are standing outside the car when the car begins to move slowly towards the edge of the hill. If you notice the car moving early enough because your introspection is active, meaning you are mindful of **all** your emotional nuances, your twinge, cringe feelings etc., you can nudge up against the car in the early stages and reach in to pull the handbrake on fairly easily meaning you change tack in your mind fairy readily or drop the subject altogether. On the other hand, as is often the case, we simply allow our mind to wander and before you know it the car is half way down the hill, at this point if you jump in front of the car to stop it you'll get flattened! Getting flattened means you are in a really crappy feeling place because the negative feeling momentum is strong and trying to think your way out is hard work or nearly impossible. Therefore, it is easier in the early stages to pull the handbrake on. Fortunately, like all cars freewheeling downhill, the hill eventually runs out as does the cars momentum. In the case of you and your negative mental momentum that could mean you have gone to bed for the night, or that you have been distracted in life by something else, as was described at the beginning of this book. Or you have consciously utilised distraction or meditation rather than trying to think yourself up the scale in these instances. Perhaps you finally drop a limiting belief and replace it with one of less limitation, therefore creating positive momentum.

Your awareness of the strength of your emotional state lets you know where you are on this hill therefore which mental tools or modalities you can use to deal with each emotional state you may find yourself in.

Obviously learning to nip off feeling thought in the bud sooner rather than later by pulling the handbrake on ultimately becomes one of your most dominant tools. This takes plenty of practice and introspective self-awareness.

You **must** make the effort to build new snowballs, deliberately thinking about things you like help to melt and dissipate your current pile of grumpy snowballs. Consciously building new momentum on topics that feel good to you removes awareness, thus momentum from the other topics that are causing you grief, try and make this your dominant practice. In other words, a grumpy snowball sits in the sun melting, while you build new ones elsewhere. Remember what your attention is on activates thought about it.

What we are doing in essence is retraining ourselves into a higher better feeling disposition, and from this higher place it is easier to find lighter points of view within any grumpy snowball that may require it. However, many snowballs will have dissipated completely thus are no longer a problem. As I've said before, at first this can be hard work but in time it becomes second nature and you can't imagine not directing your mind in this way.

So building a repertoire of tools you can use to feel better during different emotional states is of paramount value.

You need to use a discerning curious mind, not a critical mind, and follow your emotional indicators as to which tool is appropriate for you to use in any given moment. Can I simply pull the handbrake on (pivot my mind elsewhere), or is it too late for that do I need to distract myself with X, Y or Z activity instead?

This is a trial and error thing that you have to do for yourself hence where your real experience comes from, ultimately creating an inner wisdom and freedom few come to realise.

You have to make it your dominant intention to feel good and make the effort to direct thought by how it feels to you if you are to find any real zest and passion for life. This is definitely a personal journey and process, one that won't happen overnight, but it does happen especially when this inner behaviour becomes second nature and not so heady.

We need to discern where we are on the hill of negative or positive momentum and use our wisdom as to which approach to take. This really is a cure all, type of inner behaviour.

The morning after momentum.

You can evoke negative momentum or positive momentum within your feeling space through observation of things you deem good or bad. Remember in observation of anything your thoughts, beliefs, opinions and **preferences** are activated whether you are aware of it or not. For example, have you ever watched a movie which evoked horrible feelings within you in your reaction to it, which lingers long after you finished watching the movie? It appears you are no longer thinking about the movie and yet you still have this horrible feeling, perhaps you may have watched a real tear-jerker film the night before and now 11 am the next day at work the momentum is still within you. Although you may not be specifically thinking about the movie itself the negative momentum carried on after you awoke. When negative feeling momentum has a hold like this it is really hard to think positively much beyond the negative space you are in without deliberate conscious effort. Hence more often than not, you can unwittingly add more negative momentum in all other subjects that come to mind, possibly reacting outwardly in a knee jerk kind of way. Often people do this to themselves in observation of any number of subjects in life, not just in watching a movie. This is where the work is, **reach** for an emotional shift within yourself, look for relief, do everything in your power to feel better. Where are you on the hill within your momentum?

Conversely, you may find yourself in a good feeling space to any degree, rejoice in the realization of this, pat yourself on the back and **reach** to hold this space longer, milk it for all its worth, enjoy feeling good for the sake of feeling good. However, if you find yourself in a peak high enjoy it sure, peak highs are fun but not the goal for sustainable happiness. Appreciate the fact that you feel good and consciously hold your good feeling space longer but not in a hyped up sort of way. If you are one who can have manic messy highs, you still need to gain control of any messiness within the hype. Simply recognise the messiness within any hyped up experience and over time quietly learn to redirect yourself into a relaxed **appreciative** flow rather than a manic messy sort of high. Appreciation is the purest form of a steady high state.

Evoked emotion.

Emotion is evoked within us in all areas of life. It appears 'things in life' evoke emotion from us. Negative emotion is a good thing because it lets us know where our particular work is, naturally evoked positive emotion is delightful, the more the merrier! Love at first sight, a natural click, connection or vibe with certain people, a smile as you observe children at play, the ocean, lake, forest or stream perhaps, adventure and intrigue within your chosen activities, this is the essence of life. The more naturally evoked positive emotion in an individual's life the better. Life evokes emotion, it just does! The trap is the incessant association outside of self, thus the incessant chasing for outside stuff and experiences to evoke it within you. You have to get over the outside chase and allow for a positive feeling space within yourself regardless of X, Y or Z circumstance! Ultimately the embodiment of this work allows more of these moments into your experience, which continues to get deeper the more connected to yourself you become.

Also in regards to instantly evoked negative emotion within any daily human experience such as when bumping your head, stubbing your toe, something you are using breaks, or somebody criticizes you etc., it's natural to react instantly. Simply do your best to let it go, try not to hang onto it or let it upset your overall tone. Certainly endeavour not to spend the next hour in negative mental dialogue about it! In time these instant reactions become lighter and can change completely as you do this mental/emotional work in all areas of your life. Reach beyond tolerance or suppression so as there is nothing to tolerate or suppress!

Five steps to attain sustainable happiness.

1. Make it your dominant intention to feel good.

Firstly, you **must** make it your **dominant intention** to feel good **and** take full responsibility for your feelings in time discovering that you have full control.

In all life situations you always have the option of picking a better feeling thought or a worse feeling thought, you also get to choose what to give your attention too. If your dominant intention is to feel good, then you will always strive to harmonize your thoughts in conjunction with your emotional indicators. In time, you thrive inside.

If your dominant intention is something else, such as to be clever, to win an argument, prove a point, or fight against an issue of any sort, you will not be harmonizing yourself.

Create inner harmony **first** and all else follows.

Making it your dominant intention to feel good means you are more likely to build deeper levels of introspection, which means you will recognize and take notice of every subtlety of nuance, tension and twinge feeling of emotion positive or negative more readily and can therefore consciously do something with it.

2. Mindful introspection. Become aware of the times you feel good and hold it longer.

Your joy, your happiness, your overall disposition, comes from how you direct your mental dialogue your thinking relative to how you emotionally react to it.

Thinking is a focus, your observation of all things, an awareness which grows with your attention. We are usually very sloppy with this awareness, thinking all over the place with no regard to the way any of it feels. When you find yourself feeling good you **must give more attention to simply feeling good for feeling goods sake whilst looking to hold the feeling for longer consciously.** This builds positive momentum which helps us to think more positively in other areas of life, meaning we continue to build positive momentum within our minds thus state of being. When you are feeling good notice what you are thinking about and hold the attention longer by giving it **more attention,** ponder it for longer until the subject runs out of steam so to speak. When the subject that initially evoked the positive feeling runs out of steam then make the effort to deliberately think about anything else that is positive to you, again endeavouring to hold the good feeling space for even longer. Learn to do this in a natural, gentle and relaxed way.

In time with self-observation become introspective of the relationship between **all** your thoughts and feelings, recognize how you feel relative to all your habitual patterns of thought. In their desire to fix things people doing this work often unwittingly tend to give more attention to times of feeling bad, rather than times of feeling good. They may try to figure out why they feel bad and what thought caused this or that bad feeling. Although this is a required self-awareness we can unwittingly add more negative momentum to our negative states simply by giving it more attention when trying to figure it all out! Hence sometimes we keep negative momentum going for longer accidentally creating bigger negative snowballs because we were already well down the slope! Remember attention is the slope for the snowball. In these times it can seem impossible to find a lighter perspective because our thoughts tend to add more negative momentum rather than positive, hence this mental work takes gentleness, a discerning mind and experience to grasp. Our attention on any subject always expands it, expands the thought, the belief and thus the feeling.

You must use a discerning mind and **reach** for a feeling of relief if you can, if not, you are well down the slope thus you must learn to drop the subject altogether for the time being.

We all do this to some degree expanding the problem in our minds unwittingly, so learning to give more attention to good feeling thought and neat moments in life builds and expands positive momentum where we as individuals want it. Which makes it easier to think clearer elsewhere in life, because it is easier to think positive when already feeling positive. **Practice this a lot and be deliberate about it** as it truly is a powerful practice, learning to get your attention off subjects that you are struggling to make peace with, by deliberately thinking about something else to **consciously feel better first**. Because when you are feeling better it is easier to find clarity within your bigger issues you may be dealing with. Try not to seesaw between one and the other trying to fix an issue, but rather focus on finding and holding that higher feeling place as your dominant target, then see how things begin to resolve themselves in your mind. The depth of this statement can only be understood with multiple experiences in actually doing it. Holding genuinely good feeling spaces longer and on purpose is powerful work. It is a happy life we are wanting after all.

3. Deliberately choose what you think about.

You must become more discerning. Start to deliberately choose what subject you think about by how it feels, get fussy and choose everything you focus on by how it feels to you. This includes all things such as what you look at or are allowing your awareness to be on such as music, television, world events, local events, politics, people, traffic, weather, everything!

Most of us choose the clothes we like to wear with a particular discernment, use this type of discernment to choose your thoughts, your focus, the things you observe, using **your** feelings as your guide no one else's. This practice helps shift your overall tone higher thus allowing you to make peace with the subjects that interest or bug you as just discussed.

4. Find new points of view, beliefs that feel better to you.

There are of course times and situations in life where you need to think about and deal with issues because they simply are part of your life and yet they feel bad. When this is the case do your best to look for thoughts and points of view that feel better to you within the subject. Obviously use a discerning mind, reach to feel better and try not to add more snow unwittingly. Do the work you're learning here when you are faced with these moments, or at times when you are feeling good and the subject comes up in your mind. However, be mindful of your emotional indicators, if you are really upset this is **NOT** a good time to do mental gymnastics, this would be a time for distraction or meditation. Whenever you notice your negative emotion getting worse, stop! Get your mind and awareness off this train of thought ASAP using whatever means you can because if you are feeling worse you are adding more snow, more negative momentum! Remember we want to build positive momentum in nice feeling snowballs as this is where skill, practice, experience and wisdom comes from within this work, not to mention you will truly be getting to know oneself. Most people unwittingly add more snow when trying to think out a problem because they are not taking heed of the build-up of negative emotion, thus you must be mindful of the direction your emotional state is heading any time you try to figure out your particular issue. This can be tricky to learn to begin with! Remember that regardless of where you are on the scale, there is always a feeling of relief as you move up the scale. Seek this relief and when you find it smile, and recognize that you have done good work, no matter how slight.

Finding a completely different perspective on any subject that feels lighter, exciting or a breath of fresh air to you, is the work. Because a different perspective, a different point of view, is a different thought! Remembering that we all want a happy life from our own perspective and this is totally governed by your chosen direction of thought.

Often trying to mentally search your own mind for a new thought **appears** impossible to begin with. You could try asking your friends if they have a lighter perspective, but be aware that often your usual friends have a similar perspective to yourself and we can feed off each other in a negative way, thus not helpful in finding a lighter perspective. So instead try chatting to a life coach, counsellor or psychologist, start of by saying, *'Hey I have this issue, I simply want a fresher lighter perspective have you got one?'* If these people are not helpful either, or you'd rather try a different route, find something, anything that has a possible different perspective, a book you can read, or do some research on the internet for example. Constantly speaking about your issues with friends etc., without seeking genuine relief from the issue simply keeps the issue active adding more negative emotional momentum. Try and refrain from needing other people to agree and understand your pain to feel better yourself, this is unsustaining. The idea is to get to a lighter fresher perspective within yourself ASAP thus you are self-empowered!

5. Make the effort.

Actually make the effort to do the above things consistently and deliberately in your daily life, come to fully understand the three mental options coming up below and use them consciously until it becomes second nature. Many people only make the effort to do this work in a traumatic situation, but when the situation has passed they return to their usual thinking patterns thus stay on the emotional roller coaster, this makes life hard work and is not very effective long term. You must make this work your natural behaviour which creates a flow system that allows you to effortlessly process the day's events into and through your mind as you move throughout the day, and can thus go to bed with an empty head! This ultimately means you are more adept at dealing with traumatic situations should they arise.

Also if you do not redirect your mind relative to your own inner impulses, you inadvertently continue to build more congested understanding within you, blocking your own flow and therefore you can become confused, frustrated, stressed depressed and so on.

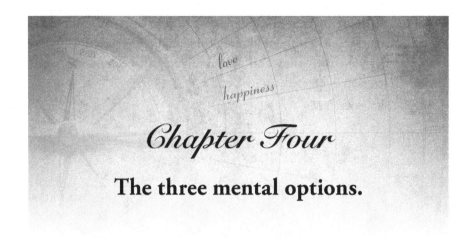

Chapter Four

The three mental options.

Within **any moment in time** you really only have three mental options to enhance your overall well-being, and they require more clarification, these are: -

- Stop thinking.
- Seek better feeling perspectives, within your beliefs, patterns of thought, your life issues.
- Think and build new thought patterns.

Understanding these three options through your deliberate use of them over time will enhance all teachings ever taught on personal well-being. These three options are foundation work to be used within **any** other technique or teaching for personal wellbeing beyond the picture I paint in this book. If you take these three options and super impose them over and within all life situations and any technique or teaching to attain personal well-being, you will develop the keys to life everyone is looking for. They really are your **only** options in any given moment. In fact, in any given moment you will be engaging in any one of these mental behaviours whether you are aware of it or not. However, it is the deliberate and conscious use of them in relationship to your emotional indicators where true power is born.

Option One - Stop thinking.

Stop thinking about that subject or looking at that subject that is giving you grief, you are only adding more snow to the snowball. Slow down thought, diffuse thought, redirect thought, chill, breathe, relax, let go, meditate. Endeavour to stop thought **which really means shifting your awareness elsewhere** especially if you're in a very crappy place. Trying to think your way up the scale when you're in a crappy mood or living a shitty situation is very difficult because of the slope you are on, the momentum in your thought and awareness. This can appear like suppression in the early stages of doing this work, however if you can completely get your awareness off a subject, the subject is not an issue in that moment and is not suppression because your awareness is off it. Hence this is why when you are no longer thinking about it, or aware of it you will feel better. Of course your physical life issue or situation may not be resolved with your awareness no longer on it, but you will feel better and you are training your state of being upwards which means you can think clearer from a higher state in more situations more often. You are shifting your overall disposition which is vital because a happy life is about holding a higher state regardless of your situation!

Most people don't consciously do this work meaning they can suppress and bottle up their issues causing problems for themselves. However, as you develop an understanding of how your mental activity relates to how you feel within all areas of your life, those areas you may have suppressed will get sorted out as your overall tone lifts. Of course getting your mind off something can appear impossible when living an unwanted experience, sort of like having your toe whacked with a hammer and then telling yourself not to think about your sore toe. It's not only possible, it's imperative that you learn how to shift your awareness to deliberately feel better. Because when your awareness is somewhere else that means you've stopped thinking about it! This is the essence of meditation in the sense of mind focus and can also be encapsulated into the saying a wise man once said which was, *"Turn the other cheek"!*

Option Two - Seek better feeling perspectives within your beliefs and patterns of thought.

Morph the thought itself, search for a lighter perspective within the subject as has been previously discussed in the five steps to happiness and throughout this book. This is distinctly different to trying to fix problems outside of self as is a habit that most of us naturally tend to do. Seek a lighter feeling perspective within the subject of life that you're thinking about or dealing with. Find a better and usually broader less limiting, dynamic way of looking at it. When life situations trigger emotion within you this is where the work is! If your dominant intent is to feel better with an ultimate goal of learning to hold a natural state of appreciation, then you are consciously seeking up the scale in all areas of life as life evokes reactions within you. Then in time the snowballs you removed your awareness from, dissipate melt or morph entirely.

Depending on which aspect of your issue is triggered, and what mood you're in at the time equates to how easy it is to do the work of option two. Because option two really is shifting limiting beliefs. You will float between all three options.

Option Three - Think new thoughts.

Build new snowballs! **Find things you enjoy and focus on them more and more. Try and make this your dominant practice above and beyond options one and two**. Study subjects you like, simply for the pleasure of it. What you give your attention to grows within you, thus takes your attention off other negative thought patterns. New thought patterns are the ultimate goal for creating any positive state which is imperative to us all. Seek new things to think about with a curious relaxed attitude.

Also consciously change the way you observe things throughout your day make an effort to look on the brightside more often than not, until it isn't an effort anymore. A practical way to look on the brightside is **learning to look for things you like as you move through your day**, whilst dropping your attention away from the things that annoy you. **This is far more important than it first appears.** This practice gets easier and easier building positive momentum within you, which enables you to do the work of option 2 more readily thus enhancing your consciousness. It is easier to think say and do positive things when you are already feeling good so focus on making it your dominant intent to feel good.

Activating thought, is really the only option.

Life is more about how we feel than is often realised and as you will come to know through doing this work, the way we feel is completely between our own individual set of ears. We all want to be happy and we all want to live and experience a good life from our own perspective. These three mental options although are normal mental habits we all naturally do as part of our thinking process, are however a whole new ball game when you are consciously and deliberately using them to think in relationship to how you feel as afore mentioned. This is huge and where true inner freedom comes from. If you take it quietly as I'm encouraging, eventually it becomes more natural relaxed and free flowing. The reality is you can only ever activate, direct, or choose thought even in the deepest states of meditation your awareness is still on something, somewhere, somehow. **The only option you ever really have is what thought do I think now.**

The three mental options simply show you different ways in which to **activate** thought by moulding, and directing your thinking in a way that **serves you better.**

Sure for some it can take a while to sort yourself out within each life experience that comes your way so try, try again.

Consciously enhancing yourself within life like this is a process that is never ending and evolves within you endlessly. **Thought is infinite** and like it or not you get to play in the arena of thought for your entire life, so consciously using a combination of all three options with a discerning mind that is directing your mind relative to how you feel will be a damn good habit to build.

The depth and power of option 3, the ability to deliberately shift to a new idea in your mind is immense, it cannot be overlooked.

There are many people who simply want to feel better and really don't want to know the depth of what I am trying to share within this book. In that instance, if you can simply realize **you have the ability to think about anything** and trust that it is your current **mental focus** that is causing

174 | *Richard Haycock*

your crappy state even if you don't know what specific thought that is. Then you make the effort to think about something else, anything else and **have actually shifted your awareness,** then you will gain insight in your own ability to create your feeling space which is all you really have to know.

Remember when something in life distracts you and you find yourself feeling better this is because your focus has changed. With this knowledge you can use tools such as mantras for example to consciously cause these inner emotional shifts, which essentially **is** thinking something else once your awareness has actually shifted. That's all you need to do, make the effort it's simple! Well, conceptually it seems easy but it still takes effort learning to focus the mind relative to feeling. It is a practiced skill which in time becomes second nature. At any rate, anyone can do a mantra, or meditate in some way that is appropriate to them distracting themselves mindfully if their dominant intent is to feel better, to feel appreciative. No one else can do it for you! Please be aware trying to figure out which thought caused your negative state, although is required in your overall redevelopment of habitual patterns, can also stifle you as well by unwittingly adding more momentum where you don't want it. Hence the work of option two can be tricky and is best done when in a calm relaxed inquisitive state. Options 1 and 3 are good for creating a higher state which in turn helps you to do the work of option 2, if you still need to. Sometimes you may be doing the work of options 1 and 3 for weeks and simply cannot get to the work of option 2 within a particular issue, this is because the issue continues to evoke displeasure within you, hence it can seem impossible to find a lighter perspective. Please relax and continue with options 1 and 3 for as long as required, sometimes you will be amazed when you discover the issue you were trying to work on is no longer an issue once your attention has been sufficiently off it for a period of time and you have subsequently raised your overall tone. Work in all areas of your life and in time you gain emotional control.

In essence you cannot really stop thinking as such, you cannot meditate all day with no thought given to your life, even in meditation your awareness is still active somewhere somehow as afore mentioned. All you can really do is choose what to think or where to give your attention. Hence when you use options 1 or 3, really you are endeavouring to think something other than the thought that was bothering you. So you can only really activate thought and these three options help you to see how to make change in a practical way. Option 2 is actually a spin on option 3 because ultimately an improved lighter thought within a subject is a new thought! You can only ever activate thought. Choose wisely.

The work of little niggles.

Strive beyond your negative little niggles, and like a dripping tap your positive state of being bucket fills!

With your introspection developing your awareness of the small little niggles, nuances and tensions positive or negative within you become more obvious to you. You must recognize these subtle little niggles and strive beyond the negative ones within each life experience that evokes them. **This must become your daily moment-to-moment work, it is very powerful work** because as a niggle brings an issue into your awareness you can reach to overcome it thus you harmonize and stabilize yourself in a very powerful way. **More importantly** than overcoming your little annoying niggles **is recognizing your positive impulses** such as peace, excitement, appreciation, happiness or whatever positive state you may be in **and deliberately try to hold the feeling for longer,** make this a more dominant intention rather than trying to fix issues.

Do not underestimate the work of small niggles, **because this is the work!** There is a gradual and permanent enhancement of yourself as you stretch out the positive moments longer whilst also reaching beyond your negative, subtle and small inner reactions. This needs to become second nature to you, make this second nature to you! Frankly, everyone, the entire world would benefit from this emotionally responsible way of being!

Furthermore, your little niggles are easier to deal with and not so bothersome as tackling our big life issues head on. Your little niggles are always associated to your bigger issues in some way at any rate so overcoming them one by one is quality work of redeveloping beliefs to those that serve you better. By doing this work you are building a deeper more enhanced state of being, you are shifting your tone your set points higher. Approach this work with an excited interest in yourself, rather than making it a big important must do with critical overtones. Make light of it and gently reach and strive to overcome your negative inner impulses whilst looking to hold the better feeling spaces longer and just like a dripping tap gradually fills a bucket, your state of being fills with more calm, clarity, vibrancy and passion etc. In other words, your tone shifts higher up the scale.

For example, any time you feel even the slightest embarrassment within you, perhaps you react around a particular work colleague or acquaintance, or public speaking, whatever the situation is, do everything in your power to reach beyond the feeling. You may simply recognize the feeling and talk yourself away from it within your mind, using comments such as:

- It doesn't matter what they think, it only matters what I think.
- Oh oh, here's that damn feeling again I don't need to feel like this, it's only self-criticism, I can let this go now.
- Ah there it is again, there is no need to feel like this, what will it even matter in a 100 years' time?

Of course you have to find words that are appropriate for you within each life situation or simply recognize an off feeling, then strive beyond it within each experience that evokes it. You don't necessarily need a mental dialogue about it, the life experience itself and your desire to improve your state of being in the moment is everything. Nothing teaches like life experience.

Please remember It Is more important to recognize the good feelings and then stretch them out longer regardless of what evoked them **because what you focus on grows within you.** In other words, positive momentum builds. We all want to feel good so notice it and appreciate it when you are feeling good. Consciously appreciate the good feeling and appreciate the experience and thoughts that evoked the good feeling within you, whilst also not associating your feelings outside of self, do not become attached to the experience, become attached to the feeling and deliberately create the feeling!

In time and hindsight, you will begin to recognize the subtleties of improvement within you, applaud yourself as you see any shift within, no matter how slight. Each drip fills the bucket!

When you feel a negative niggle, perhaps you can simply imagine feeling better, simply reach for improvement however you can within all life moments that these nuances are evoked within you. Perhaps modify your behaviour as best as you can in each moment if that is what is required, perhaps you have a habit of angry outbursts and reactions, simply reach and try again and again within each experience.

You could use a modality such as E.F.T. or perhaps you can use light work in the heat of the moment, I will briefly talk about light work shortly in the tools section. Perhaps jealousy of some kind is an issue for you, guilt maybe, anxiety, are you sensitive and easily upset, or do you have a need for forgiveness, are you feeling fidgety? It does not matter what the feeling is or how the feeling is evoked, whether by your own behaviour you wish to modify or evoked within any life situation. In all cases strive, strive, strive to move up the scale within each experience. Thus like how a dripping tap soon fills a bucket, deeper more naturally held states of **appreciation** become **your natural** experience as your consciousness expands to a less limiting appreciative state.

All the small things.

Consciously and deliberately coming to understand your inner impulses and following them all day every day, on all the little things is best. Trying to do this work only in the heat of some big issue is hard work; it must become second nature to you. Use your discernment, trying to do mental gymnastics when there is strong negative momentum on any subject usually sucks you into more negative attention thus emotion and can drive you crazy. In cases like that options 1, or 3 are better choices to engage in. This means learning to genuinely relax inside yourself, let go, and breathe.

We usually unconsciously react outwardly in some way instead of looking within. In other words, not using our inner niggles and impulses for conscious change. Thus like heat to skin, we get burnt, we inadvertently create our own issues. Quite simply as you consciously activate or choose good feeling thought, you are not activating bad feeling thought in that moment. Therefore, your emotional reactions evolve within you thus your interactions with the world around you evolve for the better.

This information can be difficult to apply to begin with, it can be a slow process because you really have to make it your dominant intention to feel good, thus follow your inner emotional indicators right down to the subtle nuances of feelings, and frankly few do. Usually we just want our issue fixed now dammit! Regardless of what the situation is, whether it is a life circumstance or a heavily held negative state, both are emotional.

That said when you have big internal pain and confusion and everything seems to hard, or a subject has permeated every area of your life, it can seem impossible to do this work to begin with. Which is why I am suggesting the use of modalities, therapy's and medication if required in conjunction with this real work to get you going. It's worth keeping in mind that if you have massive change and success with a modality, please don't get trapped in the belief that the modality is a cure all, or that you must go to this amazing healer person, or therapy all of the time. I believe in self-empowerment and **know** you can do it for yourself. Please don't misunderstand me, definitely use everything in your power to feel good, modalities can help fast track our movement into a happier freer state, as E.F.T did for me. It is also possible that you may try many modalities with little success, and this is where this perspective we are discussing is of its highest value. Because you can always do this work, and you **will** get results from this internal endeavour the more you naturalize it within yourself.

If you do get great results from a modality and you feel better than you can ever remember feeling, please also keep in mind that this is only the beginning of your new life! You have unlocked congested understanding energy, and will **acclimatize** to your new state of being fairly readily. Therefore, continuing this real work will bring you to an ever-evolving passion and zest you didn't even know existed!

Life itself will give you inner shifts, such as 'Ah Ha' moments, you may drop a concept, or belief, or simply let go of something, and you can have a result similar to what a modality may give you. In reality, in fact in all cases including within the use of any modality you may use, you have naturally done the work yourself through your desire for change, and your life experience provided the means one way or another. Don't gloss over these experiences where change has occurred, they are powerful moments in time, specific to the enhancement of your life! And that is everything to you!

Chapter Five

Tools.

The 'Imagine how it feels' tool.

I have been harping on about how thought creates all emotional nuance within you. However, instead of struggling with mental gymnastics when you feel a negative nuance of feeling within you, simply recognize the feeling and reach to feel better. Imagine feeling better, imagine letting the feeling go, imagine a different type of feeling all together, whatever is appropriate to you in the moment.

For example, perhaps a particular person always seems to piss you off, you always react around them in some way whether it's a feeling of embarrassment, anger, frustration, feeling inferior perhaps, or jealousy even. It doesn't matter what it is, it's an off feeling and you don't like it. Often you can simply recognize the feeling and reach to feel better by **imagining** feeling better no mental gymnastics required beyond imagining! **Mould your emotional state through imagining your emotional state!** Do it in the heat of the moment, as well as afterwards rather than letting your mental chatter go ten to the dozen. This is another powerful and useful tool to add to your toolbox and develop over time.

It is interesting to note that imaging how a feeling feels is still a thought.

Another way to do this imagination work is to ponder how certain feelings feel. For example, give yourself some time, just like you would if you were to sit and meditate or do a journaling exercise. Then simply pick an emotion and ponder how it feels to you. Don't rush it, just pick one feeling and stretch the feeling out for a good few minutes. For example,

- What does fun feel like to me? Ponder fun, imagine the feeling of fun, feel fun as best you are able in that moment.
- What does excitement feel like to me?
- What does freedom feel like to me?
- What does delight feel like to me?
- What does romantic love feel like to me?
- What does appreciation feel like to me?
- What does clarity feel like to me?
- What does happiness feel like to me?
- What does peace feel like to me?
- What does relief feel like to me?

Like all ideas and examples given, the overall intention is to share various ways in which you can **train yourself** higher up the scale. Thus ultimately holding a natural good feeling disposition.

Meditation and distraction; a useful point of view.

Meditation can be utilized at any time and within any emotional state you may be in, assuming the technique is appropriate to the individual within the moment. For example, **deliberate** distraction of any sort is powerful meditation when you find yourself in a place of strong negative emotional momentum of any sort, when that damn grumpy snowball is half way down the hill. Whereas attempting traditional meditation at such times can actually be too hard for some people especially in the beginning stages of taming their mind, therefore not necessarily helpful or appropriate.

Practicing quieting the minds off feeling thoughts, thus slowing negative momentum by finding what distraction tool works for you personally within different situations and moods takes practice and experience.

So distraction and meditation are sort of the same thing, a slowing down, diffusing or redirecting of the minds off feeling thoughts and awareness within you. Obviously you cannot always sit to do traditional meditation in all life situations so understanding meditation in this way and how you can make it work for you in all life situations is what I like to call active meditation. Frankly this is as simple as mentally adjusting thought relative to your emotional nuances as I have been describing throughout.

Remember the example I gave at the beginning of this book regarding distraction when you go to work, a movie, visit a friend or whatever it was you did, and you then find yourself feeling better? Well, that is a legitimate use of this knowledge. If you find yourself careening out of control in some big old grouch of a snowball (momentum of thought or awareness), and you cannot do the mental gymnastics of finding a thought that feels better due to being quite upset because that damn snowball is full steam down the hill, then this is usually not a good time to try and think yourself better. Rather do anything you can to distract yourself. Distraction really means evoking a natural use of mental options 1 or 3 through action or mental techniques in some way. This is why physical exercise is so powerful for people suffering strong states of depression, or anxiety etc., as depressed people have one or many snowballs strongly in their awareness, which **appear** impossible to get their attention off of as is normal in strong mental momentum of any kind. Not to mention once in a low state there is little motivation to actually try to do anything, a depressive state appears to suck the life out of you. But within the **mental distraction** that physical exercise evokes, or another chosen distraction technique, you are in essence meditating because you have dropped some of your negative thoughts or awareness in those moments, which really means you have naturally utilised mental options 1 or 3 Isn't that interesting?

Frankly meditation is one of the most powerful tools you can use relative to your emotional state, especially when understood from this broader perspective. It ultimately helps train you to focus your mind because that's all you can do; you can only ever activate (choose) thought. Meaning in learning to meditate by slowing thought, and diffusing thought you are gaining control of where you choose to place your awareness, which is also thought!

With everything I have been saying can you see the benefit of this education within a traditional meditation practice?

Meditation as a word and practice has vast differences in its definition from teacher to teacher, and person to person. However, from my point of view when you understand that there are only two types of thought, that which feels good and that which feels bad, then when you reduce thought, diffuse thought, or redirect thought, and then find yourself feeling better this is because you have reduced your off feeling thinking. Therefore, you have shifted your awareness from an off subject or subjects which is what most of us are unwittingly engaged in doing to ourselves most of the time!

Due to the habitual and often critical off feeling thought process we are mostly engaged in, the experience of 'feeling better' within meditation has caused some teachers to accuse 'the mind' of hindering well-being and happiness. Resistant, critical, congested and limited thinking is definitely hindering individual wellbeing. On the other hand, non-resistant, free flowing, appreciative connected thought is the **enhancer** to wellbeing and meditation is still one of the leading tools for moving you towards a state of clear free flow thinking. However, many have missed this vital point. **The point being, 'There is clear, free flow, appreciative connected thought' and traditional meditation is only one form of getting you there.** Obviously when you make a deliberate effort to guide your thought in all areas of your life relative to how it feels to you, this is of upmost importance and is what I mean by 'active meditation.'

Accordingly, a good quality meditation will linger in your feeling space for some time, sometimes even days. **This is positive momentum** and therefore it is easier to think positively after a meditation that has slowed your mental awareness in subjects that are off to you in some way.

Utilising meditation to evoke positive momentum, then deliberately choosing thoughts that feel better, whilst busily engaged in life is a powerful practice and understanding in the sense that life is not about, 'not thinking' as many teachers like to teach, **but life is more about joyously expanding and enjoying your creative thought process whilst holding a positive feeling state of being.**

Seeking to understand and redevelop your inner niggles all day everyday as best as possible with a gentle approach to it, is the most powerful form of meditation or mindfulness you can do for yourself and ultimately the world as a whole. Gently quietly shifting into free flow thinking thought by thought, day by day combined with a short traditional meditation first thing in the morning, evening or both is a habit worth considering. The more you relax your mind and just be, the more your introspective awareness of your thought develops, especially for those still on that damn roller coaster! A fifteen-minute meditation is more than enough, life's for living and living includes a lot of thought, not whiling away the day sitting in the lotus position trying to stop all thought as some believe. This combined knowledge and practice is extremely powerful to understand and utilise.

Meditation can be achieved in many ways!

My first genuine meditative experience happened whilst at Raglan surf beach in New Zealand flying my paraglider prior to understanding or working with my inner niggles. Imagine a very busy mind going ten to the dozen, one that was still quite stressed and feeling hurt in some ways, but was also fully engaged in life nonetheless. A lot of people find themselves like this in busy, stressed, sometimes hurt mental head spaces. At any rate here I was learning how to fly paragliders, imagine sitting in a comfortable armchair floating casually back and forth along a ridge top, I had no fear of heights or adrenalin junkie type reactions that some experience, just a casual appreciation for the beauty and experience of where I was and what I was doing. This was my first long flight, about one hour and twenty-five minutes. I had to be focused as flying was not second nature to me, so here I was flying gently back and forth, back and forth making what felt like graceful turns at each end of the fly zone. The conditions were perfect for flying, everything was easy, and all taking place above a beautiful surf beach on a gorgeous summers day. The gentle focus on flying meant that no other thoughts were active in my mind, possibly for the first time ever due to this relaxed focus during flight! When my instructor radioed and asked me to land, there was a profound awareness of genuine joy surging through me, this was astounding as it was unexpected. This was my first powerful taste of the release of congested, resistant, bad feeling thought, and that feeling lingered within me for a solid three days! Could this be considered meditation? Yes, it can!

Many activities can be deliberately used with the intent to be meditative. These can include but are not limited to walking, swimming, working out at the gym, or reading a book. The goal is to relax off feeling thought hence enhance your state of being, thus enjoying any activity for the sake of the activity is highly meditative if understood and consciously utilised in this way. I'm not specifically suggesting that you fly a glider to meditate, that was simply an experience I had which reduced my off feeling thought long enough by engaging in a gentle appreciative awareness of my surroundings whilst gently focused on the task at hand. The inner connection I felt (joy) was my natural reaction to getting my awareness completely off certain subjects and quietly appreciating where I was and what I was doing.

Can you see how awareness off a subject is not suppression as suppression means you are still very aware of it thus feeling it to some degree.

A traditional meditation example you can try.

If you can relax your mind thus entire self, you can allow for more positive feeling experiences due to more connected clear thought.

To begin with you need to relax, this is not a case of stopping all thoughts that pop into your mind rather a case of **relaxing your mind**, by gently letting go of your mental activity by not engaging in it as much if at all whilst still **fully awake and aware**. Simply observe thought as it passes through your mind trying not to engage in it.

I'm sure it goes without saying, try to find a time with no distractions as best as you're able, at the same time do not concern yourself with distractions either if they do arise. Just let your awareness on the distraction gloss past you, try not to engage in it. If you do engage in it don't let this annoy you just gently move back into your meditation. (Criticism is never of any value).

Having something to focus on that is gentle in nature such as your breathing, the hum of a household appliance, or a ticking clock is helpful to centre your thoughts, do your best to simply relax into a gentle focus of your breath, ticking clock, or humming appliance as best as possible. Perhaps count quietly to yourself, deliberately focusing on something inconsequential like this is relaxing your mind because your mind is focusing and aware of something of no consequence, therefore evoking no negative emotion within you. That is of course once your awareness is fully engaged in the simple act of listening to a hum, ticking clock or whatever it is you've chosen. Simply let your thoughts and awareness float by without engaging in them. Realize that if you can get fully focused on any of these examples, you have activated thought on another subject and therefore the other possibly resistant thoughts no longer have attention on them, thus you are meditating, your awareness has shifted somewhere else. Learning to focus is a big part of meditation and a big part of your ability to choose thought consciously, but don't stress over it. Just gently focus on whatever you're focusing on and **let your other thoughts drift past you.**

As previously mentioned, this is not a case of stopping thought but rather a case of slowing down, relaxing and diffusing thought, this is done by activating a gentle, non-resistant thought flow in something else such as the ticking clock or your breath etc.

You are not your thoughts, instead you will notice yourself observing your own thoughts, many call this part of themselves 'the observer.' The trick is letting the thoughts float by and not engaging. This takes practice. I prefer to call this aspect of your true self 'the director' rather than the observer because you get to direct which thoughts you ultimately engage in within any moment in time. The director (you) is where you gain your true power because you can always choose a new thought in any moment, truly you can.

So get comfortable, sit or lie down, it's completely over to you, certain positions are not as important as many believe. Often people will drift off to sleep during meditation however, this is not really the goal either. Being fully awake and conscious will garner better results because the overall education is training ourselves up the emotional scale and that can only be achieved with consciously directed thought, which we must practice.

I don't believe that there is any extra benefit in meditating for hours on end. Sure sometimes it can take an hour before you allow your mind to relax for a 15-minute quality meditation, but you do whatever it is you're inspired to do. Some people love meditating for a long time, awesome, great no problem, however fifteen minutes of quality time is actually all that is required on top of everything else we have discussed throughout. Of course with a busy mind and no experience in this entire body of mental work, 30 seconds gained in your first fifteen-minute meditation is a good result.

So do **NOT** beat yourself up with critical thoughts such as, meditating is hard, or you can't do it. Simply do as I've suggested with a relaxed attitude and try, try again. Beating yourself up that you can't do something, is highly critical, highly resistant and not a helpful thought process, cut out all criticism as soon as you are able. Criticism is still just a thought and one which does not need to be engaged in.

There are many other ways to meditate so no matter which one you use please understand this is about creating a free flow system in your mind. Once you become proficient at meditation you can often find yourself with lovely, free flowing connected thought, high up the emotional scale! Awesome! You have had a successful meditation!

That said, the simple and most powerful goal of meditation is to simply relax your mind and **feel a little better** with gentle focus on something inconsequential, that's it nothing more. This helps you train yourself up the emotional scale as afore mentioned because developing the ability to focus is key to this entire education and your life.

Although you can have a profound experience as I did flying my paraglider, everything is in degrees and my experience was powerful due to the intense degree of negative awareness on certain subjects prior to the flight. The degree of stress felt equals the degree of relief felt.

So please, please do not associate any one experience as the target for meditation beyond the simple shifting into a better feeing place to **some** degree. Understand the best meditation is achieved by slowing down and diffusing off feeling thought then pivoting into lighter feeling subjects and points of view as you move out of your meditation however you do this whilst fully awake and conscious.

I have deliberately left out the esoteric reasons why many people meditate. This is due to it being far too big a tangent for this book. Meditation has many different definitions to the word and purposes.

Distraction a most powerful tool.

Here are some examples that can be used to distract and redirect yourself when you are upset, pissed off, grumpy, depressed, anxious or whatever the negative feeling is. Even if you distract yourself all day and then go to bed. It's always a fresh new day tomorrow to try again. Actually every new moment is a new moment to try again, but if the momentum is strong a good night's sleep is often the best distraction.

Some examples of PHYSICAL distractions you can use: -

- Go to bed.
- Go for a walk, bike, run or swim.
- Play a sport of some kind.
- Pat the cat, dog, horse, goat or whatever!
- Have a shower or bath.
- Go for a drive.
- Play with children.
- Yell, scream, hit a pillow, chop firewood, absolutely anything to slow down and diffuse the negative momentum.

Find whatever that is for you. Just make the effort because there is nothing more important than that you feel good which has to become your dominant intention thus you reach to get over things or let things go. People in strong states of depression often won't even want to get out of bed. Force yourself if this is you, if you have been in bed depressed for a long time then bed is no longer serving you. Or if you have a friend like this take them gently by the hand and go for a walk or to a movie or whatever! Move yourself and help others by encouraging them to move themselves. This is powerful distraction and helps a reactivation of other thought processes.

- Breath, taking deep breaths has always helped people regain their composure, and is something you can do anywhere any time.

Many believe breath is a path to inner-peace and there is good reason for that. Your breath is in direct relationship to your emotional state, just as your emotional state is in direct relationship to your mental state, all emotion is always felt within the body and your breath is a big part of the body's reactions to mental/emotional states, thus connected to your overall well-being. So as a part of developing introspection of each feeling you feel, you can also take notice of what your breath is doing. When you recognise any restricted type of breathing and you reach to adjust your breath to something more relaxed and calm in nature which appears to be a physical undertaking you will also be doing the work of the mind naturally by now becoming aware of your breath thus focusing on and thinking about your breath. Again there is no escaping that thought and awareness is within everything we do. **You can use your breath as one of your main introspective emotional indicators if you wish.**

As you reach to adjust your breathing as you recognise an off-ness within your breath, this is in essence doing the work of little niggles. There is no separation here other than what you are labelling as a feeling within you, there will always be some form of emotion attached to all your different breathing states.

During moments when you have developed a state of pure personal harmony within, through focusing yourself into higher and higher states of pure thought, you can come to a place of simply **appreciating** the pleasure and deliciousness of a deep breath, which is far beyond deep breaths to calm oneself. Again appreciation is the ultimate target within your state of being. Pure thought means being focused in such a way, thinking in such a way that your state of being is currently in this moment in time, somewhere near the top of the emotional scale.

Some examples of MENTAL distractions you can use.

Simply try to relax and consider thoughts such as: -

- It's only a moment in time.
- It's ok this too will pass, it's only strong momentum.
- I don't have to work it all out right now; in fact, it may take time to sort this out in my mind.
- All is well really, it'll work out.
- Remember concepts such as time is a healer or it's only a thought and a thought can be changed.
- Meditate, or use a mantra even if you're busy at work, try and reduce your thought on the subject.
- Watch a movie, listen to music, or read a book. Just be mindful that some movies, music or books may negatively trigger you even more. You have to use a discerning mind and choose those that uplift you.
- Simply let it go if you can! Take a breath and let go!

Let go.

There is an old yogi analogy which helps us to understand letting go. Imagine a little old yogi sitting next to a camp fire listening to one of his students complaining about an issue he had. The student was talking about his issue, explaining his issue, arguing his reasoning for his issue and really struggling within his mind. The little Yogi sat there patiently listening and when finally, the student stopped talking and looked to him for advice, the yogi immediately launched himself on to the nearest tree and wrapped both arms and legs around the tree deliberately showing that he was hanging on tightly. Then the yogi yelled loudly, *'get off me tree, you are hurting me tree, get off me tree, you are hurting me tree.'* He stayed there clinging to the tree for several moments before quietly returning to his place at the fire.

I am sure by now you can see that the issue was always in the mind of the student and that we always hurt ourselves by hanging on to the thought longer because our hurt has been inaccurately associated outside of self at our issue, in this case the tree represents thought associated outside of self. In other words, let go of the tree, means let go of the thought that is the real cause of our issue. The immense power of letting go cannot be overlooked!

Sleep and meditation.

Sleep is not meditation but it is a powerful tool to use in a similar way to distraction, in fact it is the ultimate distraction tool. It is common knowledge that when you are highly stressed, depressed, in strong states of grief or other similar situations the body naturally wants to sleep, or conversely may suffer from insomnia. When the mind has strong negative momentum the body often naturally wants to sleep as this gives you some reprieve between the ears. An expression that captures this is 'Ahhh sleep is bliss!' So if you need to sleep, then sleep!

When you awaken it is often with a fresher outlook depending on whether you instantly reactivate negative thought patterns again when you wake up, as we unwittingly tend to do. Trying not to re-engage in these negative patterns when you awaken is highly beneficial for everyone to understand and truly is worth practicing each morning.

Blending meditation with sleep both before and after is highly beneficial. Using meditation before sleep reduces negative momentum of thought which helps slow negative momentum when you awaken also. Which in turn helps you to meditate in the morning thus builds positive momentum each day little by little. So meditate before sleep and then mediate when fully awake and conscious first thing after you wake up as well. In part meditation is training your ability to focus your mind. At any rate, when you finish your morning meditation try to consciously focus thoughts up the scale rather than engaging in the ones you know will mess with your head. Using a series of writing techniques or some other activity to aid in building positive mental momentum first thing after a morning meditation really does help kick start positive momentum.

Also don't beat yourself up for taking a nap! If you are upset in some way and you simply want to have a nap during the day, then go ahead and do it! Get up afterwards and have another crack at the day! **Naps are great legitimate distraction tools** to use, so use them as needs be.

If you struggle with sleep at night and often find yourself wide-awake at the witching hour, why not try meditating, consciously learn to relax, let go, chill, breathe…

Writing techniques.

There are many writing techniques available from many different teachers which help you grow better snowballs and melt others. **Nothing focuses the mind more specifically than sitting with a pen in your hand.** The dialogue in your head can appear hardwired yet it isn't. Writing will help you **focus your thoughts** in a way that is easier than trying to think things out.

A good morning process to make the time for, is to get up, take care of personal needs, get comfortable and meditate for 15 minutes then write using one of the following techniques for a further 15 minutes or so. After this you can get on with your day. With time and practice you will be building positive momentum in your thought forms and thus emotional space. Always consciously use the three mental options reaching to feel better within your writing and of course you can do this process at any time not just in the morning.

Sentence starters.

Using sentence starters builds positive momentum and can often be used as a process of pulling yourself out of a not so good place so you that you can then move on to doing a scripting or a mental option two technique as well if you choose too. Scripting or reaching to shift thought higher is easier to do the better you feel so using sentence starters first can be helpful in achieving this. Sentence starters is a great way to learn how to focus on the small positive things in life which again is helping to train yourself into a more positive disposition which gets easier to maintain because a series of positive snowballs begin rolling down the hill. Momentum is momentum, positive or negative. When using sentence starters, the idea is to sit and write as many positive sentences as you can with the starter to guide your direction of thought. You can use one and repeat many different lines with the same sentence starter or use multiple starters. The same rules always apply; write with an intention to enhance your feeling space.

Of course you can do this in your head at any time and is a brilliant mental habit to build, however sitting and writing with pen in hand truly helps you to focus more. Sometimes your mind will get on a runaway of fun uplifting thoughts faster than you can write, awesome, run with it, stretch it out for as long as you can.

Some examples of sentence starters that you can use:

- I like…
- I Love…
- I truly appreciate…
- I want…
- I will…
- I believe…
- Wouldn't it be nice if…
- How would it feel if…
- 10 things I like about _____ is…
- Remember when…
- I wonder…
- I am looking forward to…
- I prefer…
- I am truly grateful for…

Scripting (story writing).

The process of scripting is to write stories about aspects of your life focusing on particular details of what you personally want, without adding 'because I don't want' or adding aspects of awareness of 'what I haven't got' into your story thus limiting your feeling space. (Abraham-hicks.com teaches this far more deeply than described here.)

Just **write about what you do want and why you want it**. Seeking delight in your imagination. Fantasise and play with this, get as descriptive as you can without evoking negative emotion. Again the rule is to write with an awareness of what your emotions are doing when you are thinking about your stories.

The purpose is to deliberately build and enhance a good feeling space within, which creates a gentle shift of your beliefs which in turn sustains your higher disposition.

You will notice in hindsight after a period of time writing, perhaps a month or two, how your stories have changed and how your overall feelings have also changed. Scripting helps shift that mental dialogue that is incessant within you to something more positive **and to harmonize your beliefs with your desires** as this is imperative for personal wellbeing. There is no escaping the mental/emotional connection to your personal wants, you ultimately have to make peace with all subjects that concern you one way or another or get your attention off them altogether, but don't stress out about it because this naturally happens when working with all your little niggles as described.

It doesn't matter if you keep writing the same story every time you sit to write as long as you feel good when you're doing it. If you get triggered and feel crappy in some way and cannot bring yourself back around to a positive state, drop the writing and try meditating, distraction, E.F.T or whatever works for you. Try, try again as best you can with a gentle relaxed attitude.

The power of **recognizing the shift in your emotional state relative to your thought** is truly beyond description and is the missing link in almost all education on personal wellbeing.

If you haven't changed the way you feel about a subject, you haven't changed anything!

A mental option two technique for shifting thought to a new place.

Pick an issue you want to feel better about, preferably a little niggle not some massive life drama as your first attempt with this process. In fact, if you make the effort to ignore your big drama for several weeks whilst learning how to work with your niggles you get more skilled with the whole concept and the process will be easier to do whilst also reducing your attention on your big issue. Remember it is your **point of view** of an issue with **awareness on the issue** that is making it an issue in the first place. So getting your awareness off it altogether with mental options 1 or 3 is often a better process than attempting to hit it head on with option 2 which is what this technique does, hits it head on.

Now that you have chosen a subject look at the emotional scale and honestly decide where you are on the scale within that subject. Of course you can swing between emotions on any subject depending on your current mood and differing thoughts within the subject, this is normal as we all have different wants and beliefs tugging at different aspects within our beliefs.

It's best to approach this work in a reasonable headspace but of course that's not always the easiest perhaps build into it if needs be with meditation then a sentence starter exercise.

Sit and write about your chosen subject being aware of your current feeling about it, and the only goal you are aiming for within this writing is to feel a little better now in this moment, on that subject.

If you find in this moment that you cannot focus enough into a better feeling place on that subject and the opposite happens (you feel worse), stop and try again at another time. Trying to force it with a negative tailspin won't help you. Ideally you will be trying to feel better by one or two emotions further up the scale from what you currently feel, not aiming for the top. Trying to go from hate to love on a subject is asking too much of anyone, especially in one leap, in fact it is simply not possible in one leap.

What you write is your business, don't judge your writing by the content, judge it by the way you feel and if it feels better then you are doing good work. As discussed earlier feeling anger feels better than powerless so if you move from powerless to anger and feel better, that is good progress. When you feel you have done enough or you run out of steam so to speak, stop and forget about it then do it again another day, and again, and again until you have genuinely made peace with it to your own satisfaction. This is a process of deliberately taking thought into a new place and you will be surprised when you look back over what you have written after several months of doing it just how much your beliefs, thus points of view and tone has shifted.

You will see in the following example that the emotional set point had changed slightly as a result of the first day's effort, and on the second day the employee was able to get to a better feeling place quicker than the previous day's attempt. You can truly shift your emotional set point on any subject with this process, some people have been struggling with baggage and issues for years, sometimes it might take you 15 minutes a day for a month to truly shift an emotional set point on a subject. That's powerful when you consider you may have been struggling for years, this is far beyond unlocking congested understanding, this is a deliberate enhancement of your points of view and beliefs.

An example of mental option two writing technique.

Giving an example that all people can relate to is not possible, because everyone reacts differently subject to their own patterns of thought, their belief structure and personal preferences within their own life experience.

You have to do the work yourself because only you know how you feel and what thoughts work for you to feel better, so this example is just that, an example. You have to consciously search upwards emotionally yourself, and sitting to write is the easiest way to do this because of the mental ability to really focus whilst writing. Start where you are, if you are grumpy start writing from there but reach beyond the grumpiness, don't spiral down into more anger for example.

This example is of a common employee, employer relationship issue which starts in frustration and is reaching for hopefulness. Refer to the emotional scale as you read this.

First day's writing.

- Fucken' hell he's a prick when he talks to me like that! (Starting in mild anger with strong frustration)
- I'm bloody sick of it.
- I just don't damn well get it, there's no need for it.
- I don't even think he's aware he's doing it! (Notice the reaching here in this sentence)
- He's always worried about something and then he reacts, he's always struggling and worried I guess? (More reaching)
- He is hard to communicate with at the best of times, and this makes things worse!
- I guess he's had a run of bad luck lately.
- But this doesn't excuse him!
- I know he can be normal though. (A bit back and forth in these last few sentences but still reaching)
- He gave me petrol vouchers for my fishing trip the other week when he knew I was struggling for bucks, which was bloody good of him he didn't have to. (Good work)
- When I spoke to him about barking orders at people at the end of last year he seemed to understand. (Good work)
- But then this happened again yesterday!!!! (A dip backwards)
- But I guess I kept my cool better than usually, and that's good I guess.
- Things have been better overall I guess?
- I have been frustrated which is better than the angry outbursts I was having afterwards at other times.
- I am doing a good job, I guess it's just his inner shit he hasn't sorted out yet and he probably won't either he's so hung up on money. And he's not working on himself like I'm trying to. (Very good work, good positive momentum here)
- He wouldn't understand if I tried to explain anyway.

- I am sick of his shit though…. things are changing I guess.

Second day's writing.

- It's damn frustrating when he's being an egg! (A softer start than yesterday)
- Maybe he doesn't realize what he's doing?
- I have seen him think before he speaks.
- It was great that he gave me petrol vouchers, it helped me a lot.
- I've realized that his shit doesn't have to affect me so much.
- It's my reaction to his shit, that is the real issue.
- I know that he isn't really that bad.
- I like knowing that I can sort myself out, and help him calm his ranting in a peaceful way.
- This is a chance for me to work on my reactions. (A good positive flow going.)
- I can at least try to see the best in him.
- As I change my point of view I feel better and that's all that really matters.
- I really do appreciate the job and aspects of him.
- He does appreciate the work I do.
- I realize that for the most part, we all get along really.
- I also respect him really, just look at the business he created and he has hired me after all.
- All is working out really, I do like my job and it's really just my own reaction that's the issue.
- And I am feeling better, and getting better at feeling better
- One day soon I won't even react which is really the problem.

Mantras and Affirmations.

A mantra is simply making the conscious effort to repeat a phrase over and over again. Let's say you're at work and your mind has wandered to a subject that has got your attention and is causing a negative emotional response within you, perhaps it's the work itself, or an annoying work mate that triggered your negative emotion in some way, perhaps some other life issue has evoked a snowball that is careening down the slope. If you don't need to engage in conversation or deep thought regarding your work, you can consciously make the effort to repeat a phrase over and over again, whilst you go about your day. The phrase can literally be anything; it can be nonsensical such as simply repeating, black cats, black cats, black cats or calm blue ocean, calm blue ocean. A mantra can also have more meaning to it as long as it is using phrasing that doesn't evoke negative feelings within you such as repeating, all will work out, all is well, all will work out, all is well. This type of phrasing can evoke negative feelings as well as positive depending on your mood at the time so you have to build a repertoire of your own that works for you when your mood thus snowball is in varying places on the slope.

Repeating a song verse is another fantastic use of mantras, or putting your headphones in with an uplifting song of your taste and singing along to it on repeat. When using mantras at first your attention will still be on whatever is bugging you but within 5 or 10 minutes you will start to feel better as you consciously strive to relax your mind and thus get your awareness off the subject. In essence you have now successfully meditated whilst at work or wherever you are. How cool is that!

Mantas are a very powerful tool because of the ability to pivot from bad feeling thought to better feeling thought reasonably easily, if of course you make the effort. If your dominant intention is to feel good and follow your inner emotional indicators, then mantras are a great easy tool to use in many situations, even as a meditation practice in and of itself.

You can design many different mantras to use in different situations and they are especially good for developing new beliefs, remember as earlier discussed, a belief is only a thought you keep thinking.

When you are using mantras be mindful that sometimes a particular set of words can trigger a negative response within you, hence trying to force the use of that particular mantra is not helpful in that moment. You would be better off to realize that your negative response, your emotional indicator has triggered some limiting beliefs you may have and therefore find a different mantra to use in that instance, possibly a nonsensical one, where's that dam black cat got to! You must make it your dominant intent to feel good first which then makes finding lighter fresher perspectives easier to find later on. So depending on how you feel at the time will determine your internal responses to certain mantras. Trying to be too positive about a subject that is bugging you when you are already upset to some degree often does not work because remember it is very hard to think, say or do anything positive when you're in a bad emotional space, hence a positive mantra in an instance of feeling bad will often send you on a negative tail spin. Therefore, the use of nonsensical, more general, relaxed mantras or song verses at these times is of high value.

It's really important that you always use your emotional indicators, in other words choose your mantra by how it feels to you in the moment. This is the conscious swapping between mental options 1,2 or 3 in action.

Obviously affirmations go hand in hand with mantras. The only determining difference I will make is a mantra is one way in which you can use an affirmation. I find it helpful to write a mantra down and keep it in my pocket to memorize it, especially if it's a bit long winded, as mine tend to be!

A young boy's first mantra experience.

My first experience of using mantras and affirmations occurred when I was approximately 21 years of age. My life was great in many ways, but I **felt** trapped in a relationship I didn't really want to be in and I didn't know how to end it. I had no idea what I wanted to do with myself in the greater scheme of things either. At any rate, we had bought a small lifestyle property in the rural north island of New Zealand which I was working on every day. We were setting the property up based in permaculture principals and living as self-sufficiently as we could. It took me approximately two years to get the infrastructure, trees and gardens in. The entire time I was unemployed and spent the bulk of my savings on the property. My partner provided the funds for all normal household bills which were substantially reducing due to the self-sufficient lifestyle we were living. It was a joint decision to buy, and set the property up in this way, which meant I would not be in normal employment until the infrastructure was built. At any rate I was becoming more and more stressed and depressed although I was very focused and busy within the project. I was not self-aware enough, experienced in life enough **nor had the education** to figure out how or why I was feeling so bad. In hindsight it is obvious to me. I had an intense awareness in being in a relationship I didn't really want to be in, and I was feeling more and more stressed due to a lack of having my own income. I also had no set direction for life which was strongly in my awareness from a limited perspective which was heavily connected to that damn status quo and limited concept of success.

In due course I was getting very shaky, my hands would tremble, and I would need to eat something to stop the shakes. It got that bad that I went to the doctor to see what the hell was wrong with me. He told me that I had hypoglycaemia and that I would have it for life. He said all I could do was manage my eating to alleviate it! This did not impress me one bit. It got worse. At some point around this time we visited my partners father and lovely wife in Tasmania. Whilst staying with them I was flat out busy putting fence posts in around their garden to keep the wombats and wallabies out. On the second day the shaking drove me mental! I threw the spade down in disgust, stormed inside had a sandwich and then hunted down Louise Hay's book, *"You can heal your life."* I had heard about this book from several other sources and was aware it was on their bookshelf along with many other alternative self-help books. In due course I discovered the affirmation Louise offered for hypoglycaemia, according to Louise, there is a belief that says certain patterns of thought/belief can manifest as a particular illness within the body. In this book there is a chapter which highlights different illnesses in conjunction with what she suspected could be the thought pattern which may have caused the health issue. Next to Hypoglycaemia this simply said, "Overburdened with the pressures of life." Well in hindsight, I certainly was! But at that time I couldn't see it as clearly as I can now.

The affirmation Louise offered to counteract this belief, this state of being was, *"I now choose to make my life light, and easy, and joyful."* Well at that time in my life these words had no basis of meaning to me, light, easy, joyful were foreign concepts, they literally were cold empty words with no meaning in them whatsoever. Life was about hard work you know, hadn't you heard? I am from a pioneering farming family in a young country, so like many New Zealand families I had encapsulated the belief that life was about hard work among other limiting ideas. At this stage I had already started to ponder life deeply and could see the essence within her book regarding the power of thought. So I decided that even though the words didn't mean a lot to me I would try it out. I mantra'ed the hell out of that affirmation! I repeated it over and over in my head as an almost **full time mental dialogue**. I even started singing it to myself out loud over and over again. This meant that the constantly repeated affirmation had become a **nonsensical** mantra to me. I just did it because I trusted the concept, the words themselves were still meaningless. I was also trying to figure out within myself where this overburdened with life thing fitted in my life? It took years for the words of this affirmation to begin to have any real meaning to me; it was rare to even get a glimpse of happiness at that time and frankly happiness was a foreign concept, being productive and working hard were the ideals I had picked up and these ideals had no room for happiness in my consciousness at the time. What I did have back then was a desire to get over the Hypoglycaemia, and with this a dogged determination to do this damn affirmation thing. So on and on it went, in my head day in day out for approximately three months. Well at the end of those three months the shakes eased up and were virtually gone. I pranced around like a peacock telling everyone all about it, and that the side effect was that I was happier! I had literally shifted my state of being up the scale, and I could notice a happiness that I hadn't experienced before, to me that was somehow more exciting than the shakes going away. This was my first real taste of letting go. Letting go of negative feeling thought although I didn't realise that at the time.

Now 20 or so years later I realize that I had a desire to get over this health issue, and in essence I was meditating using mental option 1 (by doing a nonsensical mantra) with the intent to get well.

I had alleviated the issue of being overburdened (depressed) because whatever thoughts I had in my head had reduced substantially through enough **lack of attention**, which meant I was able to skip up the scale a bit. A key point here is **I made the effort to do this affirmation in mantra format.** I also now know that the happiness was the result of the manta taking my attention off other thoughts, and the side effect to this new happiness level was the shakes (hypoglycaemia) going away.

There are many books available with affirmations and mantras you can use to help yourself find new thoughts, new word combinations etc. I know how hard it is to try and come up with them yourself to begin with so rather than adding them to this book, seek out some other titles elsewhere. Louise's books are still great for offering positive affirmations. You don't need to be unwell to use the affirmations she offers, simply choose the ones that resonate with you. Also the purpose of this story is to share with you the mental work which created the positive emotional shift within my state of being, not so much the possible psychosomatic health interrelationship. There is obviously more to the story regarding psychosomatic health education which is covered very completely and powerfully within the work of Esther Hicks.

An example of Letting go, like the yogi.

This next story is also offered for the psychological shift that occurred more than the possible psychosomatic health interrelationship. This story is different in the sense that I could clearly see the issue within me when I took Louise's book off the bookshelf, her ideas helped me to **let go** by giving me self-awareness.

Here I was back in the hill country on our permaculture property perhaps within a year of the last story. I was almost penniless, I recall I had approximately $300 to my name and had spent the bulk of my personal savings on fruit trees and other required infrastructure, yet still had a bill of $400 to pay at the tree nursery, of which I had no way to completely pay. I was acutely aware that this bill needed paying and was intending to go back to employment after two years working on the property. I managed to find two scrub cutting jobs, this was not a full time job but rather this was me doing a small job for two separate farmers. I bought a cheap chainsaw at the local hardware store with the remainder of my money; these jobs would have earned me enough money to pay the tree nursery bill and more besides. In short order the cheap chainsaw I bought shit itself with long grass binding into the plastic oiler therefore requiring a new oiler. When cutting scrub off at ground level, you are also cutting through long grass, and as it turned out a cheap chainsaw wasn't cutting the mustard. So I returned to the hardware shop I bought the chainsaw from and I managed to get the oiler replaced once but they refused a second time even though this happened again over a space of a single day. They also refused to take the saw back even though I didn't get 4 straight hours work out of it! So here I was part way into a job and no useable chainsaw to finish it, and no money to buy another chainsaw either! I wondered if I could pay one off as I was intending to find more scrub cutting work so I went shopping. I walked into a farm machinery store and was eyeing up shiny nice new Stihl Chainsaws. Boy they looked great! It's a boy thing ok! In due course the salesman came over and asked what I wanted so I told him my woeful story of my clapped out cheap and nasty chainsaw and that I had a scrub job to complete, and another job to do after completing my first job as well, but I also had no money, could he help? He said well that Stihl 021 over there would be ideal, and he suggested putting a slightly longer bar on it for more reach in the steep country, and gave me a spare chain and some two stroke oil as well. He literally gave it to me and said come back and pay him when I could! He didn't ask for my name, address or phone number, he simply trusted that I would! I walked out of that shop with approximately $1000 worth of new toy, and had instantly placed that man on a pedestal! I had however just made my debt grow substantially as well. Boy did that saw go well, top quality gear is great. I finished that job fairly readily and gave two-thirds of it to the farm machinery store, and the rest to the tree nursery which nearly completed the original bill. All was well until I went to start the second job, this would have paid for the chainsaw and cleared my tree nursery bill as well, but the second farmer no longer wanted the scrub work done this season, damn! Now what? Try as I might, door knocking, asking around etc., I couldn't seem to pick up another scrub job. Uh oh, guess what my poor little brain was doing? It was intensely aware and focused on owing this great man money for the chainsaw and no work. It would be fair to say I was stressing myself out over it!

Then my back got sore. I hadn't been working for nearly two weeks and my back got sore? On top of that it was my lower back, I'd never had a sore back before and couldn't figure out why it got sore when I hadn't been doing anything physical for the last two weeks given that I had been extremely physical doing shovel work etc., for the last two years? It got sorer and sorer to the point that I didn't think I could cut scrub even if a job did come up. The phone rang, it was a local bee keeper whom had heard I was looking for work, asking if I wanted work for the summer over the honey harvest? Hell yes I said. I immediately freaked out when I hung up the phone, worried that I couldn't lift the 20 kg honey boxes as my damn back was so sore. God, now what? Ahh Louise's book! Guess what it said for lower back problems? Fear of money! Well, I wasn't afraid of money, I was acutely aware of **the lack of money** and **this awareness in the absence of money had consumed my thinking entirely.** This was a no brainer for me, unlike hyperglycaemia and the concept of being overburdened I could clearly see the money paranoia in my head and I had just secured a job starting tomorrow so I knew I didn't have to worry about money or my bills any longer. I read the affirmation offered in this instance a few times that evening. But really I had already dropped all the mental anxiety through my circumstances having changed by having secured a job. I went to bed and woke up the next morning with no sore back, it had gone just like that! Imagine that, it was so sore that I struggled to walk at times and overnight it was good as gold! From a mental point of view, you can clearly see I had returned to the campfire and had let go of the tree like the Yogi suggested in the earlier analogy. In other words, I'd let go of the acute worry thoughts. I had dropped my worry of a lack of money as I now had a job. You can also clearly see the entire time I was mentally, thus emotionally struggling through this experience that my awareness was on the lack of money, my focus was on the opposite of what I wanted. I want money, but I haven't bloody well got any! **Any awareness of something missing evokes negative emotion, this is powerful to know, this is where our ever present work lies.** In this instance it was easy for me to see where the problem was, well it was when Louise's book pointed it out to me that is! Therefore, it was also easy for me to **let go** in this instance, because the conditions had changed I now had a job.

Dropping the anxiety and worry about the lack of money allowed me back up the scale substantially. I really was quite stressed out about paying these bills. Although these bills were small on the greater scheme of life you have to remember I literally had not earned a single penny of my own for two years, so $20 was a lot of money to me at the time. At any rate the feeling of relief evoked from securing a job was palpable, I felt the unease leave me like a lead jacket lifting off my shoulders. In this case it wasn't the affirmation or mantras that gave the desired result, it was the simple dropping of a negative focus in the lack of money thoughts in my head.

Had life conditions changed to help me do this and to feel good? Of course they had. Would I have been able to drop it as easily if the conditions hadn't changed at that stage in my life? I doubt it, not without good education like offered here in this book and time to learn at least. The change in my conditions (getting a job) definitely allowed me the freedom to drop the anxious thoughts, **but it was still my thoughts causing the problem.** The association was still outside of self, I had still done it to myself unwittingly by not using my emotional indicators to reach for inner change as I had no real **education** or experience in that concept yet, life was heavily associated outside of-self back then.

A point to note here is, do whatever it takes to feel good to get you up the scale, even change conditions if you can, of course we are all already doing that as it is our most dominant tool we tend to over use, you control freak you! Remember, it is easy to feel good when everything is going well for us, but it takes skill and practice in directing one's own mind to feel good in all situations. It is so worth the effort of at least trying to feel good in as many life situations as you can. Your state of being is everything to you, it just is!

Light work.

Light work is another tool that is good to utilize in the **heat of the moment** when life is evoking niggles inside you. Light work is highly effective for many people; it certainly has been for me. It is very esoteric in nature and as I am endeavouring to keep this book as main-stream as possible, I will leave this subject and my stories of it out of this book beyond a brief introduction.

I will however recommend a good possible place to start on this subject, this can be found in the book *"Spiritual Growth"* by Sanaya Roman.

Light work is great because as I said, you can use it in the heat of the moment whilst still being fully engaged within any life experience such as when in conversation with somebody. This is because charging yourself with light is simply a thought or visualization within the mind and it can be a very powerful and useful tool for many. I have personally witnessed and experienced many inner shifts with light work and it is great given that mental gymnastics are not required. All you need is a simple striving and desiring for change, with a gentle thought or visualization and an intent to feel better, or to improve a situation. If you consciously super impose and mould the three mental options within light work you will be enhancing the power of light work techniques and meditations. For example, using Sanaya Roman's light work to simply **feel better** within the heat of the moment of any situation is enhancing her work, and super imposing the knowledge offered here within her powerful meditations and techniques. It can be done instantly within any life situation.

I have had experiences prior to my knowledge of learning to follow my inner emotional impulses where charging myself with light has resulted in a natural use of option one, my mind simply dropped the subject. Similarly, with option two, where a whole new development of thought grew within me morphing and drawing my belief up the scale to where it served me better, new ideas and thoughts simply popped into my head! This is fascinating because I was still trying to fix things outside-self at this stage in life, and yet light work resulted in moving my 'thought', thus myself higher up the scale. It caused a natural unconscious use of the three mental options. There is more than one way to skin a cat you know! In hindsight it is interesting to note that it was still my personal thought that had shifted within the use of light work due to my desire for change. Change can only genuinely come from within because everything we want, we want it to feel better, and feeling better always requires a desire for it thus a mental shift.

Use a discerning mind and play with these ideas. Remember the real work is always creating a free flow system between your ears because it is your mental response to life that is causing any and all issues, thus super imposing the three options within **any** technique grows a dynamic understanding and powerful repertoire of tools and experience over time.

Search out more options and techniques and mix them up a bit.

Another great technique to explore is Thom Hartmann's walking technique, this can be very useful especially for those that love to walk. Get yourself a copy of *"Walking your blues away,"* often a good start or end to the day is a walk whilst using Thom's walking technique. Walking itself can be very therapeutic on its own. Thom describes some of his reasoning about this within his book. The manager of the youth offender program I worked for said, that over the years he had noticed the more he walked the boys, the better they did in the overall program! Isn't that interesting?

You could try mixing walking with other techniques such as doing E.F.T, or light work, or all three whilst out for a walk. This is a lot of fun and I have found it to be very powerful for different people including myself. There really is a lot you can do to help yourself!

Walking with the deliberate intent to meditate is obviously fantastic too!

Chapter Six

Natural appreciation and perception.

There is simply nothing more important than coming to a place of natural appreciation both of yourself and as many aspects of your life experience as possible. This will gradually happen over time with the deliberate searching for better feeling opinions and points of view within all things, which obviously means dropping all critical thought. Of course the time involved can be frustrating, frustration in this instance is caused by your awareness of the time and effort involved to shift yourself toward an improved feeling state. This is obviously not appreciating your life's journey of self-discovery to some degree. Hence looking at your inner growth in a time limiting possibly critical way evokes the feeling of frustration. Isn't that interesting?

To begin with doing this work can be an effort, learning to direct and focus the mind just is, but with practice it becomes second nature. However, in many situations it is possible to simply 'let go' thus not as much effort is required as you may think in resolving many issues.

Ultimately we are striving for more moments in time where you naturally appreciate and many of life's woes no longer trigger you, therefore are no longer life woes anymore! The effort pays off, as you clean up your critical points of view and change old habitual patterns to more free flowing connected thought, everything changes. The way you perceive aspects of your life changes.

Sustainable happiness changes everything.

For example, I had a fantastic childhood (Thanks Mum and Dad, love ya's xox.) Yet I couldn't say that I had a great childhood for years. I believed my childhood sucked. This was because of my **own** inner insecurities and depression caused by my **own** limitation of thought in some subjects mixed with an oversized dose of self-criticism. All of which held me in quite an unhappy place. It was fair to say I had a low self-esteem, although not all would have known or seen that as I was and am quite outgoing and like everybody else was getting on with life. As I grew older I used to perceive my childhood as crap, this was due to my limited points of view on several subjects unrelated to my childhood which perpetuated my low emotional state into my 20's and early 30's. This in turn meant it was hard to think say or do much beyond the negative emotional state which also meant my **perception(s)** were fairly negative in some ways. Now however from being substantially further up the scale on a consistent basis I truly delight in remembrance of my childhood, truly I do it really was brilliant! I look back now in remembrance of my experiences, school friends, brother, sister, mum, dad, and farm life feeling a genuine deep appreciation, a warmth of love fills me when I stop and ponder any memories from that time which was not even conceivable before! These are not cold empty words; this is my truth about how my inner world has developed as a result of this work and I was not even trying to work on my childhood perception! My perception simply changed as I changed, as I moved higher up the scale, this is far beyond nostalgia. **Nostalgia is a blend of appreciation and of something past, something gone**, so nostalgia has an awareness in limitation, in something missing hence really still is a negative emotion! Of course nostalgia can feel good because of the appreciation aspect and thus could be further up the scale from where your current tone sits hence feels good to many people. However, pure appreciation is where it's at, there is no better state to be in, and you can drop the aspect of something missing within any nostalgia feeling, thus simply appreciate past aspects of your life, truly you can!

In my case when my state of being, my overall tone had moved further up the scale, the side effect was this positive shift in perception of my child hood. A key note here as previously mentioned is I hadn't even been thinking about my child hood! My thoughts had simply changed to that of a deeper natural appreciation of my life, past, present, and future. This is the same thing that will happen with all other issues, such as forgiveness as another example as you sustainably move up the scale by making it your dominant intent to feel and hold good feeling spaces for longer.

E.F.T initially took the congested understanding 'sting' out of a hand full of memories in regard to my childhood, although I had nothing really bad happen in my childhood. In fact, the only 'bad' thing was my own critical outlook of self and other subjects which created a low depressive state. As my overall tone moved higher up the scale from learning to follow my emotional indicators mentally, thus dropping more criticism, the result was this deeper appreciation within me which is now a natural occurrence anytime I ponder any of my memories. For anyone struggling with their past this is a huge awareness of possibility! As I am sure anyone can appreciate.

As your state of being changes, you have changed, thus your perception of all things also changes. In other words, **'If you take control of the way you feel, you will profoundly take control of all aspects of your life.'** What this example shows us is if your awareness is off a subject such as your childhood, a trauma, or a need to forgive yet you are working your way up the scale by holding and milking good feelings longer whilst also working to lift or drop each negative niggle that is evoked in all areas of your life, in time your perception of all things change for the better.

So in doing this work it is usually not a good idea to tackle the biggest issue in your life first up because that will often cause you more grief by adding more snow as we have discussed. Rather go bit by bit, gently quietly within all areas of your life and pick away at it; the slow turtle will definitely win this race!

Please note the mental work I'm talking about, raised my overall tone allowing me to genuinely appreciate many aspects of my life far beyond what any modality or therapy ever could, because that is your work of the mind! The only work of any consequence, the only legitimate life career choice!

In all of this work please prioritize 'mental option three' to build new snowballs.

When doing this work it's not always the best idea to try and figure out what off thought or awareness is causing your emotional ills because as afore mentioned we most often perpetuate and expand our problems further. Rather learn to feel better first with the use of mental options 1 and 3, and then tackle any issues as they arise **should you still need to.** If we begin this work by trying to figure out our bigger problems, we often tend to unwittingly add more negative momentum when we try to think things out or fix things. You can tell if you are making things worse because you will be feeling worse, stressed, confused, angry etc. Sure you will need to be able to nip these thoughts in the bud with your awareness of them**, but making an effort to simply feel better by focusing on building new thought forms, new snowballs, is of far greater importance**, because this shifts you overall tone higher evoking massive internal shifts over time often including a redevelopment of your bigger issues with no extra attention given to them as just described above.

Gently quietly building momentum in subjects that interest or please you are of top priority. Whilst also gently morphing old grumpy subjects quietly over time as life evokes negative emotion within you, these are your niggles. More often than not we endeavour to fix things, fix our problems throughout life in general, hence when beginning to learn this mental work most of us naturally want to start with mental option 2 doggedly trying to fix an issue like we do in other areas of life. In endeavouring to fix a mental issue through thinking it out with option 2, we often keep ourselves **fixated in our problems longer.** Ultimately we need to be consciously using all three mental options relative to how we feel in all areas of life as a natural practice which most of us aren't to the degree required, thus we can unwittingly add more snow, more momentum, more congested understanding to our issues if we are doggedly trying to 'fix' a thought with option 2.

In other words, if you change your mental dialogue to better feeling stories for yourself (option 3) as best as possible, and also stick your head in the sand as required (option 1) your state of being and your tone rises. When in this higher state that you have created for yourself the use of option 2 becomes easier to find a lighter thought within a subject that is bothering you, If you still need to! **Remember it is extremely difficult, if not impossible to think positively when you are already upset in any way.** This is why option 2 is best used when you are in a good mood. Of course this is always in degrees, and it **is** possible to find a new point of view whilst in a heavily negative state which feels like a breath of fresh air because you have made a substantial improvement in your thought, but usually there has been a hard battle finding this new point of view from a low feeling state. Hence always strive up the scale with your dominant intent to feel better first and then the use of option 2 is easier. Be mindful that when you are in a good mood and you dredge up an issue to work on you can instantly plummet from your good mood in which case this is not helpful either! Option 3 or 1 is still best practice if this is the case. In time your issue(s) will evolve and resolve especially if the work of little niggles is dominant within your overall mental behaviour. I know this sounds tricky but with time and experience this will make more sense. The power of now always lies in your ability to pick better feeling thoughts now. Like all things the deliberate and dynamic use of all three mental options becomes second nature with practice and experience.

Please remember.

Completing this work does not mean you won't ever get grumpy or upset again, but you will see how you are always creating your own feeling space in all situations. This will mean dropping all blame and gaining an ever increasing control over your own state of being. Ultimately gaining a deep awareness of how full emotional responsibility creates love within you. This will have evolved you past the point of associating outside of self that so many people are stuck on. The end result will be seen in more and more natural moments of appreciation, and thus becoming the person you've always wanted to be and more besides. Also remember just doing this work once or twice on your big issues isn't the point I'm making in this book, that would be an attempt at option 2 without the mental behaviour required for long term sustainable happiness. This is about **training** your mind thus overall disposition, your tone, your state of being, your attitude, your mood higher up the scale by consciously directing your thought within all life experience. We can all do this and frankly I cannot imagine why you wouldn't because this is the basis of creating true quality of life.

You must allow yourself and all others to feel good no matter what!

Many people believe they must feel a certain way relative to certain subjects. This is never a good idea as that can hold themselves in a perpetual state of not so goodness through the incessant association outside of self.

For example, perhaps you did something which hurt another person and you are now feeling guilty and perhaps you believe you must feel guilty, therefore you are holding onto a space of guilt for a lifetime in some cases, therefore never truly letting go and becoming your authentic self. It is impossible to love, hold an appreciative state or heal from any emotional trauma if you believe that you must feel bad in certain situations or each time you think about a certain subject. From an emotional perspective feeling better has to be considered healing. Conversely perhaps you believe someone else must feel guilty because of whatever they have done, and if they don't feel guilty then we judge them as not having a conscience and critically point our fingers at them. Of course our guilt feeling is a good thing **to begin with**, remember all negative emotion is always a good thing; it is our emotional indicator for conscious change after all! So, in this case due to our negative emotion such as guilt, we often endeavour to modify our behaviour to feel better in some way thus we often modify our conduct to become a better person, so as to not feel guilty. Modifying our own behaviour in this way with the intent of creating a deliberate enhancement in self, both behaviourally and thus emotionally is a great use of that one tool we all tend to over use, that of changing our conditions to feel better, in this case changing our own behaviour is changing the conditions.

Although guilt often evokes a desire for change within our own behaviour, **we are actually critically judging ourselves with our own opinion of ourselves hence the guilt feeling to begin with!** We must reach to find a way of critiquing ourselves with a gentle appreciative mind rather than a harsh critical mind. You can desire personal change without self-criticism being involved in the process, self-criticism **is not** self-appreciation. Therefore, you can learn to appreciate your growth process from a place of appreciation, rather than criticism. Thus you are moving up the scale forming an appreciative, positive and sustainable tone within. A deliberate and conscious change of yourself like this is great but must not be confused with modifying your behaviour to keep other people happy! Modifying yourself for others almost never works out to well for you or the others, because those demanding you to change are those whom have no emotional responsibility themselves, so if you change for their sake this is disempowering for them as well as for you. So you should consider not doing it unless you **want** to. Modifying our behaviour is constantly demanded of us by those that have not yet learned that their emotional state, their own reactions are caused by their own thought process thus they unconsciously still believe outside conditions need to change for them to feel better!

Many times we try and make amends if we have hurt someone, which is great if you can make amends and take responsibility for your actions etc. **BUT** even though you may have done something to upset or hurt another, ultimately it is still their reaction to the situation that causes their hurt emotional response. Therefore, on a deeper level they have actually hurt themselves, as you do yourself, this is always the case for all people. This last statement feels counterintuitive I know, however please reach to understand, as this is at the heart of self-empowerment and ultimately unconditional love.

The hurt party ultimately must learn how to consciously use their own emotional responses for inner growth which in turn is giving the hurt person their own self-empowerment which is everything! Plus, when you can hold an appreciative space regardless of conditions then you are unconditionally loving.

Most often people don't want to take responsibility for their own reactions meaning they still want to transfer their hurt, their anger, their disempowered feeling etc., outwardly on to the person or situation. The first step towards true sustainable happiness and unconditional love is coming to realise everything you feel comes from within you which is at the heart of emotional responsibility. Of course those that are unaware of this often flatly refuse to accept that their reaction is their reaction. Of course knowing your reaction is your reaction, and their reaction is their reaction is not an excuse to behave badly, but this goes without saying. Truly bad behaviour is largely coming from low down the emotional scale due to limited beliefs and usually a suppression in the way an individual feels regarding their own life's freedoms, hence their battling outside of self in the first place. At any rate, common kindness is natural to us all when we are connected to ourselves, whilst also realising you are not responsible for another's emotional reactions, just as no one is responsible for yours.

Often people find themselves stuck trying to 'fix' an issue that they feel guilty about, which cannot be fixed for any number of reasons. If this is the case, you have no choice but to forgive yourself, which really means drop the subject and move on. Be like the Yogi, let go!

If you believe you must feel guilty forever, or that someone else must feel guilty forever, then you do not truly have an understanding of what love and compassion are to the degree I am teaching here, nor can healing take place. You must come to a place of understanding yourself (therefore others) for your own sake, bloody hard to do in certain situations **until this work is well grounded within you.** The fact remains, that if you hold yourself, or someone else in a place of anger, resentment or guilt, **you** cannot move forward into a place of natural appreciation or love and neither can they if they believe this also. Therefore, the belief which transfers blame of emotion outside of self in **any way** creates a situation where there is limited, slow or no emotional healing first and foremost for ourselves which then transfers to society with our limiting words, beliefs and actions. If we continue to stay reactive and blame everything outside of self for the way in which we feel, the pain and horrible events will continue to happen with the development of all types of people shit. Often with an ignorant need for justice (or revenge) therefore the cycle of pain and suffering continues.

If you are critically condemning someone in this way whether it be yourself or someone else, regardless of whether it's justifiable or understandable, you need to learn how to simply **let go for your own sake!** Criticism and condemnation that is held within **your** state of being is very poisonous to **you** first and foremost, you are drinking your own poison.

This type of inner work is not excusing people from taking responsibility for their actions. For example, there are plenty of people in prison who need to stay there whom will likely never aspire to this work at all, let alone to the depth I am teaching here. Even so, a leopard can change his spots if he wants to and he should be encouraged to if he is asking for directions as to how. We all want to love, even the most heinous person who has created the most heinous beliefs within themselves, but they cannot get there if they and society believe they must feel guilty or bad forever. Where is the compassion, understanding, and appreciation here? There is not. Therefore, under these limited conditions of holding oneself in a space of negativity, and suppressed freedoms etc., there can be no change, just behaviour control in the form of society's dominance, laws and deterrents etc., which is such a limited understanding that is far too prevalent within us all.

Strive for compassion for **all** people because the inner pain of those who are hurt and hurting is often horrific, hence the bad crap that some may have done in some cases of criminal offending in the first place. Their pain, like your pain is also their guidance from within which will ultimately also be the cause for their desire for inner change and another way.

Until such time as this information becomes more widespread within the masses and people discover changing life conditions to feel better is only part of the story and rarely works in a sustainable way. We will continue to go around in circles of pain blame more pain, pain blame more pain and so on. We all want to feel better than where we currently stand. Sure there are those that appear very comfortable within their volatile and in some cases horrific nature as they have acclimatized to it, meaning they are holding multiple limiting beliefs (often authoritarian) that continue to perpetuate their off-ness and they have no desire to change behaviourally let alone emotionally, usually because they are blind to this understanding or how it feels to be in a deeply connected appreciative place, hence there continued battling outside of self for an inner connection they cannot find.

Very often those we consider as criminals may have what we consider as a broken moral compass, or perhaps they have a ridiculous eye for an eye mentality which they have acted on and has eventuated in them being in prison. There are also many people who are not termed as criminals who also hold aspects of these draconian beliefs, including much of the law system itself! Just look at laws relying on the limited belief of an eye for an eye, how well has this really served us? The eye for an eye concept is the natural but flawed result of outside of-self associations regarding **our limited point of view as a society.** Most of us consider it normal for punishment to match the crime as a form of fear deterrent etc., but we all suffer the consequences of that which is first and foremost experiencing and living a limited state of being. This is due to our negative emotion being blamed outside of self thus no improvement gained, this then perpetuates more of the same negativity in our limited belief that we need to punish people to deter crime rather than enhance our collective states of being so that crime is not inspired in the first place! The result of associating emotion outside of self affects us all to varying degrees, at the extreme end we end up with the corrupt creation of things due to authoritarian thinking processes. Authoritarians strongly associate outside of self by thinking you need to change for them to feel better, thus they like to force and impose their will on the mases hidden in an agenda of, 'this is for the good of all.' When really it never is. An example of such is the military industrial complex leading to the utter horror of unnecessary war.

The entirety of this work is experiential and trying to describe the depth of beauty that can be felt within oneself to some people is often a futile effort. Sort of like trying to describe what strawberry's taste like to somebody who has never eaten a strawberry.

In summary, expecting someone to feel guilty or bad in any way is very resentful and harms **you** terribly because if you expect this you have unresolved negativity within **you** and does nothing to help you or society!

You can feel remorse from a guilty place and desire change which we critically judge as a good thing, or you can have no guilt and no remorse from some place of arrogance or a position of self-justification and we critically judge this as a bad thing simply because there is no apparent desire for behaviour change. Thus we justify our own need for justice when people are behaving like this through our own lack of emotional responsibility.

If a person like this is bothering you in their lack of remorse, reach for understanding for your own sake, not for the person you are critically judging. You can be assured their life is not all roses even though they don't appear to care a damn about you or whomever they may have hurt. Feeling anything less than appreciation is some form of pain and limitation within your own consciousness. Finding understanding of others requires truly understanding oneself first. To truly understand oneself you must observe yourself relative to your own emotional reactions to life situations in relationship to your own beliefs and preferences within each situation, **and then redevelop** your beliefs to raise your tone and only then will you truly begin to know yourself.

What you feel is where you are, and that's ok, but anything less than appreciation leaves room for improvement!

You must allow yourself to feel however you feel **initially** thus validating yourself. Then at some point you must realize that there is no belief worth harbouring if it holds you, or anyone in any negative emotion long term. You must make it your dominant intention to feel good no matter what and consciously strive. True healing comes from within, from moving higher up the emotional scale. You must allow and encourage those you are condemning this same compassion. Because if you don't encourage those you are condemning to find their own inner connection they can never change, thus you are still part of the problem yourself. This does not mean to say that you are naïve to someone's off-ness, ignoring their ignorant disposition, or lack of moral code, it means **YOU** have developed emotional responsibility therefore; **YOU** are no longer upset by other people's actions, thus are developing unconditional love within self. This is critical for the positive evolution of us all.

To forgive someone simply means you want so much to feel good that you have no other choice!

Stop for a moment here, take a deep breath, relax and reach for a feeling of appreciation.

This is what you are truly searching for in life, not criticism, anger, guilt, resentment or revenge!

Another example of believing we must feel certain ways in certain situations.

Again when someone is holding themselves in a state of anger and justifying their anger for infinite reasons this is not allowing themselves to feel good. Sure anger and revenge may feel good if you are moving up the scale from below, but ultimately becomes your poison if you believe you must feel this way or **any** negative way for any length of time. **You must drop all justification of any negative feeling** and reach to find a way to make absolutely anything that upsets you irrelevant to you!

An emotionally healthy society can only exist with emotionally healthy individuals! I consider anyone genuinely striving to better themselves from any place a damn good thing and worth applauding, regardless of who they are. By better themselves I mean to find an inner freedom an inner connection, a higher state of being consciously. This can only come to the degree I am constantly alluding when you take full responsibility for all your inner reactions and truly get to know oneself as afore mentioned. Remember earlier I said, 'An emotionally responsible mind knows his anger, his hatred, and his revenge comes from within, thus realizes fighting others is a futile effort of less than zero value. It poisons you first and foremost (with your negative emotion) then your often ignorant actions poison the world around you.' Thus perpetuates more of the same.

This is hard to accept when we are on the receiving end of some horrible behaviour thus when we are feeling anger towards somebody or something we naturally want to blame their behaviour for our anger and seek justice, or to control and dominate those that are acting in a way that is unpleasant or deemed criminal. However, we have created our anger ourselves nonetheless and any action taken to appease this feeling outwardly is an under evolved consciousness like it or not.

It is not so much the emotional reaction in the heat of the moment that's the problem, but rather how we perpetuate it afterwards between our ears that continues to add more negativity that becomes the real problem. Because in perpetuating off feeling thought you continue to add to your own limiting beliefs, which then continues to transfer outwardly in your future words and behaviours. So rather than seeing problems as problems see them as an opportunity for personal enhancement, this creates powerful self-realisation.

Have you ever had an argument with somebody and then ended up annoyed, you then blame the other person for the reason you are annoyed and perpetuate it in your mind for a period of time, they are never the reason you are annoyed regardless of any circumstances; **your reaction is still your reaction perpetuated by your thinking process.**

As you become proficient in this work, by recognising your niggles then shifting your thought higher creating positive enhancement within several life subjects you will gain a clarity and a realization that it does not matter what the details of someone else's life is, or has been, or will ever be. It is always our mental journeys that makes us or break us, always! Therefore, there is always something you or they can personally do about it between the ears!

This is why my eyes role when people use that classic line, *"You don't know how I feel, what would you know, has it happened to you?"* and other such phrases.

Sure that's fine and fair enough, that's a normal response when someone is in pain who doesn't yet understand this broader body of work, but arguing over who's pain is the greatest relative to a particular experience is a knee jerk reaction of no value. No one needs to truly know through an equivalent experience how horrible you personally feel; we know you are hurting! We all feel, we all have emotional responses, and these responses are always relative to our thought, belief, life preference interrelationship, relative to how much we care about a subject. This means you **can** get over it and you can come to appreciate life moving forward. You ultimately have full power over all your internal chatter, which means you have full power over your life. This sounds impossible to some people relative to their particular hurts which is fair enough in the beginning stages of taking control of the way you think, when you haven't made this work second nature yet. So gently quietly reach to develop a more sustained positive disposition for your own sake as best as possible. Of course some of us often have strong emotional trauma to work through of varying forms relative to a life experience that evokes it, such as grieving. Strong grief takes time to move through, it just does, as does forgiveness etc. Go easy on yourself or others in situations like this. I am not suggesting anywhere throughout this book that you should instantly and always feel fantastic, that's naïve and large issues such as grief, guilt and forgiveness, are a process to work through, they just are. **It is however, possible to work through any grief or off feeling, and this is something you must do for your own sake!** Which may be by getting your attention off the subject whilst striving higher as previously described. Grief and sadness from a psychological perspective is an awareness in the absence of something wanted, everything is in degrees, and the more you cared about the something, the more you grieve when it is gone. This is regardless of whether the grief is based in a person, situation, or object. Grief, like all emotion is natural when in the awareness of something missing or limited hence does not need to be carried for a lifetime.

So be under no allusions, feeling guilty, grief, anger or anything like that are all detrimental to anyone if held for any length of time. So use it as it is meant to be, as conscious guidance towards appreciation by redeveloping your beliefs regarding your life experience, or let go, turn the other cheek!

Clarity of mind is really where we are headed.

Ultimately once you have cleaned yourself up, which means you are nowhere near as negatively reactive as before, but rather have

conditioned yourself to feel more genuine appreciation and are stable with more happiness, you will also be developing a stronger sense of, 'clarity of mind.' This is hard to explain but clarity of mind **from a higher state of being, from appreciation** is what we are searching for and is the result of all this work of reaching to feel better. Everything we have been discussing really boils down to your ability to focus your mind relative to your own emotional responses. Which means being able to direct and change the dialogue in your mind to feel better moment by moment as a second nature behaviour. Ultimately perhaps a year or two down the track you will have stopped using modalities and techniques because your big triggering issues, your congested understanding, **no longer exists**! You will mostly be bouncing around consciously playing with the three mental options moment to moment, constantly improving and evolving your state of being with a clarity of mind and a stable sure footed approach to life. To my way of thinking there is nothing more important to you or to our society because your state of being is everything, it just is! This means you are naturally feeling more appreciation within more subjects more often.

Many think they are already clear thinkers, but haven't really sorted themselves out to the degree that I am teaching here. That is because they haven't been dynamically recreating their beliefs with the emotional connection to thought, but rather relying on intellect alone which we all tend to do to some degree creating all sorts of limiting beliefs concepts and ideas often suppressing inner emotional reactions.

You can get very good at suppressing inner reactions, thus think that you are a clear thinker because you 'think' you are not reacting to your emotions. Yet your opinions are coming from a place of limitation. For example, during a conversation or argument you can learn to supress your negative inner reactions so that you can clearly articulate your point of view, yet in the suppression of your inner reactions you have not yet sorted out **your thoughts, opinions and beliefs thus they are still coming from somewhere limiting thus low on the scale** even though you are managing to hold an apparent steady place in conversation without losing your cool.

If you are low on the scale your opinions are often limited to a lower consciousness outside of-self need to fore full your own personal preferences even though you may be able to control oneself. Hence why the political arena is rife with people shit the same as other areas of life and society. At any rate controlling your inner reactions like this is a great skill to have (to begin with) as it is often part of the process of moving up the scale as you control yourself within conversations etc. However, more genuine appreciation in more now moments is your indicator that you have truly shifted yourself, thus clarity of mind from higher up the scale allows for a much clearer mindset from a heart centred position meaning your beliefs and opinions are developing to something higher. **If there is no negative reaction to suppress or control a heart centred conversation can ensue.** Seriously the depth of this is hard to explain because it is experiential you have to embody it to truly understand. Understanding this conceptually is meaningless until you do actually embody it, embodiment means you have **sustainably** shifted your overall tone higher thus can maintain this higher tone because you have developed your thinking process and belief structure relative to your emotional indicators becoming more heart centred and appreciative for all life. This has been called enlightenment, spiritual growth, alignment, emotional literacy and so on. If you are striving up the scale using your emotional connection to thought, **you are doing the work** that will ultimately **embody a constantly improving state of being. You cannot ask more of anyone.**

In time dramas and what I love to call 'people shit' drops out of your experience altogether as you drop your negative reactions and criticisms out of your own mind. **If you stop fighting the world, the world stops fighting you! And here, true power and real change is born!**

Many people consider their criticisms as normal as we go about our daily lives. We all acclimatize to where we are to a certain degree, and subject to our own tolerance levels of our emotional reactions. Thus criticism is rife within most of us because we have learned to tolerate the negative emotion that is attached to criticism of any sort. In other words, we have acclimatised to our critical feelings by tolerating them and considering critical thought to be normal. Most of us are still in this conditioned habit of thought and behaviour, we go about trying to discern and work out the shades of grey between right and wrong from our own point of view then point our finger at those living in a different way. Thus we acclimatize to our criticism and do not have a vibrant state of being. Of course it's normal to be this way, its copied behaviour passed on from generation to generation. However true clarity of mind must not have any criticism within it, but rather come from a place of appreciation or intrigue perhaps, from somewhere further up the scale.

For example, I was listening to a chap talking whom has never worked on himself in this way and likely never will. He is very intelligent and articulate and has a highly developed skill of controlled conversation by not allowing his inner reactions to interfere with his spoken word, thus he naturally believes that he does not have emotional issues to sort out because he simply isn't aware of them, his introspection in this regard is limited or non-existent. This has happened through a lifetime of forced emotional suppression rather than conscious enhancement as I have been teaching. I respect this man greatly but he is also quite critical as is fairly normal.

At any rate, he was complaining and criticizing about the way others were living even though he didn't know these people himself, he had simply seen their home which was a fairly nice modern home except that it was in the most appalling condition, utterly filthy and deteriorating badly. He himself is a very particular person and prefers a clean environment, therefore he could not get his head around this, *'why would someone live like that? I don't understand it? Have they no pride etc.?'* This was his train of thought thus articulated criticism. He was just making the comment in passing as we all do when we are making idle chit chat with friends and work colleagues etc., **but this is the point!** We have acclimatized to this type of criticism and are ignoring the small inner emotional nuances that criticism evokes within us, thus we consider it normal and don't usually strive beyond it mentally. Therefore, we continue to think and behave this way and like a dripping tap fill our own state of being bucket with criticism thus suppress ourselves unwittingly, which in turn holds ourselves back from a vibrant free flowing connected mind thus truly vibrant life experience. Again criticism is pandemic. A vibrant life lies in your emotional reaction to it.

Vibrancy is not achieved with outwardly presumed status or any form of perceived physical success etc. Vibrancy is an emotional state. You can drop your critical habits of thought or your 'he said, she said' negative mental dialogues at any stage in life. Reach to hold an appreciative space anyway and in time you will develop an inner vibrancy and a clarity of mind which is everything to you! You must recognize all your little niggles and seek to move beyond the negatives and focus in the positives, you must! Therefore, clarity of mind coming from a basis of appreciation means the words, thoughts, opinions, beliefs, understandings and behavioural offerings are coming from a place beyond simply controlling negative critical reactions, because you have evolved your limiting points of view higher thus the negative reactions no longer exist!

Seek a higher state of being and you shall find a higher state of being, there is nothing more important than that, for you and everyone everywhere!

Love Richard.

Part Three

Thrive!

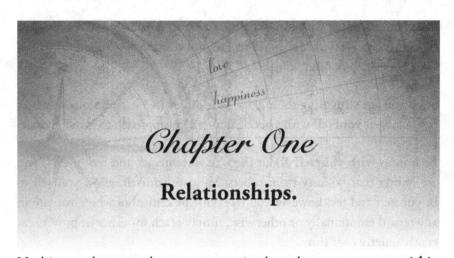

Chapter One

Relationships.

Nothing evokes more love or more pain than the way we **react within ourselves** with regards to all human relationships. Love comes from within not from those whom appear to be evoking the love within you. It is 100 percent possible to simply feel appreciation without the need of any outside circumstance to evoke the warmth of appreciation within you. This is a massive awareness that cannot be overlooked.

Said a different way nothing has to **happen** for you to love or to feel happy. **You don't need a reason to feel happy or to allow love to flow.**

So like all emotion be mindful of associating love outside of self in any regard. **Knowing** this in **all** life situations is true emotional responsibility. Developing emotional responsibility is the only way to have a genuine high quality relationship with yourself or anyone else. This means you sort out your own inner issues and baggage with a constant awareness that your inner reactions are yours to deal with, therefore you are not blaming others for what's going on within you, including when you feel any positive emotion such as deep love.

Developing full emotional responsibility translates into a substantial reduction of any arguing and bickering with others and the incessant need some people have to be right, or get their point across in an opinionated way. All these behaviours and more besides are emotional reactiveness outside of self, which you can **feel** whilst in the middle of the experience thus take responsibility for and work beyond. Ultimately becoming someone whom has a better manner with others because all your outside of-self reactiveness (buttons) has evolved higher. Thus, quality relationships of all kinds is a natural development in your life.

So, if you are struggling to interact with others in a harmonious way best take a look at **yourself** with a gentle non-critical approach to **inner** change.

Be **honest with yourself** about the way you interact and feel, even if you are hiding that honesty from others. Validate yourself, allow yourself to be yourself and feel however you feel don't be critical of where you are in any regard emotionally or otherwise, simply reach for inner improvement gently quietly over time.

To truly be your authentic-self you have to let go of all your internal issues finding ever increasing levels of self-esteem within each life experience. All your emotion is yours, so as part of this process of building your relationship with yourself, learn to **appreciate** all negative feeling spaces of any kind and to whatever degree that you may find yourself in. Without the negative emotional indicators bringing to your awareness that an off thought or two is active within you, you couldn't possibly realize you have some work to do within your consciousness, your belief structure, your active thought patterns thus resulting behaviour.

Consider how interesting this statement is, **feel appreciation for your negative feeling emotions.** This is no small thing; truly reach to feel appreciative for your negative emotion. Build a better relationship with your negative emotion, in other words appreciate it, it is an integral part of who you are and your life. Negative emotion is as important to you in the same way as your sense of touch is at guiding you away from an injury. Make peace with negative emotion and use it as it is intended, to guide you in harmonizing your chosen patterns of thought.

Anything less than the warmth of appreciation leaves room for improvement. Choose to become heart centred with deliberate evolution of your points of view and opinions by utilising your inner emotional niggles as indicators for **your own** conscious change. Rather than labelling outside circumstances as 'bad' when feelings such as disgust, anger, rage or sensitivity are evoked within you in observation of something horrible. Reach for a deeper awareness, reach to understand yourself and others, reach to appreciate all life and experience. In this way you **are** building your relationship with yourself as you become more appreciative, centred, assured, confident, relaxed, at peace and so much more.

Regarding relationships, people often run around doing all sorts of things to keep others happy, bend and change and behave themselves to suit another and pronounce that they have nurtured a relationship therefore believe that they have quality relationships. Yet these same people are often living on an emotional roller coaster seemingly at the mercy of other people's behaviour, walking on eggshells etc. This is always in degrees, and of course it is nice to do nice things for one another and although it is possible to have some relationship success in this way, **behaving in a way to keep others happy is extremely limiting for all involved** compared to the quality of relationships that can be achieved once you stop this appeasement dance. Behaving in such a way to appease others is only adding to any outside of-self associations others carry, which is extremely disempowering for all involved because others need to learn for themselves that their reaction is there reaction therefore find a steady place in their own skin also. Once you have cleaned up your reactive niggles there is no effort in being kind or nice or doing something for somebody else because you **want to** rather than doing these things from some place of agenda, obligation, limitation, or to appease an inner niggle of your own, or to appease another's inner niggle. Appeasement or P.C behavior is not a solution it is an utterly limited Band-Aid.

Imagine standing completely secure in your own skin, you are not upset by another's criticisms, you naturally have a steady emotional space within without effort to maintain, also any tolerance or suppression of negative emotion you may have had is leaving you or gone because you have learnt to take responsibility for and direct thought thus emotion as we have discussed. In this state where your niggles are no longer affecting you badly and what niggles you do have you are working with consciously, then the types of relationships that you will be experiencing goes infinitely beyond bending and changing to keep others happy.

Within human relationships there are all sorts of emotional reactions (niggles) going on to various degrees. For some people whom have not worked beyond their inner niggles as we have been discussing, their inner issues can appear overwhelming making it near impossible to create any easy, genuine, or effortless relationships because of their own inner battle which is most often associated (blamed) outwardly on to other people and situations, thus reactionary behaviours of all kinds occur. This often stifles an individual within life in many ways, for example some people whom blame their reactions outwardly can get hung up in petty dramas causing all sorts of grief for themselves etc.

However, as you move beyond negative reactions, whilst consciously enhancing all positive reaction, you become more appreciative and react less negatively. This then means you are more accommodating, compassionate and understanding of those around you in a self-empowered appreciative way. Not in an assertive way either because you are not struggling within yourself feeling uncomfortable around others thus being assertive is not necessary! This means you are relaxed in the presence of your friends and co-workers you are not worrying what others think thus you won't be reacting to negativity or criticism as badly as before if at all. **Plus, your opinions and attitudes are developing to something of a higher nature.** Most people drama will be dropping out of your experience because you won't be reacting to others, nor adding to it. This is not a small thing, this is huge because now it is natural and normal to effortlessly be within quality relationships because you are not as negatively reactive within **yourself.**

The biggest cause of negative inner reactiveness which transfers outwardly through your words and behaviours is, **limiting mental dialogues** which you may spend a lot of time thinking. Two such examples of limiting dialogues go along the lines of, he said, she said trying to figure out what to say next time etc., or the kind of mental dialogue where you are trying to figure out how to manipulate, force or argue your point of view over another's point of view and beliefs etc. Both of which and more besides really are limiting emotional roller coaster type thinking processes which transfer to all kinds of manipulation, bickering, arguing and one upmanship.

As a result of introspectively noticing the off-ness these types of thought patterns evoke within you, and your conscious nipping them in the bud early because you have made it your dominant intention to feel good no matter what, your entire thinking process changes. Thus you are simply getting on with life in a reasonably effortless way.

Battling or tolerating negative emotion is a fruitless effort it makes life hard work, you must learn how to use emotion consciously as we have discussed throughout. The only relationship you have consistently through your entire life is the **mental emotional** relationship with yourself, fairly obvious I know but important to note nonetheless. Nurturing and enhancing your relationship with yourself by working with all your emotional niggles as life evokes them is the singular most loving thing you can do for yourself and everybody else in your life. Because the ease that you feel in your own skin, in your own company is directly proportionate to the ease in which all your relationships flow.

In fact, until you can see in depth how you truly do create every emotional nuance within yourself, and take some semblance of mental thus emotional control, you don't really know yourself that well. Your relationship with yourself is everything.

Your ability to feel more appreciation naturally both within life circumstances and without life circumstances to evoke it is true success.

Loneliness for example, is an inner void that must be replaced with an inner-calm, with a genuine appreciation of being in your own skin, truly comfortable within yourself, vibrant and connected. You do not need others around you to fill the loneliness void. You must find a self-esteem within yourself which simply replaces any outside need to fill any loneliness feeling. Of course to do this like overcoming any limitation of self, takes life experience, an endeavour, and an understanding that you **can** replace **any** negatively held space with one of ever deepening levels of appreciation. This entire book is about a lifetime of self-exploration. The better you get at holding a pleasant state the easier it gets to do, to the point that it is simply natural **but ever evolving.** Thus the more your entire life and all relationships you engage in are enhanced and you are the main benefiter of that, because life is largely about how you feel.

So in summary, can you see that to have quality relationships in the first place, you must be a person whom is non-critical, accommodating, understanding, yet not worried about what others think of you, thus non-reactive within-self first? Therefore, it is not the relationships in and of themselves that are evoking your happy place, because if you are dependent on others behaviours to keep you happy then you are still trapped associating happiness outside of self! Of course quality relationships are often a life preference, and it is easy to feel good when a preference is met. Whether quality relationships are your preference or not **you cannot have a sustaining happy relationship with another until you have some semblance of sustainable happiness within yourself first,** this is a fundamental fact! Your relationships with others has more to do with the way you feel yourself than it does the other person, regardless of their behaviour. This is why the degree in which you are inaccurately associating your inner reactions on to others is directly proportionate to your ability to experience quality relationships with others. For example, that person who is pissing you off, isn't actually pissing you off, **you are pissing yourself off each and every time!** Coming to understand this comment is 100 percent emotional responsibility. Reach to really understand this statement! This is a fundamental fact of all human interaction which almost nobody wants to accept at first because of their incessant associations outside of self.

Accordingly, true sustainable happiness thus quality relationships with others can only come from nurturing your relationship with yourself, and this is an endless evolution.

Appreciate yourself and others. Diversity is the spice of life.

Intellect is great if you are blessed with it, but an individual's state of being is far more important than intellect, because state of being defines quality of life no matter who you are or your circumstances. You simply have to find a way to feel appreciative within your own being for yourself and all others, to be secure in your own skin without any need to find this outside of self. Build deeper levels of self-esteem from a basis of appreciation dropping criticism of yourself, others and all situations. Reach to appreciate.

For example, do you cringe when you see someone suffering from mental illness, or someone who has Down syndrome or any form of mental handicap, do you feel superior to a work colleague that does not seem to have the same intellect as you, or a different opinion to yours. Conversely do you look down at yourself in any critical way what so ever? That cringe feeling, criticism, or arrogant superior feeling or any other negative feeling such as embarrassment or anger is really your **inner knowing** telling you your mental perspective is not quite right, your perspective is not up to speed with appreciation, hence you feel the negative feeling in the first place. Any time you don't feel good this is your inner knowing telling you to shift your perspective somehow, reach consciously for a deeper perspective, a broader perspective, an appreciative perspective, or turn the other cheek shift your awareness elsewhere.

Conversely any time you are feeling better or good in some way this is your inner knowing telling you to keep moving in that direction consciously. Obviously a discerning mind is striving for this better feeling between their own ears, rather than having a negative behavioural reaction outside of self to appease an off feeling, such as when arguing, bickering or fighting with others.

We must simply do the best we can to uplift ourselves first and foremost, and then each other through example whilst also understanding that we are not responsible for another's feelings, that is their responsibility so teach them, uplift them by giving them their own self-empowerment! Most of us care how others feel and of course that is a natural caring part of life, the problem arises when you constantly try to keep somebody else happy which isn't actually teaching them how to maintain their own happiness! You simply have to find a way to be authentic to yourself, and kind to others **without disempowering them** by unwittingly teaching them that their happiness depends on your behaviours and kindness! Again this is a powerful awareness that needs to be fully understood for social and individual wellbeing.

If you come to the conclusion that your behaviour does not matter (which it does), because another has to sort out their own reactions (which they do), then you are still coming from some lower consciousness yourself. You do however have to do what is right for you, what is appropriate to you, whilst not falling into the trap of constantly modifying your behaviour to keep other people happy. If you are behaving in a way to appease another this disempowers you firstly and disempowers them by unwittingly training them that their happiness depends on the behaviours of those around them. Therefore, ultimately all people have to develop emotional responsibility for themselves if they ever wish to maintain their own happiness. Of course use your discretion and act in a way that is appropriate to you.

As this inner work becomes more conscious within society, as more people take emotional responsibility for themselves therefore are looking within rather than blaming outwardly, then people will interact in a more conscious manner without the ridiculous tit for tat behaviours or brownie point system some people live by. (She did this for me so I will do that for her. He did that for me so I will do this for him.)

What replaces the brownie point system of living is an inner harmony where you freely give and receive because you **want to** with full **appreciation in the giving and in the receiving** with no obligation or agenda involved. (I would love to give this to you. Wow I love this that you have given me.) Again simply appreciate, love is the incessant answer to all things.

People working within themselves will move past individual hurts more readily showing others that there is a path beyond pain. Helping yourself helps others by default!

There are children whom naturally understand how to maintain their inner balance who then simply do not develop inner emotional problems for themselves in the first place, observe these children, see how they do it, cherish these kids they are teachers by example.

Making the deliberate conscious work of utilising little niggles second nature within oneself is growing within society far more than many realise!

I am constantly meeting people like this from all over the world although they may describe what they are doing differently to how I describe it; it is essentially the same. This realisation that there are many others striving consciously for inner harmony with this type of education is very inspiring given the immense power of this understanding! When ideas build momentum within the many paradigm shifts occur in society, do not underestimate the power of your own happiness.

So don't blame away any negative emotional niggle because you think it is understandable, justifiable, or normal by attaching it to a **'reason.'** Get excited about it by seeing it as your guiding light to improve your own consciousness towards a higher state of being, because without your inner knowing telling you that your point of view is off through your little and not so little niggles how could you possibly know? Like heat to skin emotion to thought, again anything less than appreciation leaves room for improvement.

When you begin to climb the emotional scale consciously therefore **embody** this work within the experiences life provides, you will really begin to understand yourself relative to how you think and believe in relationship to all your personal desires for life.

Which means in understanding yourself more you will **at least begin to understand** the lying politician, criminal or terrorist more readily making it easier for you to be at peace within big subjects such as these in a way that is appropriate to you.

It's no small step to expect to hold steady with full emotional responsibility when observing disconnected people behaving in atrocious ways but **you can** and you must seek this higher path for everybody's sake especially your own.

Also please consider how often over the billons of people on earth the average person is actually faced with a genuinely horrible person in life for real, sure of course it happens but consider how often within the time frame of any individual life, over billions of lifetimes? Not so often statistically I don't think. (Plus what is your definition of horrible?) Virtually all of us are good reasonable people wanting to get on with one another whilst living a good happy life from our own perspective. **Yet many are blind to the inherent goodness of mankind** due to what they allow themselves to focus on, thus think about which very often builds blind bias.

If you are constantly focusing on any negative subject such as within news media for example, you will often build this negative bias unwittingly which doesn't usually serve you and those around you with your negative and often limited point of view. So if you won't use mental option one in regards to negative media by not looking at it in the first place, then consider using negative media as a life experience to see if you can develop your point of view to such an extent that your emotional reaction is redeveloped to something more positive, in spite of the negativity you are observing. Again not tolerance, suppression, or desensitising, endeavour to seek out a deeper perspective of life.

When you can truly see how your state of being is utterly created from within regardless of circumstance, because you have consciously begun climbing the emotional scale yourself you are in the process of redeveloping your belief structure to one with **less limitation from an unconditional appreciative perspective**. This means your thoughts and opinions will be changing to something higher and less limiting for yourself and others. You can see the beauty in the diversity of other cultures and the interesting characters the world offers. Including when observing big world issues such as an activism subject that you may be passionate about. With, the experience of self-improvement this work provides, you will begin to see how those few that are operating from such a disconnected place have become this way because of their individual mental patterns. These people's patterns of thought for the most part are not consciously chosen with any link to emotional knowing, or lacking any form of conscious striving for something higher because for the most part their desire, their freedoms thus feelings have been associated outside of self.

As you now know, what you look at evokes feelings which are actually caused by your personal opinion and preferences (wanting and desire) of what you are looking at. Understanding that if a preference is suppressed in any way, we associate this as a suppression of freedom which none of us tolerate well, hence many horrible reactive and aggressive behaviours are created.

With regards to horrible subjects of any kind, it may appear all too hard to redevelop our point of view or our beliefs and that's ok. Often this redevelopment requires a much broader perspective of life on a whole which is no small process or undertaking. Which is partly why a wise man once said, *"turn the other cheek,"* which really means utilizing mental options one or three, stop looking at the issue or thinking about it!

You must make it your dominant intention to feel good no matter what, because the better you feel the easier it gets to find higher perspectives and solutions to problems within mental option two.

Find appreciation by looking elsewhere first therefore feel appreciative and hold that space. Then from here reach to understand if you so desire. It's not a case of appreciating bad behaviour, it's a case of understanding bad behaviour and not being upset by it whilst continuing to hold an appreciative state of your own regardless of circumstance.

The conundrum of loving more than one!

As you move your overall tone higher in more subjects you ultimately have more natural moments of appreciation in more and more areas of your life. Your perception shifts for the better regarding many subjects and memories etc.

This can also become a conundrum, simply feeling appreciation, love naturally when you haven't adjusted any past mental associations you may still be carrying regarding what you have associated the feeling of love too. For example, regarding romantic love we often believe we must only love one person which may become confusing as you find yourself appreciating many. If so then you will need to reassess any confusing out dated associations, you may have. An example of this is the limited belief that people are only allowed to love one person. Love truly does come from within! This of course does not mean that you will want to be in a romantic relationship with everyone, but you may find yourself appreciating many more people and experiences which is great once you've redeveloped any funny little beliefs, ideas and associations you may still be carrying.

If you are in love, you have a problem with love.

If you only see love in terms of being in love, can you see if you are associating your feeling of love to the person you are in love with, that this is still outside of self? Thus you have a problem with love! Your love always comes from within you! Of course it's great when we have a beautiful person from our personal perspective who naturally evokes love within us, there is everything nice about **wanting** a person to naturally evoke the love within you thus you can say you love them. **However,** if you need this person or any circumstance so you can maintain your overall appreciation, your love within self then you are still trapped by associating your love outside of self, therefore you have a problem with love! **You must simply love.** This does not detract from romance in any way. In fact, as you develop and hold more natural states of appreciation you will enhance all your relationships romantic or otherwise.

Everything in life is relative to your personal preferences, your tastes, your wants including relationships of all kinds. Any one individual has many aspects to their character some of which may fit your personal preferences some may not. Usually you can easily appreciate (love) those with character traits that fit your preferences. However, you can also appreciate the diversity of those that do not fit your preferences, this truly is an awareness worth pondering. The diversity of all people is a wonderful thing. It takes more than one to build a world you know!

Often (but not always), your romantic partner has many aspects of their character you personally prefer which you can then naturally appreciate with ease, thus say that you are in love because it is easy to hold an appreciative state when your preferences are met. However, this can also be a trap such as when a character trait not to your liking rears its head and you focus on it, then how do you feel? Again this is outside of self, be careful what you focus on **because what you focus on can become all**

that you will see. Consciously strive to look for the character traits that evoke warmth within you. Even if you cannot find any positives within some people's character strive to appreciate all people's **being-ness** whoever they are and how ever they are regardless of their character, a step in this direction can be termed as seeking unconditional positive regard for our fellow man. **Diversity is the spice of life!**

An individual whose character traits match our personal preferences are easy to appreciate and that is what we all naturally tend to look for in a romantic partner. However, strive to look for the good in all people as just mentioned, consciously try to focus on and appreciate the character traits of your taste, of your preference within all the people you interact with thus helping teach you to focus your mind and thus state of being positively.

This is a practice worth considering for us all because all too often we do the opposite of this, we tend to zero in on the aspects we don't like and then moan and groan about this and that aspect of so and so. Criticism even of a mild nature is still criticism so cut it out! It takes a bit of practice in swapping from the negative nit-picky focus of what we don't like in others to a positive focus of what aspects we do like but the rewards are monumental for all involved. This level of consciously directed thought is part of the process of moving up the scale therefore, your romantic life and all relationships are enhanced one hundred fold as you learn to look for the good in **all** others **and** because of your overall work moving your own tone up the scale in all other areas of your life.

The way you feel about all subjects regardless of the subject is really in direct relationship with yourself first and foremost because it is you that is feeling! This means in doing this work within-self by endeavouring to feel better in all subject's life presents you are ever increasingly becoming stable and secure within your own being; with a genuine appreciative self-esteem few adults realize exits, thus you are simply loving!

Without the depth of self-esteem and self-empowerment that love and appreciation from within brings, the type of relationships I am referring to cannot ever be in your experience to the degree I am alluding to here.

This is because you are still reactive outside of self to some degree. All your relationships are always reflective of your reaction to them within self, therefore the better the relationship with self the better your relationship with all others.

This means that if you are holding any sort of disgruntlement towards another and you believe the relationship has been scarred for life this is untrue. When you release the disgruntlement within you there is no issue! Learn to relax and **genuinely** let go of any inner worry of how others think and also release any ill feeling directed at others even of a mild understandable or justifiable nature, in doing so all your relationships enhance for the better. This is powerful to experience and see within yourself over time; you have full control over all your relationships because you have full control of all your inner reactions which is really the only relationship you can control, the relationship with yourself.

Some people are not 'in love' per say with their partner or spouse, they may be going through the motions of relationship for infinite different reasons and degrees of feeling. Many people wish for, or long for something better, this can be in any subject not just relationships.

The bottom line is this, if you are looking for or longing for something better **it is simply because you want to feel better**, you long to feel love flow through you and are possibly trapped in the belief you need a better partner or circumstance to evoke a better feeling.

This conundrum many find themselves in evolves for the better one way or another as you endeavour to consciously work your way up the scale in **all areas** of life. Either your love for your current partner is rekindled and develops as you learn to really focus on the good in others, or you simply move on. As a result of your **continuing movement** up the scale and should you move on to a new romantic relationship your next relationship is often an improvement, not necessarily because you are with a different person, but mostly because **you are a different person!**

Unfortunately, if you are not doing this inner work then people often bounce from uncomfortable relationship to uncomfortable relationship and build a resentment and bitterness within themselves blaming the opposite sex for all their woes whilst coming to the incorrect assumption that all relationships are hard. Clean **yourself** up mentally thus emotionally and all relationships around you become easy!

If you currently do not have a partner, but want one and are a bit of a mess inside yourself, this is a great opportunity to sort out some of your issues first. That way you do not bring as much baggage with you into your next relationship, which inadvertently causes issues within this next relationship. Of course our work of inner niggles always requires experience within all kinds of relationships and life experience. Regardless of the details of what's going on the work is always the same. Take notice of your niggles and reach beyond the negative impulses whilst building the positive ones, thus ultimately finding a constantly growing warmth of appreciation within yourself which evolves for the better endlessly.

Chapter Two

The pain of not living the life you want, and that damn success belief!

What are your beliefs about success? What does it mean to you? Be very careful with the idea of success. You must mould any belief that is causing you grief, and societies status quo limiting beliefs about what success is can be a lifetime's struggle for millions. The majority of beliefs regarding success are mostly **'limited concepts'** that have been perpetuated by mass consciousness and that is all! You get to mould any belief you want. This means you do not have to accept any belief if it does not serve you personally. If a belief is causing you inner strife, then try to harmonise it with broader perspective or drop it altogether, be like the yogi "let go." A less limiting definition of success is much the same as developing sustainable happiness, meaning you have more moments in time which feel good to you, regardless of life circumstance. **A happy-self equals a happy life thus a truly successful life** because whatever you define 'success as' is always wanted for the better emotional feeling you believe it will bring you, so why not learn to feel good regardless of your current life story? Happiness is after all the only legitimate life career choice!

However, now that I have suggested that a happy life is a successful life, those that don't have society's concept of success and are also unhappy may struggle even more to deal with this new concept. For example, if you are not feeling good for any reason, if you are suffering long term depression, anxiety, fear or any other low emotional state which is hindering your quality of life, please don't go criticising yourself because you are not happy!

244

This is like double whamming yourself with negativity thus making things worse for yourself.

For example, some may think *"Well I'm not happy dammit and haven't been happy for years, I haven't got what I want in life either and now you tell me happiness is success! Then I must not be successful in this regard either!"* If this is you please take the pressure off yourself go easy and learn to let go, relax, breathe. To learn how to apply the work of the mind in relation to how you feel to the degree I am portraying in this book takes time to learn and to embody. Usually several years with much life experience just to get the hang of it! So give yourself a break.

What most of us believe success to be is so actively thought about within mass consciousness belief structures world over, it can certainly take some figuring through to make peace with. Those around you will likely hold some version of the status quo as their truth, thus possibly won't understand what you are going through as you redefine your concept of success. Some simply may not understand you. This is normal any time you buck the current of any status quo thought. Just ask my father the amount of times I've caused him to roll his eyes with my thoughtful ideas! So go gentle with yourself and others. Perhaps even keep your thoughts to yourself no point trying to convince others of your new point of view unless they are genuinely interested.

At any rate, true success is within you, within the creation of your state of being, the way you feel and the way you perceive is a massive part of life and you ultimately have full control over all of that even if you haven't quite got the hang of it just yet.

So be careful with the concept of success, if you believe you are not successful and are aware of where you don't want to be within any aspect of life you can drive yourself crazy chasing an elusive ghost outside of self all in order to feel good. You must mould your concept of success to suit **you** better. Of course when you are not successful from your own point of view because of the limited belief you may carry regarding success, or when you are in **any** unwanted life situation, you may feel stuck in the grind of life. You may find yourself bashing your head against a brick wall wishing for things to be different. Usually the 'so I can feel better' aspect isn't even recognized, **because we just want things different now dammit!**

For example, perhaps you're in a go nowhere meaningless job on basic wages thus living hand to mouth from your perspective. You don't like your job, money is a struggle, therefore freedom seems impaired through a lack in finance and time availability and it pisses you off, you **want** something different. Perhaps you know what that is and cannot figure a way to it yet or you have failed in your endeavour towards it. Perhaps you're stuck in the conundrum of not knowing what to do but you know you don't want this current situation. Over all, things may be going ok even though you don't like your job. You may be very engaged in life and active outside of work, but still your awareness is on a big chunk of unwanted life experience, a job you don't like. Or perhaps you haven't got a job and you're on the bones of your arse, or you're utterly sick of working hard for little return and you've had a gutful. In any case, or rather in **all** cases, it is your point of view within your **awareness** on the **unwanted** situation which is causing the not so good feeling, and we tend to write these feelings off by considering it normal to feel this way under these conditions thus strive to change the conditions rather than working with our emotional indicators as discussed throughout.

Almost everybody in the situation of not feeling successful whom is aspiring to status quo success will try and figure a way to a better paying job, another way to make more money, or perhaps try to generate more time for themselves. This could look like someone buying a business, or someone endeavouring to find their life path and many other situations. Many have been down this path and have failed or not found peace within it thus have given up on life and **tolerate** a negative state of being thus suppress themselves terribly. Tolerance has its place but often goes hand in hand with suppression and giving up. Never tolerate any negative emotional indicators for too long, use them as we have been discussing, aspire to enjoy your life regardless. If you don't these emotional indicators will likely get louder and louder causing some form of pain!

Please understand there is nothing wrong in striving to achieve your wanted goals and dreams financial or otherwise, except of course if your predominant reason you are striving for these things is to gain some sort of self-worth or emotional state from **outside of self!** Of course, there will always be some degree of this everything we do we do to feel better in all life situations and that's ok, even when you pick a thought to feel better you are still doing it to feel better (obviously) hence there is no escaping this fundamental truth. Love is the only answer hence anything less than appreciation leaves room for improvement!

Thus learning to enjoy your life **now** rather than waiting for something to **'make'** you happy is worth considering! Seek to appreciate what it is you are already doing.

Then through experience and time show yourself that the real reason you are pissed off or whatever negative feeling you feel, is caused by **your mental awareness in the absence of where you want to be** within any subject however slight or intense that feeling may be. More attention, more awareness relative to the degree you care usually equals more intensity. Understand you can redirect any awareness and shift perception more than you realize, thus consciously finding a much more comfortable place in your own skin. You **can** find a steadier place within yourself regarding all life subjects truly you can.

At the root of this issue of success or any issue that annoys you is the desire to feel better, and now that you know how your mental activity, your mental awareness, is the real cause of your pain even though your pain is intrinsically connected within your preferred life experiences you **can** do something about it sustainably. This is huge, this is where the real skill comes from within this work, gently quietly doing the work in all life situations as best as you can, getting better at it with experience.

Many people whom are not aware of this inner work and hold some aspect of the status quo belief, often assume that simply getting a job or a different job, a business or whatever will **'make'** them feel better and therefore there is no need to bother with any of this mental work.

Hmmmm, Really? Will you? Well of course when things are going your way relative to your preference it's much easier to feel good, hence a large part of the misunderstanding of what brings happiness in the first place. However, after you get a new job or change your circumstances in some way unfortunately before long you usually end up chasing your tail again, around and around in circles trying to fill that inner void with all manner of things, except the only thing that actually can fill it which is cleaning up **your mental behaviour by aligning thought with emotion, gently quietly over time.** Therefore, if we don't at least try to do some conscious work of aligning mind with emotion within life as well as whatever else we are doing to feel happy, we can often live a mediocre state of being and blame, blame, blame.

It is easy to feel good when things are going your way hence the constant chasing of outside circumstance. Some people in a good position who have achieved some semblance of status quo success but who haven't done this inner work or are even aware of it, can sometimes be self-righteous or not understand why others are struggling and therefore sadly miss the depth of this work. They may say, *"See I worked hard to get where I am and I feel good, you just have to work harder to succeed then you will feel better."* Can you see the limitation in that common statement? Of course the one saying a comment like that may see no limitation in the comment because their success has added to their incorrect belief about success and happiness. It is easy to feel good when things are going your way, when your life is aligning with your wants and desires, however as anyone who has lived life can tell you, this is not always the way life goes! Everything in life is in degrees; how good does the successful person really feel? Even if somebody has status quo success and says they feel good, do they? Really? How much joy and genuine appreciation are they really experiencing? Happiness and joy, clarity and passion all the positive emotions are true success and are within you, within everyone regardless of circumstance. Strive to embody a higher state of being and you will achieve a higher state of being.

Societies pressure on people to conform to this limited concept of success starts at a very young age with that often destructive question, *"What do you want to be when you grow up?"*

Remember 'society's pressure' is just a lot of people with similar beliefs within them which we then take on board and pressure ourselves with. We always do it to ourselves, create our own negative state, usually unwittingly. This process of mental work never ends, it is not a case of suck it up and tolerate issues, it is a case of moulding yourself from the inside out which creates a constantly improving perspective and demeanour. Once you have cleaned yourself up from your big issues by using emotion as discussed you will be consciously skipping through life directing thought by the way in which it feels, then you simply cannot fall into deep emotional traumas of any kind, thus you will clearly see the true value within your negative feeling impulses. A life without emotion is like a car without a steering wheel.

Having moved myself out of what can only be described as a long held depressive state heavily connected to my old status quo belief about success and several other life subjects, my own mental gymnastics continue to develop for the better with practice and experience, which has meant I can clearly see that through this work I will continue to improve day in day out, year in year out, I expect to be even happier and clearer in 10 years' time, **because this is what is happening!** This deliberate seeking of **a thought** that feels better really is your cure all, your all-encompassing box for a more vibrant life!

I know for certain that those actually using this different interpretation of emotion, this overall perspective, will be creating a sustainable happiness few are experiencing.

Your inner world has got to be your top priority, firstly for yourself, and then and only then will you have authenticity to share with others anyway. So in practical real terms, you are enhancing the world around you substantially by doing your own inner work.

I talk to a lot of people in passing from many different countries in my own travels and those that are touring here in New Zealand; almost all of them are struggling with this issue of success and life path, and what they **perceive** is expected of them. No matter what country we are from, most of us are searching outside of-self due to our natural misinterpretation of our emotional responses. Hence we chase our tails in all areas of our lives, and around and around we go.

True success really is feeling good in more moments in time regardless of our personal circumstances! There are those with plenty of status quo success that are certainly not happy, you only need to look as far as some celebrity disasters that happen with drug addictions etc., to clearly see that. Change your thoughts and you change your inner world, thus you change your perception of your life, the better you feel the better your personal perspective. That's huge, that's everything! No matter what age or stage of life you are in and whether you have money and society's definition of success, or you consider yourself an average Joe is utterly irrelevant to creating your own state of being, your own happiness, thus quality of life, because quality of life is more about how you feel than anything else and that is always generated between your own set of ears.

It's none of your business what others think!

Then there is that other doozy of an issue we all have to contend with in one way or another, and it is usually intrinsically connected within any limited concept of success we may hold, and all other areas of human relationship. This is worrying what other people think, worrying what you perceive people expect of you is also the same thing.

Let's say you are not overly successful from your own point of view, life's a bit of a drag. You're not where you want to be and some self-righteous person who thinks they are clever, or has a few more bucks and a nicer house, critically judges you. It's natural to have a hard time not reacting negatively at times like this. You've got a lot going on within you. You're not where you want to be, you've been critically judged and you are likely taking on board another person's criticism thus worrying about how they think, probably criticizing yourself as well in multiple ways. Thus there will be inner reactions firing off in regards to multiple subjects within you, your emotional niggles are fully activated letting you know where your work is.

Learning to find a happy place in all of this mess, is definitely a process you have to work through. It's a process that takes time. You have to find a way to make peace with the usually limited concept of success, as well as cut out self-criticism and let go of worrying what other people think. Therefore, develop a steady self-esteem within. At first this seems a lot of work, gently quietly will get you there the tortoise very definitely will win this race! Without these types of experiences, it is difficult to develop the self-esteem I am teaching without the experience to learn from in the first place! Remember any criticism someone is directing at you means **they are feeling criticism** therefore they are drinking their own poison so to speak! Hard to remember this when you yourself are reacting negatively to the criticism.

I know not reacting negatively in situations such as this is hard to do, especially when you perceive that some arrogant pompous type of person is looking down their nose at you, who may never understand this work you are doing within yourself anyway. Remember this is not a case of not reacting, this is a case of redeveloping your negative reactions gently over time to those that serve you better, each drip fills the bucket.

At first you may suppress your inner reactions in these situations as you gain control of your thought process, but in time as you move up the scale and your overall self-esteem grows, you simply don't react, or can redirect your mind fairly readily which is not suppression!

Be mindful that you don't make stuff up in your head by imagining what others may be thinking, because it is irrelevant what anybody else thinks! Any off feeling you feel you are completely doing it to yourself. It is still **your thoughts** causing all connect or disconnect within **you**. Not what someone else may or may not be thinking, saying or doing.

Again bare in mind the critical nature in the way people think only ever hurts the person thinking the critical thought! This is because the feeling of criticism is emotional pain regardless of degree, be under no allusions of that!

Many are hung up worrying what others think. There are very few who are coming from a place of non-critical appreciation within their life whose **self-esteem is developed** to such a degree that there simply is no longer any worry about what other people think.

Please note, there's a distinct difference between someone ignorant, or arrogant at the bottom of the emotional scale who doesn't care about others or what others think, compared with someone nearer the top of the scale who cares about others, but who is also not affected negatively by what other people think. The difference within these two states of being is as vast as the Grand Canyon.

When you finally move through this issue of worrying what others think, most of your people shit problems vaporize with it. You will find it a breath of fresh air and an inner freedom of self that you simply must experience to know what I mean. Many people are hung up in worrying what others think to varying degrees, some have let it permeate their entire life in extremely limiting ways.

Here are some extreme examples; the person that works excessively hard to keep the front of his property tidy in fear of what the neighbours might think, the person insecure in themselves to the degree that they struggle to be in their own back yard because they may simply be seen by someone, an inner anxiousness when talking to certain groups of people, a fear of public speaking or any nervousness in this regard, not wanting to use a public toilet because you feel shy or embarrassed, feeling bummed out at your high school reunion because you're not secure in where you have ended up regarding that damn stupid limited concept of success. Many feel this way daily which is utterly horrible.

Any of these examples and thousands more often evoke the feeling of embarrassment. **Embarrassment is 100 percent self-criticism** regardless of circumstance evoking the feeling. Even when you are embarrassed for another such as when observing a comedy for instance this is linked to your own self-criticism. Again of course, getting over these negative feelings in these situations is a process for each of us.

Without the feeling you wouldn't be aware there is something to get over. The feeling of embarrassment like all emotion is simply guidance, not good or bad in its own right simply guidance letting you know to work within your own consciousness. When you are feeling embarrassed, or cringing inside with worry of what another person may or may not be thinking at any stage in life, do everything in your power to evolve yourself beyond this inner reaction. Do the work of little niggles, strive beyond this feeling.

Whilst in the heat of any experience that you recognize an off feeling, try and release it in any way you can. This is the work, and it is powerful work. **The more experience you get releasing off feelings in the midst of life experience the more emotionally literate you become,** and you begin to thrive! Again this is not to be confused with suppression or forced control over oneself. Although in the early stages suppression and forced control may be needed before your overall tone has risen. Mental option 1 can seem like suppression, until your awareness truly has shifted elsewhere.

Other people's thoughts, and arrogance.

There is simply nothing you can do of any real value or merit in trying to control another's thoughts or perception of you. Sure you can manipulate and behave in a way to try and influence or coerce others thoughts and perceptions, however why would you want to in the first place? Usually because you are trying to appease an uncomfortable niggle within self with an outside manipulation of others. People shit of this type is utterly valueless. Relax and let go, it really doesn't matter what anyone else thinks, it is their right, and their freedom to choose whatever thoughts they want, just as it is yours. Realize the only reason you feel the niggle within you in the first place is because of **your** thoughts, your lack of self-esteem. You have to come to the realization that it is none of your business what rattles around in someone else's head. Hence any time your negative emotion is evoked in situations of this nature, **you will be aware,** and thus be able to try and let these thoughts thus reactions go. Many people wear masks to hide their inner emotional niggles as an endeavour to portray something which isn't really who they are, you know if this is you because you can feel it within yourself when you are trying to appease outwardly or suppress inwardly. For example, some people sometimes wear a false mask of boisterousness to suppress feelings of low self-esteem by outwardly wearing a mask of self-esteem in an extrovert fashion. In other words, some people's boisterous behaviour can actually be an unconscious masking of a feeling of insecurity within. Sometimes people wearing a mask of this nature are trying to create a perception in others of a demeanour they wish to present which isn't really authentic hence they are worrying about what others think. Of course this is only one example of the infinite examples possible.

Have you ever been to a large gathering of some sort where everyone is new to each other and you have noticed the awkwardness of those around you? This is a lack in self-esteem due to inner insecurities many of which relate to worrying about what other people think. Of course it usually doesn't take long for people to interact and relax, but that doesn't detract from the insecurities that actually existed a moment ago. So if this is you, strive for inner harmony so as the insecurity is no longer active within you in the first place.

Perhaps you have been to a community gathering of some sort where everyone knows everyone and there is an undercurrent of tension between people, for infinite 'reasons.' This too, is due to inner insecurities and a lack in self-esteem, holding grudges etc. (Holding a grudge is an immature association outside of self.)

Also understand that the arrogant one standing there in their arrogance, which can appear as self-esteem or self-importance, is actually woefully lacking in self-esteem to the degree I am portraying, thus not actually that happy either. Arrogance can often be a self-defence mechanism, this can be worn as a mask covering individual insecurities, sometimes for a lifetime, and often the individual is utterly oblivious to this. So develop some understanding for their pain even though they may be oblivious to it themselves, don't let it upset you, their arrogance feels better than the insecurities they are masking; thus a feeling of false-empowerment is felt and displayed as arrogance. So strive to develop an understanding of all others and give them a break. Hard to do if somebody is looking down their nose at you from their arrogant self-superior disposition, but this is your work. We all want a happy life and we can only ever do the best we can from whatever our thoughts/beliefs allow! Any time you move up the scale you feel better, hence self-belief combined with criticism of others often evokes a false-empowerment feeling which is arrogance. Arrogance is usually not very nice to observe in others because of the criticism of others within arrogance. Arrogance is a negative emotion but can feel empowering to the arrogant one because of the self-belief within the arrogance. There is nothing wrong with self-belief, there is everything good to be found in self-belief. It is the criticism of others and the attitude of knowing best from a self-superior vantage point that makes arrogance so ugly. Arrogant people must overcome this sort of inner pain if they ever want a truly vibrant life, be under no allusions any arrogant feeling is an inner disconnection. Even though arrogance may feel good at the time because of the self-belief aspect, or the moving up the scale from a place of insecurity aspect. You are suppressing your state of being far more than you realise if you are holding a space of arrogance, meaning you need to develop your insecurities higher thus the feeling of arrogance is sustainably worked past. Arrogance is nowhere near appreciation and appreciation is what we all seek, you can develop an appreciation of others within any self-belief rather than criticism, which is simply that, an appreciative state of being. This is far more valuable than any arrogance.

Conversely, if arrogant people annoy you come to understand the deeper reasons given here as to why those whom are arrogant are like this, thus relax any negative reaction that maybe evoked within you in observation of them. It really is their problem, their limitation of thought. Kindness, understanding and compassion is the answer here, just as it was with the child abuse example given in part one, we need to support all others in their endeavour to move up the scale and not be upset by those whom aren't trying or even aware. Be under no allusions, 'arrogance is emotional pain' just as criticism of any sort is, and yet again neither good nor bad in its own right, but rather inner emotional indicators that perspectives need tweaking.

Self-criticism, embarrassment and being like the Yogi.

I overcame a huge amount self-criticism, embarrassment and worrying about what other people think in four days flat. This resulted in the development of a much deeper self-esteem, which was a momentous inner shift in short order! Before this point, there had been years of hanging on to the tree like the yogi, nothing teaches like life experience. Remember criticism is nothing more than habitual patterns of thought of which we unwittingly cling to because we are tolerating the negative feelings critical thought evokes. (Hence tolerance is not always helpful.)

At the time I was still in the early stages of this work, I was seeking to see the link between thoughts creating all feelings. I was fully engaged in the mental seeking of this link and hadn't fully developed this awareness in all areas just yet especially in the area of self-criticism! At any rate the following story vividly **showed me my criticism** which gave me much experience within my thought to feeling self-analysis, as well as a letting go, an ah ha moment. At the time not only was I analysing my thought to feeling relationships as best as I was able, this was also amongst an ample dose of congested understanding which makes these links tricky to see. However, as a result of my ongoing inner work I was becoming more aware of my inner world. I was doing my best to overcome and understand any negative states I felt by knocking the thoughts on the head **when I recognized them** with my ever developing introspection, and then reaching for different perspectives. I had an intense desire within me to not only get beyond crappy low emotional states but to also understand how I created them. (Which I then unwittingly perpetuated in my desire to understand.) I had worked through many of life's issues pertinent to myself at this stage but that damn self-criticism was still alive and well and was heavily suppressing my state of being as it does everybody within these habitual mental patterns.

So here I was working with youth offenders. Part of the youth program included driving the lads into town to do a morning's schoolwork with a provider who offered education outside the school system, this was only one morning per week the rest of the week was made up of work experience in their chosen industry. On this particular morning the bulk of the boys didn't want to do any schoolwork, this meant they played up merry hell, achieved little and thus created a struggle for themselves and staff. These kids for the most part needed love, understanding and most of all a build-up in their self-esteem. This particular environment was not overly conducive to achieving any real academic value, nor self-esteem from my point of view. Other educational approaches were more effective in that regard which ultimately happened within the program as the program evolved.

At any rate here I was in a situation I didn't want to be in. I had driven the lads into town and several of them had been playing up all morning from the moment they were out of bed in a way only youth offenders used to the institutional life can, it got worse when we arrived. There was one lad in particular who was being extremely difficult of which I was criticising myself about my inability to get him to see some sense. Yet they had all been expressing their discontent in having to do school work in rather colourful ways. I didn't want to bring any of them here given their extreme discontent that morning let alone when they flatly refused to engage. I was winding myself up! I was only a little angry at being in this situation but the real battle was that I was critically beating myself up for feeling angry about it! I was also criticising myself for my inability to control the boys, in particular the lad who was really stirring everybody up. On top of the critical beating I was giving myself about my anger I even criticised myself for criticising myself about all of it! Can you follow how much self-criticism upon self-criticism was going on in this experience? My god if I wanted to know where my self-criticism was here it was in all its undignified glory. I lost my lolly!

The inner fury, and self-directed rage pointing at myself was insane! My entire body felt like it was on fire, this was the depth of my emotional reaction. Have you ever seen vampire movies when a vampire is burning in the sunlight? Well, that's a fair description of how I felt. Although the lads new I was grumpy, most of my inner shit was hidden within myself in my self-directed condemnation. I made an executive decision on the spot that there was no way in hell under these same conditions that I was ever going to take kids here again. I told them in a not so polite way to get in the van and we would leave. They were quite unsure as to what to do, I was meant to be Mr. calm, and here I was not so calm. Some of them freaked out thinking the course manager might kick them off the course for being unnecessarily difficult, this was a genuine concern for them because if they got kicked off in many cases that meant going back to a juvenile detention centre, youth jail so to speak. I assured them that that wouldn't happen as it was my decision to leave regardless of their behaviour. You could say I had their undivided attention! So on the drive back I was battling myself, here it was in all its glory, my self-criticism.

I wasn't battling my decision to cut short this part of the day as anyone dealing with youth of this nature knows things can change on the spot for various reasons. (Imagine a chimpanzee tea party as that would have been easier to deal with compared with these lads that particular morning.) At any rate as part of my personal inner work I had been wanting to understand criticism and to know where my criticism was. I knew I was overly self-critical but hadn't quite figured it within my self-analysis that well at this stage, and here it was in my face vividly clear and horrifically painful! The inner work began in earnest. On arriving back at the youth home I off loaded onto the shift supervisor who was going off shift. This evoked embarrassment within me during my off loading, because now I had lost my cool in front of someone I respected, that damn worrying about what other people think thing was alive and kicking. He stood up, put his hand on my shoulder and said with genuine care, *"Don't be so hard on yourself Rich"* and went home to his family leaving me to stew in my own juices. Luckily it was a Friday and I was going off shift too not having to work the weekend hence I had the weekend to get myself together. You simply cannot work with kids like this when you're in such a bad mood.

I hit the road immediately after work and began the four-hour drive north to hang out with my oldest friend, we went to kindergarten together! I was doing everything I possibly could between my ears to sort this issue out, mostly only using mental option two of looking for lighter perspectives. Which of course was difficult because of the current negative momentum which was bashing the hell out of me, yet I was determined it was not going to beat me. I gave myself a break in my mind by taking a step back, then by looking for and finding thoughts and points of view within the subject which eased my mind, plus the relief of being out of the place for a couple of days was great, the drive was helpful in its distraction as well. Upon arriving at my mate's place battle weary mid evening on a Friday, we did what mates do, boy those rums tasted good. The inner burn had subsided to a light sunburn by the time I went to bed that Friday night. Over the next two days I was processing continuously, reaching and seeking to let go, as well as developing a different perspective which was tricky. I had started the process of dropping my critical view of myself, I had also spoken to the other shift supervisor regarding the Friday incident in regard to reassessing the value of taking the boys to the education provider at all. The conversation evoked embarrassment which I was finding noticeably easier to release as I strived to release it. I took particular notice of that release of embarrassment and saw it for the progress it was. I was making good progress within my overall state of being and come Monday I was feeling myself again.

Upon returning to work on Monday fresh and ready to go, I found the two shift supervisors and the course manager struggling with the same lad I had been struggling with on Friday. Despite there being three talented and far more experienced youth workers than I doing their best, in that moment in time they had not a hope in hell of turning this kid around in that particular moment. He was having it his way hell or high water. If all three of these brilliant youth workers couldn't redirect that one kid in that particular situation effectively as a team of three how the hell could I deal with the Friday incident? In that moment in time first thing Monday morning I finally let go of my self-criticism. The yogi returned to the fire so to speak, there was a noticeable click within me, a letting go, some may call this an energy shift, a realization, a release, an embodiment, a relaxation, or a breakthrough call it what you will but I have no longer held self-criticism of that magnitude ever since, in fact hardly any at all because I can now **clearly see and feel the thoughts** as they arise and knock them on the head before they build momentum. The feeling of embarrassment and worrying what other people think is virtually gone within me in almost all life situations since then, when it rears its niggly little head it is so mild and easily deflected that it is simply no longer the same issue for me as it had been. I had embodied a new level of self-esteem in that moment in time. A new freedom within-self such as this you have to experience for yourself to truly understand. It took me a while to acclimatize to this new higher state of being, to get used to it. Self-esteem at this level was a whole new experience! My god this work of self is really, the only, legitimate life career choice!

Habitual self-critical thought is no longer a snowball of any consequence in my mind, thus my ability to direct my mind has improved substantially. In fact, it has flipped. If you have experienced doubling up of criticism, even tripling up, or worse such as described in this story, you will be amazed to hear the complete opposite happens as a result of this work. I now often recognize a good happy place within me, and rejoice in the fact I'm happy and then realize I'm happy for being happy! So you can double up or triple up in a good way as well, which is brilliant mental work well done! Remember that the more we direct our mind in a better feeling way, and then consciously rejoice in the better feeling, then the easier a good feeling demeanour is to maintain because positive momentum is growing.

Also please note, you won't necessarily have a big instant shift such as described in this story, usually your movement up the scale occurs bit by bit, brick by brick, as you build yourself from the inside out. As mentioned before, ridding yourself of criticism is a process of consciously recognizing the critical thoughts as they occur and doing everything in your power to think something else, anything else. Many people usually notice their inner change in hindsight a year or two down the track.

Of course the details of my story, or any details of any person's story **really are irrelevant** apart from for use of explanation, this is because of the infinite possibility within all human experience. What is relevant however was my desire for inner change and achieving that change, this means everything and is relevant to everybody's life story! In other words, it was my desire to move beyond my negative inner reactions from within, and achieving that change from within, that was of true essence here. The improvement in your state of being is everything!

Chapter Three

You can overcome any emotional trauma.

In the case of long standing emotional trauma due to a horrible past experience can you see that the more an individual understands and works with their thought emotion inter-relationship, the sooner they can move beyond such horrible things? **The horrible thing is only a horrible thing until such time as you overcome your inner reaction to it.** Of course that doesn't change the fact that the horrible thing happened or is still horrible. However, when your negative reaction to it is improved or gone altogether you are now not hindering your own progress in life from this point onwards; developing an appreciative state of being is everything to you.

If you believe it is normal to feel bad about such and such an issue (forever), then you are limiting yourself in the most limiting of ways. For example, if you believe you must feel grief for X situation or person whom is now gone, how can you let it go if you are believing grief must be felt anytime you think about that subject? You can find a way to simply appreciate the gone person or situation, to fondly look back with a smile and appreciate the time spent, truly you can. Of course there is a natural and normal process of grief recovery. Moving beyond any trauma is a process per person and issue and may seem impossible to 'appreciate' when the hurt is still strong within you, but in time it can be done. Grief is obviously only one example of emotional trauma. At any rate as has been discussed, when this inner work becomes more common practice in daily life, more known and talked about, then big subjects such as overcoming trauma are much more readily dealt with because more people can teach each other from their own experience of consciously creating their own vibrant state of being, regardless of their past circumstance and thus develop stories others can relate to as is the purpose of any story. The freedom you are looking for is within your mental attitude and approach to all things relative to your own inner emotional indicators, period! This whole book is based on the fact that you have ultimate control of your **overall emotional state** even though it often does not appear that way in the beginning stages of this work. Several years can be considered the beginning stages, before this overall practice becomes second nature. So of course it can be a bit of a muddle embodying this into your life to begin with, but you can figure your way through in a way that is appropriate to you.

There will always be some who flatly refuse to accept emotional responsibility even within something as simple as blaming emotions felt on the person they are in conversation with, let alone a horrible event that upsets them and that has to be ok with you, that is their choice although it is very disempowering for themselves.

Some believe there is no way they could ever recover from their particular trauma, perhaps believing that they have to live with it which is completely understandable, the horrors some people have experienced don't bare thinking about. However, sadly a few counsellors and psychologists still think this also mostly due to observing people struggling for years with an issue with no apparent improvement. But what limitations are being placed on yourself or others in this limiting belief? Each individual must do their own inner work themselves and must firstly come to understand that they create all their inner reactions within every moment in time before they can even begin to work within this mental emotional realm to this degree. No one can think for them. They must come to realize that they can actually do something about it gradually thought by thought, bit by bit, filling their state of being bucket so to speak. I believe anyone can overcome any emotional trauma with the application of this type of education, given time the wherewithal and professional help as required. Knowledge is power, sure not necessarily easy to apply, but still possible. Of course not everyone is ready or willing to take the step of developing full emotional responsibility for multiple reasons and that also has to be ok with you. Kindness and understanding go a long way.

How do you react when aspects of your character or behaviour are pointed out to you?

People often point out aspects of our behaviour and character traits, sometimes this is done from a genuine desire to help you, sometimes from a critical stance and neediness on their part for you to change to keep them happy. This is their need to control things outside of self and often takes place even if they were coming from a genuine place of care as well. In any case it does not matter the intent of the person pointing out your flaw or whether there is an actual flaw or no flaw is also unimportant. Even if they were completely wrong, coming from some limited point of view or miss understanding, this does not matter either. What matters is how you are reacting to it and what you do with it between the ears.

A fairly good approach to changing behaviours that you personally don't like about yourself is to simply keep an eye out for your behavioural responses within each life experience and do the work of change as best as you are able as it occurs and then try again and again as required in each experience as you move through life. I am sure this is fairly obvious and most of us are naturally doing this anyway, however who are you doing this for and how do you feel when you are doing it? Authenticity and kindness towards yourself within any work of change is highly beneficial to develop, rather than a critical must change myself because of X, Y, or Z reason. A self-critical approach just makes hard work of personal change, be gentle, go easy, relax, breathe, let go…

The concept of now!

The power of now or being in the present moment is an interesting subject. From our **human life experience** point of view how can it be anything but now, it is always now, in any given moment it is now, hang on a minute it's now again, wait a minute its now, oh look it's still now!

Of course you can get into deep philosophical and scientific discussions about time and space but when it comes to our personal wellbeing it is always now therefore, there is always a new powerful moment now. A new moment to focus a fresh new thought that feels better now, a new moment to relax now, a new moment to appreciate, a new moment to simply be, a new moment to take a breath, there is always a new moment.

Being in the now or being present means many things to different people and teachers.

From my perspective the degree you are connected to a good feeling place, the more present in the now moment you are. Can it be anything but that? **To be truly present simply means you are feeling some degree of appreciation within any given moment.** That's it, simple as that!

Think about it, do you remember a time when you were in a state of natural appreciation? Perhaps walking along a beach, or trail during a beautiful time in the day and you found yourself in a natural state of appreciation, this is truly what being present is. Perhaps when you are focused at the task at hand whatever that may be whilst you are holding some degree of appreciation, this is being present in the moment.

In other words, the depth and level of your state of being is always the dominant factor in any given moment. The more connected you are means you are higher up the scale thus the more present you are. The lower you are the least connected, thus least present. Ponder this because your state of being truly is everything.

I love the thought **'It's always a powerful new moment now,'** it is a great thought to have as part of your repertoire of thoughts for personal well-being. If you find yourself careening down the slope in some big old snowball of a thought form, simply stop take a breath and ponder, 'It's just another moment now,' so relax and let go, do whatever you can in the moment to feel better.

As you know we get to choose and direct our thought and thus create our state of being, so whether you are thinking about the past, present or future you can choose and focus thoughts that feel good **now**, no matter which part of time you are thinking about! Therefore, the power of now really boils down to what you are doing mentally within any given moment. Are you hindering your tone, or enhancing it? It's your choice you get to mould the way you feel within each new now moment bit by bit, even when you think it just happened to you and life's issues seem to have taken over. In fact, when life's issues have taken over so to speak this is indicative that this overall inner work is not yet second nature to you, hence it **appears** life has taken over due to feeling horrible about things outside of self, this is where the work is, life.

I can appreciate that this is really hard to hear and accept if you have been on, or are on the receiving end of an unwanted life experience, but **it is a new moment now,** and you get to choose, and it is a new moment again **now**, and you get to choose, again and again and again.

From the point of view of self-empowerment, peace of mind, self-esteem and happiness etc., it's nice to know that gently quietly over time, over lots of new **now** moments, you can direct and take control of your thoughts thus state of being. In the coming days, weeks, months, years, the rest of your life, it is of value to build a repertoire of your **own thoughts and tools to use in the now**, to enhance your state of being in different given moments **relative** to your current mood.

It's a new moment now, relax breathe pick a better feeling thought, it's a new moment now, relax breathe pick a better feeling thought, it's a new moment now…

Chapter Four

It's hard to think positive when feeling bad.

It's really hard to think, say and do good feeling things when anyone is feeling bad. This is the case even if we don't realize that we feel bad. Perhaps because we have acclimatized to our belief structure thus state of being. Perhaps we believe we must feel certain ways in certain situations therefore don't realise there is another way, such as when feeling angry. Although anger may feel good if it's a move up the scale from powerless we may also be justifying our anger outside of self because of something.

We often cling to our beliefs and opinions without any self-examination as to why we think and feel the way we do, or without any reaching for better feeling perspectives. This is part of the reason for things such as harm crime and heinous acts, as people unconsciously try to find their own freedom from outside of self, rather than having the conscious realisation that our universal and incessant draw from within to feel better is really asking us to develop our own individual belief structure, our own consciousness, our own opinions and points of view to that of an appreciative nature. Anybody's true freedom can only ever come from readjusting any limiting and powerless patterns of thought thus beliefs which holds them in such a constrained and limited feeling space.

The following is a common everyday example of a time when it is hard to think say and do anything positive which most of us should be able to relate to.

Often we wind ourselves up, we get grumpier and grumpier as the day goes on, the day is just like any other day not really anything wrong with it other than we have worked ourselves into a foul mood one way or another. At some point in the day somebody asks you how your day is going, you know your day isn't really bad but you are grumpy so you usually respond saying how crappy your day is **because you are grumpy in that moment.** It is usually a struggle to authentically say that you are having a great day; in fact, it would be quite a struggle to say your day is great with any authenticity while you are in any type of low mood.

Conversely when you are in a more stable, sure footed, good feeling place and therefore higher up the scale it's really hard to think say and do bad feeling things.

So let's reverse the above example. Let's say your day started out badly, things were happening that was upsetting you in some way thus you ended up in a fairly grumpy mood because of your attention to the negative aspects of your day. Then as the day goes on, other events take over perhaps totally unrelated to the previous issues and your attention is now focused on this event which is evoking positive emotion within you, or perhaps the events that were upsetting you resolved themselves for the better. The point is earlier in the day there were a lot of annoying things that happened which you reacted to, then later in the day you found yourself in a very good mood, then someone asks you how your day was and you know your day was pretty bad mostly, but you are currently in a good mood hence your response to the question would likely be much more positive in nature.

There is nothing more important than that you feel good, which means all of us!

As you become introspective of your moods and how you **behave, react and think** within your moods, this awareness will come clearer to you in all areas of life. It is important to develop more and more **thoughts** and tools to draw on to aid in shifting yourself out of any grumpy upset moments, regardless of any situation that evokes it, thus sustain a more stable disposition. Otherwise you will be feeling as if you are at the mercy of life events around you, and this is never the case it just appears that way to those whom are still associating outside of self.

Here's a more complex example.

So imagine a situation that is important to you, perhaps a political movement or protest of some sort, a social problem you wish to help change for the better. Obviously when people are feeling sensitive, stressed, angry, disgusted or fighting against any issue whilst holding any form of negativity within their feeling space, their words and actions are vastly different to somebody interested in the same subject whom is holding a genuine steady appreciative space within themselves. An appreciative activist's words, actions and ideas will be vastly different to an angry activist, and yet still interested in the same subject. I wonder whose ideas and solutions may be worth more time listening too? **Reach for appreciation before acting within any situation.** If you are trying to change a situation to suit your own sensibilities, understandable, justifiable or not, this is not usually of a high nature; this is usually trying to force outside conditions to change to suit your own emotional reactiveness regardless of the aid you may wish to offer.

Obviously sensitivity, anger, disgust, fear, stress etc., although are naturally evoked in observation of others doing horrible things from what we perceive as a lower consciousness behaviour which we ourselves cannot understand, our feelings are still **our** feelings. Often we may believe negative feelings are driving us for positive change of some such issue this is because of our incessant association outside of self. This means negative feelings are still not that conducive to higher practical solutions because they are very much **linked** to **limiting thought** in some way. These negative feelings really are drawing **you** for a deeper growth within your own consciousness! These limiting thoughts may be as simple as utter frustration in not being able to understand a horrible person's actions. Hence endeavouring to truly understand yourself to this level helps aid your understanding of others. Reach for conscious creation of higher states within all life then solutions of a practical higher nature can be found more effortlessly as you yourself raise your awareness. Remember your negative feelings really are evoked from a **'limited point of view'** regardless of circumstance therefore there is work to do within self. Again I know how hard this is to figure out in the early stages of this work, especially in something as emotive and complex as activism and geopolitical tensions. However, reach to feel better no matter what, don't associate your feelings outside of self and when you get good at this, your observations of other people's behaviours become clear regarding a deeper understanding of emotional responsibility. Which in turn allows you to see the depth of this within all social problems regardless of each issues complexity. Higher states allow for better quality solutions to find their way into your awareness. Appreciation, love and deeper understanding truly is an all-encompassing solution, disgust of another's actions is not love nor higher understanding. Again, relax, breathe, let go, whilst gently reaching for a higher state of being.

More about wants, desires and freedom.

All of life is intrinsically connected to your individual personal desires which can be described as your preferences, tastes and wants. Every individuals sense of freedom is connected to their personal desires within any experience, if we cannot do what we **want** then we feel constricted in some way, our freedom feels suppressed. How many freedoms (desires, wants and preferences) can you suppress in another before they rebel or shut down within themselves?

Many teachers and religions have tried to steer people away from desires saying all sorts of interesting things, however there is no getting past the fact that all of life is about your own personal preferences within all situations. What you wear, what you eat, what your interests are, what you prefer within your opinions of any subject, what you do for work, how you want the wider world to be, even when you are engaged in what is deemed as a selfless act because a selfless act is still a personal preference. You may see selfless acts as a positive behaviour because you are helping others, which of course is usually the case, however this does not remove selfless acts from being a preference, a desire. Hence, when you are engaging in your personal preference of behaviour within what you see as a selfless act you are still doing it for your own emotional gain, because it is **your preference** and there is nothing wrong in that, it's just the way it is.

This does not mean to say that you are wearing what you want, eating what you want, working at what you want, have the freedom you want, or as selfless as you want.

What this does mean regarding thought and emotion as an individual human being is, in the awareness of anything there is always two sides of the coin, meaning your awareness is either on your preference, or your awareness has some **limitation** regarding your preference.

- Any time your awareness is on the absence of your preference with a limiting perspective you feel some form of negative emotion relative to the life situation you are in or thinking about and to varying degrees.
- Any time you are living a preferred preference or thinking about a preferred preference with some possibility of your preference materializing or with less limitation in your mind, you feel some form of positive emotion.

All aspects of life are linked to how we feel regarding our personal desires, preferences, tastes and wants in every moment in time there is no getting past this.

A path to sustainable happiness is by **not looking** outside of self for these desires to fill an inner void, but rather consciously seek to appreciate what you do already have and appreciate every little aspect of what desires are already fulfilled. Appreciation is love, and love is the answer after all. However, before we discover and use this conscious work of redirecting our patterns of thought we tend to unwittingly allow our mind to develop a strong awareness (momentum) in the **absence** of some desire or another whatever that may be. Hence this work can be a bit hard to do in the early stages simply because habitual thought pattern(s) have momentum in the opposite direction of that which we prefer.

This work is certainly hard to do initially because of this mental momentum and especially when mental momentum is kept active due to living any unwanted experience, consequently the value and power of meditation and distraction. However, this same mental momentum is what makes it easy for us to maintain a good happy demeanour once we have shifted our mental focus to that with less limiting perspectives.

Every aspect within every subject in your life has the smallest subtleties of your personally preferred (desired) experience from the smallest of things such as how do you like your morning cup of tea, through to the big subjects in life such as the desired character traits of your life partner. Some people who have given up on life may have suppressed their desires perhaps because life has not delivered them.

You cannot suppress a desire without it affecting your state of being, draining you of your zest and your passion. If this is you, you must move past the suppression by truly getting your awareness of it altogether or looking at it with less limitation whilst simultaneously **learning to appreciate what you do already have.** The lack of zest you may be experiencing as a result of your awareness in any unfulfilled desire (wanted experience) can be causing you untold grief in other areas of your life by holding you in a negative feeling space. This means 'It is really hard to think say or do anything beyond your negative feeling space.' Hence, the worse you feel the worse it gets, the better you feel the better it gets, momentum works both ways. You must learn to redirect negative feeling thought process or awareness's for your own sake. Consciously use the three mental options relative to your state of being, hone this skill, realising within the three mental options you really only have one option and that is, **which thought do I think now, where do I give my attention now.**

I have met people who have retired young but have no passion or zest despite having money and success from society's point of view with no more need to work. Often these people can't actually stop working because they don't know how to entertain themselves between the ears, they are at a loss as to what to **do** because **'doing'** has been associated to things such as self-worth, or **'doing'** holds feelings of boredom at bay for those that haven't made this inner work second nature. In some cases, work itself has become a form of meditation and distraction from other aspects of life they haven't yet made peace with. At any rate, this is not the problem it appears to be, it's just mental snowballs that's all nothing more. Melt the thought forms that aren't serving you by engaging in mental option three as much as possible because as mentioned, you can only activate thought which means you can only choose and direct which thought you wish to engage in, so the more you develop new patterns the better off you will be. Get out there and live life, try new things and experiences but this time with the mental tools to back it up! Seek out things you actually **want** to do. Seek to appreciate. Always reach beyond your negative niggles and stretch out the positive feeling spaces for longer.

Find new subjects to engage in, ditch criticism altogether because when you are critical you are feeling critical, stop worrying what other people think. Can you see the whole process of letting your mind spiral into any awareness of something missing, limited or critical only holds you in a low state hence it gets very hard to think say or do anything positive? Even though this is the case, you can reach upwards gradually bit by bit. Perhaps spark up old subjects of intrigue, play, have fun, mingle, and **find many something's of interest that occupies your mind,** do this for the simple pleasure of it. Perhaps this whole concept of 'Shifting your state of being' could be your new intrigue as it has been mine for many years. Now that's an idea worth considering don't you think? Everything we do we do to feel better, so why not simply learn how to consciously feel better anyway. Life is after all, an adventure of self.

The problem of 'life not turning out all roses' becomes a non-issue if you can embody a higher state of being because that was always the unconscious target anyway!

Within all of this we are freedom-seeking beings, it is the way we are wired. We **want** the freedom to do what we **want** when we **want**. No one likes to feel constricted, restrained or told what to do, we **want** the constraints of limitation removed from our experience.

Our life experience is intrinsically connected to this, and our life experience is really about moving from personally wanted experience to wanted experience. Our emotional response to thoughts are inherently connected to our own personal desires within every experience life presents.

For the most part, we have associated our freedom to our ability to attain wanted things and experiences, to freely move about and do as we wish and hence those of us that use money in modern society have unconsciously associated our freedom to money. Even in suppressed social environments where civil liberties have been taken away from the populace, money is still required in most cases to do what we want to do to some degree or another. Therefore, we naturally unconsciously believe more money equals more freedom. Yet look how much of a trap an individual's **awareness** in the absence of money is, as a result of **associating their freedom to money alone**. Hence the term 'money doesn't buy happiness.' Thus true freedom is within developing emotional literacy, always has been, always will be. Also understand that **life experience expands individual desire** from the most basic through to the most extravagant. For example, imagine somebody living in extreme poverty with no money or apparent means to acquire any, their desire may expand from their current situation of living on the street with cardboard as a blanket in a cold damp area, to wanting a sleeping bag and a warmer drier area to sleep. Or somebody just bought a new car but would prefer the other model with a more elaborate fuel injection system. Desire for more expands subject to experience regardless of experience.

Your happiness, your freedom, your ability to appreciate is inherently connected to your ability to focus your thoughts in a way that pleases you which allows for deeper connected moments. When you feel at peace, content, appreciative, passion, intrigue or adventure you **are feeling free** in those moments. All negative emotion is a result of awareness in the absence of something personally wanted caused by a limiting belief structure of some sort. Hence, when you are focusing on what you don't want you are focused in the opposite direction of your personal preference whatever that is for you. Thus you may feel less than **free** to experience what you would prefer especially when in any unwanted life experience, but this is the work, reach to feel better regardless of circumstance. You don't need to figure out the depth of this in every life example, just realize that your anger, jealousy, frustration or any other negative emotion is telling you your current point of view is limiting **you** in some way in this moment, thus you need to do something to feel better from **between your own ears** using ideas from this book and many more besides.

More examples linking niggles to thought.

Remember how the stubbed and bleeding toe on the carpet example earlier in the book showed how anger was evoked with **instant mental awareness** in something unwanted.

Here's some more examples displaying our thought, desire interrelationship creating emotion within life situations: -

- Have you ever been pushed for time perhaps during a lunch hour when you were busy at work and needed to get back, but here you are stuck in a queue at a store of some kind? The person serving customers is relaxed and in no hurry making idle chit chat with each customer thus extending the time delay for you. You are becoming frustrated, pissed off or angry. This negative emotion, this niggle, this nuance within you **is your awareness in the absence of time available to you.** Your desire, your **wanting** is to get through the queue in a timely manner, but you are not getting what you **want**. Your anger is not evoked by the person taking their time serving the customers in front of you as is often believed by our association outside of self, but rather from your awareness in the opposite of your wanted desire, which is an absence of time. You must do the work in all situations like this. Reach to feel better, relax and let go. This is the work.

- Let's say you have a partner you genuinely love. It's a really great relationship but then your partner does something that is not to your liking and you become upset in some way. This is because you didn't **want** your partner to behave in this way to begin with. In essence you are **aware** of an aspect of behaviour, a character trait you do not want, you **wanted** that behaviour to not exist in your partner's character in the first place. You are now aware of, and looking at an unwanted life experience hence looking and thinking about the absence of your desire.

- Many people hold strong resentment towards money in some way. Perhaps our corrupt global financial system bugs them or particular taxation laws may be unfair etc. Some also have strong opinions about corporations and individuals who have immense amounts of money and point their fingers in anger, resentment, criticism or jealousy. Can you see that in reality all of that is an awareness of what you **don't want**, which means in observation of such things there is an awareness of something else that you would prefer to see. Thus you evoke negative emotion within yourself because what you are looking at is not what you want. When we are observing big situations that we cannot do that much about as individuals such as taxation laws, big global systems of finance, or any subject that is unjust, criminal, environmentally damaging, war etc., it is easy to inaccurately blame the situation for the negative feeling within ourselves when really it is our own limitation within our perspective of the something we deem as unwanted that is really evoking our individual feeling space. Obviously we naturally think the big situation out of our individual control needs changing from our own perspective. However, whether it does, or doesn't is irrelevant to your emotional well-being, don't go giving your power away in these situations by blaming the issue for your feeling response. Reach for complete control of your own inner emotional world regardless of circumstances to the point where that control is natural and easy because momentum has grown in better feeling less limiting thought patterns/beliefs. This is our never ending always evolving for the better individual work.

In some cases, this may mean using mental option one of sticking your head in the sand until you feel better before you can reach for a less limiting perspective with the use of mental option two.

Please note, you don't have to make peace with all subjects. You can simply get your attention off a subject altogether if you don't want to figure it all out, in other words turn the other cheek. This truly is a powerful understanding to see in oneself as you gain experience observing your state of being relative to thought. Less attention means the thought thus negative state dissipates. Bearing in mind the difference between suppression and awareness off a subject are two different things.

- Some people struggle with indecisiveness while others feel overwhelmed and want someone else to take control of their decision. When someone is feeling lost they often **think that they want** someone to give them direction and tell them what to do. We all **want our freedom** to choose, but sometimes we feel lost in ourselves and don't know what to do, so we think we **want** someone to just tell us what to do! Many people have had this experience at some point in life which is fine at the time, but if it continues for a longer period you may feel lost, confused and frustrated. If you have put pressure on another to make decisions for you often resentment may grow towards the one(s) you put this pressure on to decide for you. We are freedom-seeking beings therefore we **really want** to be able to make our own minds up, we really **want** our own ability to be self-directing. Self-direction, is a natural by-product of learning how to direct thought **and action** by how it feels. We are inherently freedom seeking beings, the clearer, cleaner and less limiting your thinking becomes by guiding your mind as we have been discussing, the more natural in the flow of life you become, therefore the need for outside direction is no longer required to the same degree if at all. Emotion really is your consciousness steering wheel. Everybody has some degree of **desire** to be self-directing even those feeling completely lost, don't want to be lost, they **want** to be free.

- In summary, any time you are **aware** of not being where you **want** to be from a **limited** perspective in **any** subject or aspect within a subject you will experience some degree of negative feeling. Work, health, home, partner, world events, success, status, your life etc.

Chapter Five

Where is there emotional gain in doing things I hate?

The psychological truth that says *"Anything anybody does, they do because they believe they will feel better in the doing, having, or achieving of it"* can be challenging to see sometimes. However, reach to see this powerful truth within yourself in all situations that challenges this because it will help you to sort out and understand yourself more deeply over time.

For example, when you feel as though you have to do something that is not to your liking, perhaps you may feel obliged to or believe you must because of any number of **'reasons,'** or when you are stuck between a rock and a hard place with no way out that has any apparent pleasure in it. You can be challenged to understand where the emotional gain is when there is no **obvious** pleasure in any action or decision. Especially when you feel utterly horrible in some way, perhaps when you are doing something you hate as one example, or being forced to as another. How is this doing something because you unconsciously believe you will feel better in the doing, having, or experiencing of it when you clearly dislike it, are forced to do it, or hate it and yet you are doing it?

Accordingly, until you truly understand your belief structure relative to your own actions and preferences (desires for life), hence truly understand yourself, you can challenge this concept and say that it is not true, because where is the emotional gain in situations such as the few just mentioned?

This is a great question and needs to be understood relative to life and the actions we take and the decisions we make.

Firstly, consider that each **personal preference (desire)** you carry regarding all subjects in life is where your value system is created for the most part. For example, your preferences about the way you want to behave as a person yourself (such as in selfless acts), or see others behave are always your personal preferences which is often labelled as a value. Essentially personal preferences and values are the same thing. This means, when you value a behaviour in yourself and others you are essentially saying you prefer that behaviour within yourself and others.

Secondly, consider that through life you have built beliefs (patterns of thought) about all aspects of your life, other people, cultures, religions, parenting your worldview, in fact anything that you have ever thought about and/or experienced. Therefore, when we have any experience moving through life we then perceive and interpret that current experience subject to our beliefs which were created through previous thinking and experiences, and we also interpret our experience via our personal preferences, our values which evokes a feeling response within.

Very often our beliefs are limited in nature which often means we do not allow ourselves other options within certain life situations because of the limitation within our beliefs. This limitation may also be in conflict with our personal preferences, our desires, our values for the situation at hand.

As I'm sure you can appreciate within any individual, their belief structure and personal preferences (values) can be very complex and are never identical to anyone else's. Also each belief you carry interconnects with all other beliefs you carry in some way, and when you are living any life situation several beliefs can be triggered at once which are also intertwined with what you would personally prefer to see happen within the situation at hand (your preferences, your values.) Hence this is how we can end up feeling like we are stuck between a rock and a hard place to begin with because becoming stuck like this is a result of belief(s) that are limiting you in relationship to your value system, your personal preferences, desires within the physical experience itself. Therefore, you can feel as though you are dammed if you do, or dammed if you don't, with no apparent pleasant options to choose from.

However, life moves on and you **would have taken a path** relative to what your beliefs and preferences (values) **allowed** you to do in the situation you were in. The best term ever offered for this is, 'The path of least resistance,' meaning that no matter what situation we may be in, we will always take the path of least emotional resistance that we allow ourselves access to due to our beliefs and preferences thus our values.

In situations where you are stuck between a rock and a hard place where there are no apparent pleasant options, or in doing things you dislike, hate or are forced the best way to see the emotional gain in the action you took is often in hindsight by understanding this term within the ultimate decisions and actions you have taken. You will always take the path of least resistance, even if that path **appears** harder, a sacrifice, or more painful than the one you are not taking. This bodes the question why are you taking that path? Look deeply at yourself. Whatever path you are taking or took is subject to what you are **allowing yourself access to** within your belief structure and personal preferences (values) as afore mentioned. The path of least resistance is really an emotional path of your **best available option,** this is the path of **least emotional pain** that your beliefs and preferences (values) are allowing you access to within the situation at hand. In all selfless acts, or self-sacrifice, or when you feel obligated, or doing things you believe you hate, even when you are forced you are still choosing the path of least resistance. In other words, you took the action because it felt slightly better to you than the other options that your beliefs and preferences (values) would allow you to take. **Meaning, everything we do we do to feel better!** There really is no escaping this.

As you get good at recognising your own thought to emotion interrelationship and therefore understand your own beliefs and preferences (values) relative to the actions we take, you will be able to see this for yourself, in fact you can only truly see this within yourself as you get to know yourself better as we have been discussing throughout.

There is no possible way of writing a specific life example detailing this concept to this level because our belief structures and preferences (values) relative to life experiences are so vastly different from person to person, let alone religion to religion or culture to culture. This means any example given will only be understood by the **few** whom have similar experiences, beliefs and preferences (values) within any example given. So again the best way to see this for yourself is through self-observation over time from this overall interpretation of thought to emotional link. Sure this can be challenging to see, but true nevertheless.

It is interesting to note that the more you develop yourself mentally/emotionally by re-developing beliefs and choosing thought that feels best to you, these challenging situations reduce, morph and often disappear entirely as you move through life. This is because you are no longer negatively reacting to outside circumstance due to the inner work you have done. **You will be aligning thought and beliefs with your preferences (values) so that the internal conflict is reduced and ultimately gone.** This means your beliefs are more in harmony within their interrelationship relative to your personal preferences, desires, your values.

You may find new values, redevelop your existing values, or even drop old outdated values which no longer serve you.

When you reach for higher emotional states within your mental work as discussed throughout, this results in less internal conflict within life actions because you are clearer within yourself in many areas of belief and **wanting**. You are making peace with many life subjects and developing lighter less limiting perspectives within your belief structure rather than operating from a position of obligation, or a limiting value that you may have imposed on yourself. This means you are less likely to get stuck doing something you hate as you may have been before. Which means when you do something you do it because you **want to**

do it, thus you are not stuck! True power is born where action is clear and inspired from a higher appreciative space. Remember a challenging situation is only challenging if you are struggling emotionally within it, which of course we all do from time to time.

Health and negative emotion.

When you are not well in some way and your awareness is on the fact that you are unwell, it is natural to be worried or concerned in some way however, from a psychological perspective can you see that yet again the emotional feelings within you are caused by your mental awareness in the absence of your personal preference for life? Meaning you prefer to be well but your awareness is mostly on the opposite of your preference, you are more aware of being unwell. Of course this is normal but there is huge limitation for multiple reasons within **any** worried state, you can however reach to find hope and inspiration which is highly beneficial for any unwell person.

Within all aspects of human negative emotion **regardless of circumstance** there is always a limitation of belief regarding the absence of something personally wanted. Do you remember the description of the angry reaction to the stubbed toe, this was an example of instantly activated thought in opposition to your wanting. These instant reactions cause us to think it is normal to feel certain ways in certain situations, however true inner power is in your ability to hold a steady emotional space regardless of circumstance due to having developed a deeper self-awareness and appreciation for life and yourself thus a deepening understanding of others from a less limiting belief structure.

In the case of health where I want to be well, but I am not well naturally the bulk of us begin to fret and worry because we are aware of, 'not being well.' However, surely you have seen someone positive and reasonably upbeat who is unwell but is focusing on getting better, opposed to someone worried and fretting focusing on still being sick although wanting to be better? Once this work is **second nature** within you, the naturally positive person is more likely to be you! Again, the awareness in the absence of something wanted, or an awareness of limitation within self which is really the same thing, is always present in all negative emotion. In time as you get to know yourself better by seeing how your own patterns of thought work regarding **this perspective, this interpretation of emotion,** you will see for yourself how 'limited thought' always goes hand in hand with low emotional states regardless of circumstance, therefore guiding you in building a self-awareness and sustainable happiness of your own as you choose thought with more discernment by the way in which it feels to you.

Health and hope.

Of course when an individual has been given a disconcerting medical diagnosis this work can appear like whacking you on the toe with a hammer and telling you not to notice. Bloody hard to do! Anything relating to your health and body is hard to not focus on if it has your attention, **but you can go into a bad health situation with hopefulness truly you can.** Remember the analogy I gave in part one of this book under the title of 'The energy connection?' Often the difference between survivors and those that thrive is this ability to work yourself into and maintaining a good mood or a state of hopefulness rather than fear worry or panic. A positive authentic emotional state is very medicinal for us all. So if you happen to have a troubling illness of any sort, simply do the best you can to find hopefulness **or any good mood about any subject whatsoever however you can** because a good mood is a good mood however it is achieved, hence the cells of the body are positively influenced which is very medicinal. Try to maintain an open damper on the fire so to speak.

I find it interesting that in many situations in life, not just within health that people endeavour not to get their hopes up just in case they don't get or achieve their wanted outcome whatever that is. They actively suppress their potential positive emotion by suppressing their hopefulness in fear of the potential negative emotion, disappointment, or let down that they may experience if they don't get or achieve their wanted thing or experience.

I say, get your hopes up! Learn to deliberately feel good, allow yourself to get your hopes up whilst being prepared to mentally deal with any disappointment if it should come. Disappointment is yet again awareness in something not going your way, awareness in the absence of something you wanted! Therefore, there is a limitation within your point of view. That's all, no big deal, in time you will figure it out if you want to, or you can simply learn to shrug your shoulders and get on with life without the disappointment ever being an issue for you.

I think it is a shame that within the medical profession there is often a deliberate suppression of hope, this often takes place when people with a serious condition with low medical success outcomes are told not to get their hopes up due to a perceived fear of disappointment, or a need to be 'realistic' etc. If an aspect of medical liability is part of this suppressing of hope, I wonder if there is a way to allow the patient to build hope **if they want to** as is appropriate to the discernment of the individual, then this could be a good thing. Of course many people are not doing this mental work to this degree in all other areas of life as a mental practice, so dealing with disappointment can seem an insurmountable task if they build up hope in the face of extreme adversity such as in the case of ill health.

As we now know the better you feel the more you are allowing more vibrancy within your being thus helping yourself to heal, hence any good mood however it is attained is beneficial from my point of view. Hope is further up the scale than fear! When hope is suppressed within healthcare this often holds us in a perpetual state of fear which frankly is utterly limiting for all involved. It may also suppress or hinder an individual patients reaching for alternative solutions to their problem. If you look hard enough every illness has an exception, someone who has recovered, again I say get your hopes up, try everything in your power to feel good and find a solution. Even create a better mood from a completely different topic altogether thus keeping the damper open. Obviously any disappointment is still an individual's responsibility to deal with. Actively suppressing hope in the fear of disappointment is not at all helpful from my perspective. Of course someone who has been actively working within the realms of emotional responsibility for a while will be better equipped to deal with times of hardship such as a troubling health issue. Sometimes it takes a troubling health issue for people to come to the work of the mind in the first place, this means there is usually a steep learning curve learning this mental skill whilst also trying to deal with being unwell. Often this learning curve involves going around and around in circles trying to fix things within mental option 2 thus perpetuating our pain for longer unwittingly.

Starting this process of seeking to change thought relative to its emotional connection is no easy feat at the best of times. However, beginning to learn how to deliberately feel better emotionally whilst you are unwell is as good a time to start as any, because it is another aid in your healing process. Of course if you are unwell or within any unwanted circumstance, don't go putting all sorts of mental pressure on yourself within this work to be able to do it all right now, relax, smile take a breath and breathe, allow yourself to recover gently. Allow your mind to be gentle, be kind to yourself, find a good mood thinking about something unrelated to your health issue. Meditate, relax, breathe, let go...

Have you given up on life, stuck in a rut, or bored.

Many people have given up on life. They may have **decided** this is the way things are and have resigned themselves to a mediocre experience due to interpreting life through a flat state of being. Over the years they may have wanted things but have not experienced them and in time this awareness (habitual patterns of thought) of having 'missed out' permeates their existence. Some may be experiencing a flat, suppressed, depressed, de-sensitized, grouchy or numbed state of being with no zing, there are a large proportion of people living a life like this. They may argue that they don't feel anything anymore which is an emotion in itself; a feeling of flat or numbness. Perhaps they struggle to find any excitement or interest to anything like they may have had in the past.

In other words, their state of being is not remotely close to vibrant when they say they feel flat they **feel** flat! This entire book is an endeavour in helping you realize that you **can do something about it,** and it is worth it! You have to make the effort. **Nothing has to change around you for your life to change, only you need to change and only you can do the work!** Sure it may take a year or two of sorting yourself out but what have you got to lose? A mediocre emotional state where you're living out your life in this type of pain truly is far too great a price to pay given that there are many ways to improve your emotional state.

Be under no allusions, a mediocre state of being is pain! There is nothing more important than that you feel good period! Life is about a string of happy moments, many people are looking for a happy life and thus miss happy moments!

This flatness or de-sensitizing to life often tends to happen to some folk later in life, many people have experienced a lot of things in their life and then find life to be simply dull now because while they were experiencing life in the past they were also associating their pleasure outside of self. Therefore, they often believe nothing excites them anymore. Please continue to seek out new experiences and subjects of intrigue as well as engage in past activities, just do a little head work of aligning mind with better feeling states everywhere else in your life as an ongoing inner process. **Life is a combination of mental focus relative to feeling and enjoying the physical activities we choose to engage in.** Boredom will no longer be a factor for you if it ever was because there is always something to ponder or consider in a positive, intriguing light. Life can be of constant interest to you. See if you can learn to treat life like an exciting treasure hunt just like the treasure hunt games you may have played as a child, regardless of your age and stage in life. Of course this often takes a shift in mental momentum to find the excitement of treating life like a treasure hunt, but you **can** do it in time, we all can.

Chapter Six

The happy pygmy.

Desire (personal preference) is an interesting thing, what you personally want in life is ever changing, morphing, evolving and is distinctly different for all people, even though there are common similarities. We all want to live a happy life from our own perspective. If you are living the life you want where things are unfolding as you would like them too then it is natural and easy to have a fairly good demeanour. **Desire expands within you as life shows you possibility.** Life continues to show you many possible things to experience, some of these things are to your liking, some not so much, this is how your desire, your preferences are created. For those of us whom live in the modern world with jobs, possessions, reasonable income, and a constant bombardment of media showing us infinite possibility, some of our desires can expand to a point where we may feel that it is unattainable. We may have all sorts of limitation in our minds regarding money, success, careers, relationships, health, sex, time left in life etc. Thus we really do struggle within our state of being.

People have often wondered how it is that those who live in different less modernised cultures such as some primitive tribes around the world often appear happier on the whole. The happiness of these people and **all people** is dependent on the 'stretch' created by limiting thought within your mind regarding living your desire. A tribesman whom has not been exposed to the modern world has an entirely different thought process, thus set of norms and desires for life than someone who has grown up in a modern culture. A happy tribesman's desires within life has not been **'stretched'** to far beyond his beliefs and physical capabilities to live his desired life due to a lack in exposure to other possibilities. Therefore, the tribesman is more often content in his lot because **he has little limitation in his thought** regarding living his personal desires for life, his mind is not as bogged down with all sorts of expanding desire and limiting thought as those living in the modern world may have. On the other hand, some people whom perhaps live on the fringes of modern life but who may have very little and can see others with much, often struggle to make peace with life because they can see the possibility around them beyond what they are currently living, hence are not entirely happy as they perhaps cannot fathom a way to living their own desired life.

The degree in which you allow the focus of your mind to be aware of any **absence** of any wanted thing or experience will always determine your overall state of being. For the bulk of those reading this book they will likely be living in cultures where their desires have been stretched beyond that of the happy tribesman, this is not as bad as it appears. This really is a good thing because once you figure out how to **naturally appreciate your lot** like our friendly happy tribesman, your life truly becomes amazing because when you are in any good feeling space there really is nothing better! Learn to enjoy your life because life really is a blend between physicality, thought and feeling where positive feeling is the ultimate goal.

Having stuff does not make you materialistic.

There are those that continue wanting more physical things to feel better. People like this are often attempting to fill their inner void with, 'stuff' by associating their need to feel better outside of self. Thus, they are constantly looking for more things, more dollars from a neediness position to feel better. This is often called, 'being materialistic.' Many get trapped in this neediness side of life chasing their tails outside of self.

There is absolutely nothing wrong with having nice things and money in the bank. You can have what many would describe as an extravagant lifestyle and yet be content in your own skin, with or without, 'stuff.' Therefore, even though you may have plenty of awesome things in your life you are not actually materialistic, because you don't need this outside stuff to fill a void within, because you are content with or without, 'stuff' due to there being no void to fill.

So being materialistic is really someone trying to fill their internal void, their internal unease, with stuff from outside of self. This is regardless of your current attainment, or lack of attainment of stuff. Someone with very little possessions can be very materialistic and vice versa, because it has nothing to do with 'stuff' but has everything to do with personal contentment within self.

Crying.

Crying is a natural **release** whether **tears of joy or tears of sorrow**. Please don't suppress tears allow them out if you can. As you move up the scale embodying a higher state of being your tears become less this includes tears of joy. Of course to embody a higher self-esteem, a higher state of appreciation to the degree I am alluding to, there are many stages of development as you progress and you may have times where you are crying a lot for many reasons, even stages of tears of joy. Each stage is a process per individual to work through therefore when life evokes them from you, allow them out if you can and if the situation is appropriate to you, suppression is not a good move here if you can avoid it. Many people experience an inner shift or a breakthrough, an ah ha moment or release whilst crying far beyond the natural state of simply feeling better after a good cry. So allow yourself to cry if you feel an urge to cry.

Sometimes when doing this work and have developed more **introspection** of your emotional nuances, you may notice an inflow of joy, of warmth, or love/appreciation welling up within you which appears to be pushing the tears out in front of this inflow. It feels like love is pushing the off-ness out of you. Allow these moments to flow if you can because an embodiment of a higher state of being is in play, your tone is shifting which is everything to you.

Vulnerability.

Many people believe vulnerability is a good thing, of course sharing with your nearest and dearest is a part of life and sometimes we may **feel** vulnerable whilst sharing in various life situations. However, any feelings of insecurity or vulnerability are still indicators that there's work to do to develop even deeper levels of self-esteem within yourself.

Of course everything is in degrees and there is always a process of conscious growth within any life experience so again, please understand I am never wronging any feeling anybody may feel. The way a person may feel is always natural and normal to them and is never wrong, how can your emotional indicators be wrong, how can your steering wheel be wrong? It's our outside of-self interpretation of our emotional indicators that creates internal mess.

Regarding the feeling of vulnerability, sometimes we may complain that our partner or friend is not vulnerable enough or is too emotionally distant. We may wish that they could just open up to us and really tell us how they feel and what they think, yet they are not allowing themselves to do this, hence we may wish that they would face their fear and do it anyway by being vulnerable by opening up to us.

Usually the person whom isn't able to be vulnerable or open up is struggling an awful lot within their emotional world. The niggles and nuances they feel are often all consuming and overwhelming with a strong dose of worrying how others may think or how others may react. Fear is often quite an issue to contend with for these people. So opening up and being vulnerable is fearfully difficult as they cannot yet deal with their inner emotional issues that well. A person like this who starts this work of self-development may move into a place of vulnerability as part of their process of cleaning up their inner world thus of moving up the scale which is great good work, and of course this often naturally happens through life experience.

Vulnerability is better than a complete shutdown of oneself such as those who simply don't communicate because it hurts too much, or are fearful etc. However, there are still aspects of a lack of self-esteem within any feelings of vulnerability.

Interestingly often the person complaining that their partner is not vulnerable enough to open up to them also still needs external change by way of their partner behaving differently or saying something so that they too can feel secure themselves, hence they too still have some inner work to do.

If you have a friend or partner like this it is a process for them to overcome for themselves, you cannot do it for them, but you can be gentle and kind whilst encouraging them and aiding them on their journey.

There comes a point as you continually develop higher states of self-esteem where vulnerability simply does not exist in your feeling space any more, you are secure within your own skin hence there is no need of your partner or anyone else to do anything for you to feel secure. Any form of vulnerability has become a thing of the past due to developing a higher more stable self-esteem.

So to sum up, an emotionally distant person is often very seriously struggling within their own skin, thus may struggle to communicate because of the inner turmoil they are dealing with, or not dealing with as the case may be.

Henceforth, any person whom is '**reacting**' to an emotionally distant person may be wishing that person changes so that they themselves can feel secure. No matter what the story is, it is the emotionally distant one's job to sort themselves out for themselves. Likewise, it is also an inner job of your own if you need the distant one to change so as you can feel secure. In either case you must sort yourself out for yourself and whether the other person sorts themselves out or not is up to them. You must learn to be at peace regardless of what any other person does or does not do. The **feeling** of vulnerability is neither good nor bad, right nor wrong it is an emotional indicator like all others, a part of your conscious steering wheel towards appreciation, that is all!

Nothing teaches like life experience.

I love the term, *"Feel the fear and do it anyway"* from the book of the same title by Susan Jeffers. Often we have many fears holding us back from taking action within many areas of life. Our fears and insecurities often hinder us in enjoying or even partaking in some of life's activities. I clearly place fear and insecurities under the same label of, 'our niggles' that I have been fondly using as a general term for all our inner emotional indicators regardless of which emotional label we may use. At any rate I love the term "Feel the fear and do it anyway" because it encapsulates the term, 'nothing teaches like life experience' beautifully. Most often we can overcome many fears and insecurities regarding life subjects by simply feeling the fear and doing the activity anyway! Which life then teaches you that there was nothing to worry about in the first place hence you get over your little fear or insecurity.

Nothing teaches like life experience so feel the fear (niggle) and do it anyway! Obviously use your discretion wisely!

The pain does go away.

An example of what I'm trying to teach can be exemplified in a social media meme portraying someone who has not yet sorted themselves out. The meme usually has an interesting photo of an older person with words similar to the following. *"Hey all you young people out there complaining life is hard, buckle up cupcake life hasn't even begun to fuck you over yet"*

Regardless of the traumas anyone may have faced has life really fucked you over? Many will obviously argue for the answer yes to that question, especially those who have suffered extreme adversity or those who may still be in a horrible situation, or life is not the way they want it to be and have not yet made peace within themselves.

Of course not all have suffered extreme adversity. Yet for many of us life **appears** to grind us down as we get older which is 100 percent due to our own habitual patterns of thought which are kept active through attention on them that is really grinding people down. Not their age nor life experience past or present.

If you open your eyes and look around, you will find those that have had horrific experiences or abuse of some kind and have **fully** recovered from those experiences and are thriving inside themselves. You may find these inspirational examples in the form of actual people you meet, from books, discussion groups, the internet etc. This should be evidence enough for anyone to seek a way up from their own lower feeling tone. You can do it, we all can! I do not for a single moment believe that classic line which says, *"The pain never goes away you just have to learn to live with it,"* this is utterly disempowering and totally incorrect if you are working your way up the scale in all areas of life the pain does go away and is replaced by a deeper inner connection of your own.

Sticks and stones may break my bones but names will never hurt me!

This old gem usually learnt in primary school when you were getting bullied in some way never used to make any sense to me as a child because the name-calling and teasing bloody well did hurt, hence the beginning of outside of-self associations began the process of disempowerment!

Do I need to explain how it actually does make sense now that you have read this book?

Once you get a handle on your state of being through using this work within life experience thus creating a **solid foundation of self-esteem**, your inner reactions have evolved to something higher hence sticks and stones may break my bones but names will never hurt me!

Remember this next time somebody is opinionated or critical towards you and you feel your reactions brewing!

(This so needs to be nipped in the bud by teaching emotional responsibility classes to every year group in all school's world over, in an appropriately progressive way per age group.)

Forgiveness.

Forgiveness is a problem that many struggle with for years. Your personal need for forgiveness is an emotional indicator that you need to either let go or find a completely different perspective, one or the other or both. Many believe they must hate the person that caused them harm, many believe they are justified in their anger or need closure in the form of justice being served or apologies etc. But in reality who is this hurting? **Only you!** You are the one feeling hurt, angry, resentful or whatever other negative feeling is active within you which is not a good space to be in. You are drinking your own poison by yet again associating outside of self or by accepting that your reaction is just and right! I ask you this, do you want to feel at peace, vibrant, excited for life or hold a grudge? It's your choice.

The question is how do I forgive? The answer is when you want so much to feel good you have no other choice but to let go. Of course the process of coming to a place of forgiveness is a process per individual just as grief recovery is, again gentleness and kindness towards self and others goes along way.

Remember we need to make it our dominant intent to feel good and strive forward with a gentle increasing of our tone over time in all areas of life. The operative point here being **you want so much to feel good that you have no other choice!**

It also means you no longer think about it and if you do the memories no longer evoke negative emotion. When you truly embody this work in all areas of your life forgiveness also becomes a non-issue for you in time. Remember how my perception of childhood changed without even trying to change my perception? Sometimes if you put your forgiveness issue out of your mind whilst continuing to lift your overall tone in all other areas of life the forgiveness issue simply disappears as does many other issues!

Most of us consider it normal for our memories to evoke certain emotional responses and of course it is, but most of us do not also realize that these emotional responses to memories can change for the better. This is the result of lifting your overall tone by taking charge of your mental patterns gently over time. Or of course you may get results like this with the use of modalities such as E.F.T or letting go like the yogi etc., which is all part of lifting your overall tone! Also consider that forgiveness is really a heavily associated pain that you are blaming outwardly. I know this can be hard a pill to swallow given how horrible some things are but truly your reaction is your reaction thus you have full empowerment over it.

Chapter Seven

Appreciation is caring too!

Due to our natural but inaccurate association of emotion outside of self, we unconsciously think we must feel certain ways when in certain situations as mentioned in various examples throughout. Thus when you are trying to decipher and figure out how to hold and enhance a steady emotional state, this can be a little confusing because of these attachments. For example, the subject of caring. In sad situations if you are not displaying sadness some may presume that you don't care. This means the feeling of sadness has often been associated to caring. As was discussed in part one within the angry man and child abuse example, there are often feelings of worry and concern being associated to caring and yet we can care without any negative feelings. Therefore, we can be coming from a genuinely connected place once we move higher in our overall consciousness thus tone. Sometimes we find ourselves in circumstances where we are not actually sad and we may wear a mask of sadness to display that we care even though we ourselves are not actually sad. This means we may have all sorts of funny emotional niggles going on within us as we try to wear an unauthentic mask of sadness. Again sadness has nothing to do with caring. It is in times like these you need to do the work of niggles.

To be truly authentic to yourself can be difficult if you have not yet truly found peace and an overall higher tone. For example, when you are genuinely at peace and appreciative you can interact in a loving way without showing sadness thus you are being authentic from a higher place. Obviously sadness is sadness, it's a feeling and that's ok. If you are genuinely sad then that's fine and fair enough. But if you are not sad when dealing with other people in their times of sadness, then faking sadness is unauthentic and awkward, even if you do wear a fairly good mask of sadness. That being said, you must use your judgement to behave in a way that is appropriate to you as you strive to develop a higher appreciative state yourself, meaning this is all part of the overall process of embodying a higher state of being and dropping our masks.

When an appreciative space is genuine within you thus you have made peace with many of life's issues because you have developed broader less limiting, appreciative perspectives. Then you happen to find yourself in situations where others are sad and you are not sad because your inner-peace hasn't been rattled by the circumstance at hand. Then this may be misinterpreted by others that you don't care because of their inaccurate associations. When in actuality you may care greatly. We can only ever do the best we can, so use your discretion as is appropriate to you. Placating people to appease their feelings may appear to be caring and is often a part of empathy, but in reality is extremely disempowering for the people you are trying to help because at some point they really have to understand their emotional indicators for their own personal empowerment. However, this does not mean your natural support of others in their time of need isn't loving and warranted, of course it is, nice caring behaviours such as kindness, understanding, treating others well is for the most part personally wanted life **preferences** either received by you from others or offered by you as your own behaviours. Still, within all of this you feel and your feelings are yours alone as are everybody's. With this realization self-empowerment is born.

Learn to drop your worry of what you **presume** others may think of you in all life situations, your worry of others opinions **is feeling worry** and therefore not feeling peace, contentment or appreciation in self, which is really a lack in self-esteem to some degree.

Ultimately love is the answer to all personal and social issues which hopefully after having read this book you can see that link more clearly thus is not such a cliché after all. Love has practical useable applications within any moment in time, because the feeling of love and appreciation is linked to higher consciousness where all practical solutions reside. Therefore, anytime you feel a negative inner niggle, these niggles are indicators for personal change towards higher less limiting appreciative perspectives regardless of outside circumstance.

Unconditional love is unconditional appreciation regardless of circumstance thus is unconditional! This means if you are not feeling love, you are not loving. Therefore, be careful associating any negative feeling as caring or loving as this is a misinterpretation of emotion, mostly outside of self. Love is an unconditional appreciation within all things, so feeling natural and genuine appreciation within self not only for life but for no reason whatsoever because it is your now natural state to be in is unconditional love.

Fix Panic attacks with no attention to the thoughts that cause them.

I spoke with a person whom was struggling with panic attacks. He told me that his panic attacks induced chest constrictions which felt like his heart was going to pop out of his chest. He initially did think he had heart issues and went to his doctor whom accidentally confirmed this which was unfortunately an incorrect diagnosis. More fear and panic resulted, thus the panic attacks got worse for him, understandably! At some point he got a second opinion, this second doctor realized he was having panic attacks not heart problems and totally refuted the first diagnosis which was a breath of fresh air for the patient, a relief as you can appreciate. This alone reduced a lot of the **new** negative mental activity from the first incorrect diagnosis resulting in a reduction of his worsened panic attacks, but of course they were still a problem. This second doctor told him to talk to a counsellor and that he should learn how to meditate etc. In due course he asked me if I had any ideas which would be able to help him. Whilst chatting with him it became obvious that he had an **intense** awareness of **where he didn't want to be in life**. He was very much struggling with society's limited concept of a successful life. He wanted to be financially free and living it up sharing his success with his family, which again is understandable and fairly normal. Yet here he was stuck in the same old **mental** drag of work, eat, sleep do something on the weekends. His awareness was very much critically focused on the fact that he wasn't successful to the degree that he wanted or where he really wanted to be in life. He also believed that time was running out for him, this obviously perpetuated more awareness of limitation thus causing intensely horrible feelings within. I believe he had acclimatised to these feelings considering them to be normal relative to his circumstance. Thus the negative feeling momentum built due to no heed given to each niggle as a niggle was evoked, which ultimately resulted in this persons panic attacks.

The details of someone's life and thoughts aren't so important as this is infinite amongst the billions of lives being lived, meaning the subject of discontent and complexity of belief relative to life's desires will be different per person. However, the momentum of negative limiting awareness relative to desire is causing the negative feeling space. Therefore, each individual can develop full control through using emotion consciously as discussed throughout.

Of course his story is all very understandable and of course it is very difficult for people to see how their thoughts are causing them their grief when life isn't the way they want it. **We just want things different now dammit!** Which is obviously emotion intensely associated outside of self. We are all hung up within our own personal experience of life to some degree, there is nothing wrong in that except for our incorrect emotional associations. At any rate I managed to persuade him to some degree to see how his thoughts on the subject were the real problem and discussed the use of mental option one suggesting the use of mantras as one tool for achieving this. In his case given that he is a singer and already has a repertoire of songs in his mind he could readily use them as mantras by singing to himself as required. This would require becoming aware of the negative feeling thoughts to begin with thus nipping them in the bud. We also had a discussion about the limitation of the status quo concept of success and I offered some of my points of view about this hoping that this may have helped in his process of, 'mental option two' where he starts to redevelop his thoughts about the subject of success aiming for a lighter less limiting perspective. The panic attacks reduced fairly readily at the time. Of course to really thrive and truly move beyond panic attacks completely he will have to continue with the work of self in all areas of life thus reducing the negative mental momentum whilst also finding some way of making peace with the limited status quo concept of success. Hence continue to find more comfort in his own skin. This is something we can all do regardless of our age and life circumstance it only requires the **desire and the wherewithal** to do it, and then to actually do it! Work with our negative niggles small and large. Therefore, making this work second nature is of high value to us all. Panic attacks really are a result of strong negative momentum within certain patterns of thought and belief which are left unchecked to run rampant through the mind.

Remember my first mantra experience where **I committed** to repeating an affirmation from Louise hays book as an almost full time mental dialogue for three months solid. In hind sight this was a deliberate use of mental option 1 (Active meditation in mantra format.) This reduced my negative mental momentum even though at the time I wasn't even aware of the thoughts causing my negative feeling, because I was heavily associating outside of self. So stopping momentum with options one or three may be required for a month or two before any ability to work within option 2 becomes even possible within a subject that has this level of negative momentum, this intensity. If you keep thinking the same thing you keep getting the same results. Again meditate, relax, breathe, let go...

Having doubts and making decisions.

If you have doubts about something listen to your inner voice or gut before you act. Does it resonate with you? If no, then best take a step back and reconsider your next move. If yes, then you can build trust in yourself over time as you act on these decisions in a way that is appropriate to you.

Making decisions can be quite a pickle for us mere mortals yet learning to be decisive is like all other mental gymnastics it is a skill learned by practice on all the small things as you move through life, therefore the bigger decisions get easier to handle. Most of us have been taught to use the pros and cons approach to making a decision, we go about trying to figure it all out bit by bit and often drive ourselves mad and still not make a decision either way. It is interesting to note **that not making a decision is still making a decision in that moment.**

Often option one of not thinking about it by putting it out of your mind is a good approach. Sometimes the decision simply comes to you when you stop worrying about it or thinking about it.

Alternatively use your emotional indicators within the pros and cons approach. Ponder each option on **separate** occasions while deliberately trying to make peace with the idea. Try lining up with the decision, see which feels the best, lightest, or the most exciting rather than relying on intellect alone. Usually the one you can make peace with the easiest and/ or feels the most exciting to you is your path **in that moment**. Also keep in mind that nothing is permanent, you can often always change your mind again later. Sure there may be consequences to your decision or changing your mind, however no matter what path you take constantly continue with the inner work of lining up your mind with feeling thus enhancing any path you take. Constantly do your best to make peace with every aspect of life and move forward as best you can, always do the inner work, whichever decision you make. In other words, if you have made a decision and are in the middle of living that decision and you find there is still some uncertainty lurking within you, then do your best to make peace with it as best as you are able. If you can't, then see what other idea you can make peace with. There are no wrong decisions. All of life is an opportunity to reach for something higher inwardly. Learn from it and move on. There will always be a new moment to try again now, oh wait here's a new moment again now, oh and another now... So try not to make such a big deal out of things, go easily tread lightly be gentle with yourself.

Fear does not drive you, love draws you!

Some people believe if they weren't driven to succeed by fear in areas such as business or careers that they wouldn't be where they are today. Some say that fear is driving them. This could be seen as someone being fearful of having no money hence feel their freedoms may be supressed due to the need for money to fore fill their desires. Money almost always has some association to freedom as money and time often equals the ability to do what you want. Hence we may feel fearful of being trapped without money and therefore feel that fear is driving us to succeed financially.

We could be fearful that our life won't mean anything if we don't achieve a particular type of status whatever that may be business success, land ownership, a particular role in our chosen career, sporting prowess etc. Perhaps you may stay in a relationship that is not serving you because of a fear of being lonely, fear you won't find anyone else, financial ties etc.

Fear is not driving you because *"Anything anybody does, they do because they believe they will feel better in the doing, having, or achieving of it."*

Thus we are being drawn forward with this constant desire to feel better than where we currently stand. The actions we take inherently have a desire to feel better as our driving force, albeit unconscious for the most part.

Some believe that fear is pushing them because that's how it **appears**, it is the way we are **interpreting** the experience. Often this is talked about as moving away from pain and towards pleasure when really our consciousness is being drawn forward by our incessant desire to feel better! Fear is at the bottom of the emotional scale; the actions we take coming from this position are often to alleviate our fearful feelings with our outside of-self action, thus it appears fear is driving us. We are striving up the scale outside of self by acting in a way to appease a lower feeling. When really **the constant desire to feel better is drawing us to make inner conscious changes.** Your consciousness is being drawn upwards from the top of the emotional scale! Love is calling you, calling all of us, to develop our conscious belief structure to less limiting, appreciative and unconditional perspectives! The constant desire to feel better is the driver within you, not running away from fear as it may appear.

Appreciation (love) is a powerful magnet quietly sitting there calling you forward for inner change. As a thought begins to feel better it is getting closer to appreciation, reach to harmonise thought with higher emotion thus you are moving towards appreciation and your inner world accelerates for the better quite dramatically opposed to somebody not reaching in this way. Your state of being truly is everything!

If you consciously move up the scale within some of your low emotional set points you will clearly see what I mean because to truly understand this information is experiential through embodiment. Conceptual understanding is valueless without embodiment! In essence this means when you hold a space of genuine appreciation you feel full, you feel complete, you are whole in that moment.

Feeling anything less than appreciation (love) consistently is why we have the incessant desire to feel better in the first place. At your core you want to love, to appreciate life and **all** experience thus all that is. It is up to us individually to allow it into our experience, into our feeling space. The only thing hindering appreciation (love) into anybody's experience is limiting patterns of thought and now you know these can be redeveloped to less limiting appreciative patterns allowing for your state of being to simply be this way, no effort involved.

Effort is involved initially due to momentum that already exists in the form of limiting thought patterns which needs to be let go as discussed throughout, then when there is positive momentum there is no effort. Stopping thought or diffusing thought through meditation is only part of the equation, redirecting thought and belief relative to your emotional indicators brings truly sustained inner power (love). Allow yourself to connect to yourself regardless of who you are, where you are from, or your circumstances, this is your work, our work, reach.

But what about fight or flight fear?

All emotion is guidance and it takes a discerning mind time and life experience to figure through all our inner niggles whilst considering our beliefs in relation to how they feel. This last concept that fear does not drive us can also seem to be a bit of a pickle to understand conceptually if you're freaking out within a physically dangerous situation because it appears that fear is driving you.

If you are in a dangerous situation and you are fearful this is likely your emotional indicator to seek a safer alternative, which of course feels better! The fear is still your guidance to run away from the man with the gun hence it appears fear is driving us!

Emotion is always our guiding indicators as to our thoughts **and actions** in relation to our **desires** (preferences) within the current life experience. Understand that action is a projection of our **thoughts** and **desires** for life. Thus action tends to be, 'thought, desire' generated!

Your options may be as simple as stand here and see if I get shot, which may be fearful or run away, which may feel like relief and possible safety. The action you are drawn to feels better, it is drawing you from higher up the scale, although we naturally interpret this type of experience as fear driving us. Of course each situation is unique unto itself. If you are taking any action within any aspect of life and it feels off to you, stop (if you can) and reassess your action. Take action when things feel lighter, freer, more exciting, **more right** to you. Obviously the example of a man with a gun is an extreme example!

So here's another more general example, perhaps you are fairly happy things are pretty good overall and you have made good progress with this over all mental emotional work but you are in a situation that's not 100 percent ideal from your perspective, not entirely what you want within the situation whatever that situation may be. At any rate here you are endeavouring to make peace with it mentally/emotionally as we have been discussing throughout. Perhaps by trying to line up your thoughts with the decision to carry on in this particular life situation, and yet you still don't feel quite right in some way, you've tried and tried and you still cannot find peace. Often this is your inner emotional guidance letting you know your current **actions** are not in harmony with your **true wanting, your true preference** for your life in this situation. In other words, staying in this situation is not in harmony relative to your desires for life. In this instance changing your physical conditions may be a good option. It takes a discerning mind experience and time to figure out the depth of this relative to everything else written in this book, it may sound like a contradiction in some ways but it is not. Everything (actions included) is thought, desire (preference) generated relative to your personal life experience, thus produces emotion.

Don't stress over this expanded definition, simply look to feel better in every situation mostly using mental gymnastics and in so doing use your discernment as to what action to take that is appropriate to you. If action feels exciting to you but fear is holding you back from it, you have work to do in figuring this out for yourself.

Physicality itself is the wonderment to life, it is our physical experience combined with our mental activity thus emotional degree that we feel within any experience that makes up our life after all.

If both your physical action and thoughts are lined up, you thrive inside. (Thriving is an emotional state felt physically yet derived mentally more than many are willing to accept.)

To simplify; strive to feel better internally as much as possible whilst taking the actions that feel better to you using a non-critical discerning mind.

Chapter Eight

I want to be happy, but I'm not happy. The conundrum of awareness!

Many therapists, counsellors and psychologists have noticed that there are some people that want to be happy so much they simply cannot be happy. What? How can that be?

I was one of these people before I discovered what I have now embodied and written here in this book. My earlier life was fraught with depression, frustration, intense self-directed criticism which resulted in suicidal feelings also.

I wanted to be happy but I was very aware that I was not happy. I want to be happy, but I'm not happy, I want to be happy, but I'm not happy, all I want to do is love, but I am not happy, life sucks! This was the cyclic conundrum I was in. Many people in this puzzle find themselves stuck wondering how to break the spell so to speak, *"Just tell me how to do it, and I will do it!"* they may implore. I know for absolute certainty that the education offered in this book **is telling you how to do it** from wherever you are, from whatever emotional issue or situation you may be in. Everyone is able to learn how to **direct their own mind** in relationship to their own emotional niggles big **and mostly small** from the perspectives I have offered here throughout **all** areas of life. Of course this will take time, practice and in some cases of strong negative momentum, modalities, therapies, medication and professional help as required.

As you now also know the perspectives offered here start with a 180 degree turn in how we have unconsciously interpreted our emotional responses to life circumstances outside of self. This is what initially makes this perspective so hard to grasp and feels so counter intuitive to begin with, it can turn you around inside trying to understand how your feelings really are your feelings created by you.

So why is it that intensely wanting happiness and yet not having happiness is a conundrum in the first place? Because **what your awareness is on perpetuates more of what your awareness is on!**

An individual's awareness (remember awareness is thought) is strongly on the **opposite** of their desire. Their desire is, 'I want to be happy,' therefore they get more of what their awareness is on. They get more moments of **not** happy because they are focused and aware of being not happy. Their awareness is on the unhappy emotional state in and of itself considering the emotion as a condition. Their thought, their awareness is on the emotional state of not being happy whatever the negative feelings may be for the individual. Be it anxiety, anger, depression etc., all of which and more besides can be labelled as unhappy. Of course the person wants to be happy but have gotten into a cyclic mental awareness of an unwanted emotional state in and of itself. This is also a pattern of thought in its own right!

Of course there will be other thought patterns that initially created the not happy feelings to begin with which then kicks off this cyclic conundrum of awareness that 'I am not happy.' Which in turn perpetuates more not happy!

So become aware of this pattern of thought (awareness of not being happy), as a pattern of thought in and of itself and deliberately nip it in the bud, learn to pull the handbrake on so to speak as you continue the ongoing inner work **in all other areas** as we have been discussing. In other words, don't get upset even more when you notice that you are not happy, simply acknowledge it as your emotional friend nudging you to let go or shift perspectives.

The conundrum of awareness playing out can be tricky for many people not just those stuck in the cyclic pattern just described. I have been teaching you to be aware of your emotions and to make seeking higher, lighter, better feeling spaces within yourself your dominant intention. However, this level of emotional self-awareness can become a conundrum in the same way as those stuck in the I want to be happy, but I'm not happy cycle of thought. Let's say you become **aware** that you're not feeling so great in some way and **you now care** about how you feel because you are seeking to align thought with your emotional indicators. Now that your introspection is developing your awareness may now be more on the negative emotion itself, meaning you now have thoughts and awareness about the negative emotion in and of itself not necessarily the thoughts that created the feeling in the first place! **Thus your awareness, your now thoughts, are also focusing on your unwanted negative emotion** so therefore you stay feeling not happy! I find this fascinating.

You need to get your attention off the overall not happy feeling ASAP recognizing I'm not happy is good but keeping your awareness on that realization is not. Therefore, I want to be happy but I am not happy plays out over and over again to varying degrees.

By now I hope you can see that **sustainable happiness is always in your ability to focus your mind in an overall direction that pleases you in multiple areas of your life gently quietly over time.** At first learning to focus, learning to think deliberately with this degree of introspection of the smaller inner niggles is an effort because of our current mental momentum in many areas of life, this is why it takes practice to slow and redirect habitual patterns. We may also have momentum in negative thought with the awareness of 'I'm not happy' adding to the problem as just discussed.

At any rate, next time somebody asks you why you're upset or in any negative feeling state, instead of trying to explain all the usual 'reasons,' the physical life details, issues, dramas and stories as to why you think you are upset, you can now more accurately simply say 'Because my head is up my butt!' just like everyone else on the planet who is upset, or angry, or grumpy in whatever way for whatever reason. Seriously it is that simple, happiness is a process of the mind always has been, always will be.

Happiness and heart centeredness has always been the work of the mind.

With a discerning mind that takes **full responsibility for their inner reactions** we can now do the only work of any true value. That is the work between our own ears of harmonising our thoughts our beliefs with our hearts. It has always been the work of the mind to move up the scale, in other words to harmonise mind with heart however many try to separate the two which doesn't work as they are really a cohesive whole, one cannot go without the other. To be heart centered the mind must align with the heart. To be heart centered really means coming from a place of appreciation. Happiness comes from your ability to focus on your personal preferences and areas of intrigue without any limitation or awareness of these interests being missing or lacking in some way within your experience. If you can put a less limiting swing on any awareness in something lacking, you will find some form of positive emotion. Your heart has no fear, no limitation, and is eternally free, hence any time your mind thinks something of a limiting nature you feel the discord, the negative emotion, your heart is not agreeing with your current point of view on the matter! The negative emotion you feel is your heart letting you know you have some conscious work to do because your mind is not aligned with the **freedom of unconditional love.** Unconditional love means aligning mind with heart so that you can feel and hold more moments of natural appreciation regardless of circumstance, therefore it is unconditional. Henceforth, the moment any aspect of awareness is in the absence, or limitation of your personal preference, you will feel some form of negative emotion because this is conditional and stifling freedom. This ranges in all degrees from massive trauma to the smallest often ignored little niggle because heart sees no limitation. I see no difference between appreciation and happiness other than the degree in which positive emotion is felt. Happiness is only slightly down the scale from appreciation, in fact the scale really is that, a sliding scale of moving from the degree of most pain upwards to the degree of most appreciation.

Of course to become truly heart centred this will mean cleaning up your points of view, your opinions on subjects that interest you with a deliberate attempt to feel better about them by shifting your thoughts within any such subject rather than believing that you have the 'right' or are 'just' in feeling angry or sensitive or any other off feeling because of X, Y, or Z reason.

Highly opinionated people are often ignoring their subtle inner impulses letting them know to make conscious changes. Usually they consider them normal given what they are observing and have an opinion about. Are you feeling appreciative within your opinionated rant for example? Realize your heart never feels angry, never feels sensitive, never sees limitation, it is always free, and it is always appreciative. **This means you choose to feel how you feel by accepting your point of view as the right point of view, yet your heart has other ideas!** Your heart is unconditionally appreciative it is you whom impose conditions mentally. Recognise any negative feeling for what they are, indicators that your current point of view is not serving you nor coming from the heart so to speak. Also as you will see in time and experience looking within yourself from this overall perspective, your points of view in all things have **aspects of your personal preferences within them** because everything in life is relative to your own personal preferences, your wanting, your desires.

To begin with this work is easier said than done because this perspective turns you around inside as you endeavour to re-interpret life and emotion in this new way. For example, when we see some horrible person do something which evokes anger we often self-righteously believe our anger, or sensitivity, or whatever negative feeling we may feel is justified and is a good thing because we look at a horrible person doing a horrible thing! Thus we often think we have the right and are just in feeling this way. Yet we have again associated outside of self and are not centred within self. Again our hearts have other ideas about this situation you are not feeling good or coming from the heart at all. So reach consciously to find understanding, appreciation and peace from within. Because when you do embody this interpretation of emotion you find a freedom in self truly unsurpassed. **Every one of us thinks and we all have the ability to direct our thought.** Be the director of your mind that you were born to be!

Quite simply, happiness comes from what you choose to think about and how you choose to think about it. Which is the same for all people world over!

I know I have said all this before yet this time I have given it a slightly different swing by binging in the concept of heart centeredness. There are many ways to perceive and describe this broader subject of well-being, spiritual growth or emotional literacy. My intention here is to clarify the concept of heart centeredness for those who think in this way, although I am aware it can come across a little flowery or spiritual in language and I do wish to keep this book as main stream as possible. However, the more analogies, concepts and ideas you can look at a subject from, the more dynamic your mind becomes which in turn helps you to use mental option 2 of redeveloping thought to something higher with less limitation thus feel better!

Emotional responsibility is no small thing to fully understand within yourself. It truly can turn you around inside trying to interpret how feelings like anger or sensitivity are telling you your own perspective needs addressing rather than wronging what you are looking at by inaccurately associating these types of feelings outside of self, this can be a hard pill to swallow until you truly can take a step back and understand life from a deeper perspective. Your state of being is everything to you, your ability to stay heart centred (appreciative) regardless of circumstance is everything, seek to understand this perspective. The utter depth and freedom **for all** within this understanding is worth stretching your mind a little. Reach to fully understand yourself first then you will find deeper understanding of others.

Pigeon holes.

The Myers Briggs system (which is a brilliant system) does a good job of deciphering and pigeon holing you relative to **your personal preferences**. This can be useful in many ways such as helping you to choose work or career paths that fit your personal preferences etc. It is also very useful in helping you to get to know yourself better because it can help you to understand your desires, preferences and values. However, desire and preferences morph and change over time through life experience and you change as a person in an accelerated way if you are consciously striving higher. It is interesting seeing the difference in yourself within systems like this if you test yourself again after several years of inner work, this can help build your self-awareness even more.

I see pigeon holing people from a psychiatric perspective as having limited value unless there is a simple getting on with and enhancing individual state of being regardless of which other pigeon we may sit next to. That said the Myers Briggs system can really aid you in understanding yourself and giving you more thoughts and perspectives that you can use in your work of mental option 2, thus feel better. All awareness is good awareness for inner development, I see this as the greatest strength given by these types of tests.

Who said I am wrong?

There are people who are quite different to what is often perceived to be normal with all sorts of mental and physical disabilities they may have to contend with as individuals. Just because somebody is living a different experience to you does not make them wrong or less capable of experiencing joy, appreciation or love which is really what life is all about. Again appreciate the beauty of diversity. It is enough to simply be. Reach to appreciate another's being however they are. Again state of being is everything to all of us.

Wearing masks and acting.

The fact that many people act or wear masks is a concept that has been discussed at length by many teachers over the years. Wearing a mask is always an endeavour (often unconsciously) to alleviate the subtle and not so subtle emotional nuances felt within you during various life stages or situations. These include but are not limited to, an attempt to fit in or look cool, pretending to act like something that is not naturally who you are, hiding your true feelings etc.

Obviously this is a lack in genuine self-esteem although it is possible for some to act in such a way as to look quite comfortable in their own skin when really they are not. In every case of mask wearing there is always insecure type niggles within.

An example of this mask wearing can be seen in a group of youths who are being excessively loud and boisterous whilst slouching around town acting cool in some way, perhaps they are banging windows, doors and walls, spitting and acting tough etc. Obviously there is usually a bit of pack mentality going on when people are in groups acting like this with a group confidence. In reality this is a false confidence, an unconscious reaching up the scale usually from a position of powerlessness trying to find their **own inner freedom**, meaning comfort in their own skin.

A group of people like this who are often trying to find their own inner power, **trying to find their own sense of freedom,** are doing so because for the most part society and or their upbringing has knocked it out of their individual thought patterns about-self one way or another. For the most part their self-belief has been knocked down with criticism from others usually from a young age with comments like, 'don't do that', 'behave yourself', 'how do you think that will make me feel', 'do as your told' and so on.

This intense criticism is then copied by the individual which manifests in many negative ways such as becoming critical of themselves and others. We are freedom seeking thus when you have critical constraints put on us from those around us we tend to rebel from these restraints or suppress ourselves.

Our emotional response to life always comes from between the ears and criticism restrains our feelings of inner freedom thus is one of life's biggest suppressors of self. We are all freedom seeking therefore a group acting like this is completely understandable. This is just kids growing up who need support in building their self-esteem not more knocking down from authoritarian's or the critically minded.

If a young person understood this work they could possibly relate to feeling varying insecurities, feeling controlled, or constrained, worrying about what others think of them etc. Obviously there is a lot of self-criticism and reaction to criticism going on in this. Some may carry strong arrogance and a 'fuck you' attitude in defence of themselves thinking they know everything. This type of attitude is also as a result of criticism of self and others which is manifesting in this defensive possibly aggressive way. Understand that a strong aggressive attitude like this is very often based in criticism with a reaching for freedom from outside of self by battling the world around them. Although an individual like this may think they are empowered in their battling this is extremely detrimental to this type of individual for all of the previous mentioned reasons in this book. Whilst feeling critical and defensive this type of individual often exerts a false empowerment behaving badly in an effort to find their own inner freedom from outside of self. Hence there is nothing more important than that you genuinely feel empowered from within, from higher up the scale.

Many people act their entire lives worrying about what other people think, either in an insecure recoiling way or perhaps in an aggressive defensive way.

We may also behave in certain ways to try and create and coerce a perception within other people. In other words, we may try to manipulate what we perceive to be another's perception of us because of our own inner insecurities.

For example, the classic strut of someone trying to act cool as they walk down the street, the good old chewing of gum in a cool sort of way, the hand slouched high over the steering wheel with your shoulder high pose and I'm sure you can think of many others. All of these are natural attempts at trying to find comfort in your own skin. Most people grow out of these simplistic examples to some degree with life experience. Everything in life is in degrees and yet most adults don't have adequate self-esteem to the degree I am teaching in this book and yet obviously have more than perhaps the slouchy teenager. If you are one who is becoming introspective of self on this path, you will always notice these behaviours within self because you can **feel** it. Therefore, do something about it that is appropriate to you, strive up the scale, work on yourself in the social gathering whilst feeling the insecure feeling, or arrogant self-superior feeling, the frustration whilst stuck in a queue, or the anger you feel in an unjust situation, or when you criticise anything etc., etc.

This brings me to a different type of acting which is the technique of 'fake it till you make it'.

A great tactic if you are understanding and doing this inner work but not so great if faking is all you're doing, then it really is just wearing another mask. Healthy fake it till you make it is acting to evoke a good feeling within you with deliberate intent, rather than unconscious masking. Again in doing this you would be training yourself to hold a higher place up the scale. All of this in turn ultimately allows for a natural flow of **appreciation** and more peace and happiness.

The Ego does not exist!

Ego is another word and concept that has many different definitions and education streams just as meditation has many differing definitions and education streams.

Yet ego does not exist as a tangible aspect of anyone's character. It is simply a word and concept used to describe someone's personality traits that we consider to be egotistical, or broader concepts such as the I am-ness of me.

Many of us are struggling (emotionally) within all manner of life subjects and experiences, although the word 'struggle' may not apply to some that are labelled egotistical. What I mean by this is we often become set in our beliefs, ideas and perceptions about life considering them to be 'right' and 'normal' and 'the truth' and in due course acclimatise to the state of being these limiting headsets create which then means there is no struggle because of the acclimatisation combined with no striving for higher change. Thus you may be called egotistical, arrogant and so on. Often an egotistical one is unaware of their inner niggles through a lifetime of suppression and incorrect outward associations, often displaying quite limited authoritarian and draconian beliefs. So in this sense of the concept of ego it is simply that, a concept to try and describe people whose belief systems thus behaviours and opinions may be set, hard, limited, ignorant, arrogant or narrow etc. At deeper levels belief systems like this are linked to insecurities that often aren't realized as insecurities, we just see the hardness of the character traits and label it egotistical.

People talk about letting the ego go and moving past the ego. Which is why those who are on any path of personal development by working on themselves, dropping masks and ultimately building greater states of self-esteem are considered as people who are moving past their ego. Or you could as accurately say anyone working on themselves is someone climbing the emotional scale within life subjects. Meaning the ego did not exist to begin with, all that was really going on within one who could be labelled as egotistical was their emotional reactiveness and controlling natures relative to limiting beliefs and set ideas as I've described throughout. Egotistical people could be coming from a false empowerment vantage point, arrogance, self-superior, self-importance etc., due to these set hard beliefs thus are labelled as egotistical.

Therefore, it is not ego you have to work past as such because ego doesn't exist beyond a label you can use for certain behaviours and character traits, which are really due to limiting beliefs and set ideas, opinions etc., which in turn is keeping them fairly low on the emotional scale.

Building an inner harmony, a genuine inner-peace, thus developing an appreciative sense of self-esteem is required of us all, just as it is one who is considered egotistical then they are no longer egotistical!

In other words, the label of ego really is associated to character traits that are linked to a lack in self-esteem to the degree I am portraying. Self-esteem to this degree can only be achieved by consciously working through niggles as life evokes them, rather than suppression, outward manipulation or self-righteous belief that their point of view is the only accurate point of view as is often the case for an egotistical type of character.

Doing this work will mean that as each issue is resolved a mask is dropped because a mask is simply an insecurity which is often hidden behind draconian "I am Right" ideas which could be described as ego. Of course you have to be aware of the mask in the first place and wish to move beyond it hence introspection is a powerful tool to constantly enhance within self so you can overcome all masks or aspects that could be described as 'ego.' All masks and insecurities of all degrees will ultimately feel off to you as you strive up the emotional scale. (Usually an egotistical person's introspection is not that well developed.) Ultimately anything less than appreciation is lacking in some way, therefore you can feel the difference. Strive.

Chapter Nine

The common thread within all emotion.

From a psychological point of view there are four things that go together to make up the degree of emotion felt positive or negative. These are: -

- The thought itself.: - Which either has some degree of empowerment (freedom of self, freedom of desire) within the thought, this creates positive emotion.: -or limitation which suppresses freedom, suppresses desire creating negative emotion.
- The momentum of the thought. How much it is active in the mind.
- How much you **care** about the subject you are engaged in thus thinking about.
- The above three all link together with regard to your personal preference, your wanting which is your desire within the subject at hand hence you care. (Is the thought/belief empowered regarding your preference, or limited regarding your preference?)

Strong states of depression, intense anger, not forgiving somebody and any other strong negative feeling states that may be held for any duration, always have strong **mental momentum** within limiting thought patterns. This means all negative emotion regardless of the degree of feeling felt has some aspect of limiting self within the currently active thought thus belief structure regarding personal desire/preference within the subject that is active in your awareness thus mind.

So the degree of feeling felt positive and negative is partly due to the degree of mental momentum i.e. how active it is within the mind, in conjunction with limiting or empowering perspectives. This is also relative to the degree you care about the subject which is in relationship to your preference, your wanting, your desire.

Again this is why distraction and meditation are powerful to understand from this broader perspective, simply letting go is often the best thing you can do which means pivot your thought and awareness of the topic thus slow momentum.

So, all strong negative feeling states go hand in hand with strong mental momentum even if the subject that evoked your negative reaction suddenly just happened. Instantly evoked strong reactions are due to your already ongoing momentum in your patterns of thought and beliefs within all things. Hence any strong negative states may take an effort to redirect to the opposite. Just like it takes greater effort to slow a speeding train (strong complex mental momentum), compared to slowing a speeding skateboard (not so complex mental momentum).

For this reason, a good place to start this inner work when momentum is already strong is often meditation, meditation retreats and or distraction techniques like adventure therapy programmes, getting a job etc., combined with advanced mindfulness education such as this Book! These approaches reduce strong negative momentum with little mental effort thus the ongoing inner work becomes less of a mountain to climb. If you could just engage in mental option 3 for long enough you will be surprised how many belief based issues vaporise with no air time between the ears.

The opposite of negative momentum is creating strong empowered positive momentum where a good feeling state is **now easy to maintain.** The train is now a happy train so to speak! So mental momentum is a good thing when working in your favour.

The emotional scale is a sliding scale which is directly related to mental momentum within all subjects in life regardless of life circumstance that may be evoking your reaction, either positive or negative. A happy train is at the top of the scale; an upset train is at the bottom of the scale.

Of course trying to figure out what and where any limitation is within your thought can often be hard to see and understand in the early stages of examining your own thoughts to this degree, especially if you are already in a strong negative state of any kind, or living any unwanted experience. We simply want to feel better now dammit! Hence creating an environment that naturally evokes mental option three such as high energy activities as part of a therapy regime of education and medication is of high value for those suffering strong states of depression for example.

So to reiterate, the degree of negative **mental momentum** is always proportionate to the **degree of pain felt** however you wish to label the negative emotional state be it depression, anger, anxiety etc. Also the **degree** of emotional pain felt is due to how much an individual, 'cares' about the subject(s) that are active in the mind. Understand that when you care about a subject this is because it has aspects of your personal preferences, your wanting, your desires or lack thereof within it.

In a general sense the more you care about or desire something and the more your awareness **builds momentum of a limiting nature,** the worse you will feel as the momentum gets stronger from a **limiting perspective**.

Hence, strong negative feeling states can seem utterly overwhelming and out of control such as in strong states of depression. It can appear as if the thought is thinking you rather than you are thinking the thought when the momentum is so strong, especially if life has a lot of unwanted experiences happening. It can **appear** out of your control.

The stronger the negative mental state the more the biology of the body is influenced as can be observed in cases such as that of clinical depression. Hence the flawed yet strongly held belief that biology causes the depression when really the biology is a reflection of the mental momentum. This is empowering to understand and I know this challenges strongly held medical belief. Of course please do not miss interpret this statement and shun medications that you may require, that would be like shunning other technologies that aid us in the modern world. You wouldn't go home each night and try and light your fire with a flint and steel and cook your evening meal under some pretence that your electric oven is wrong for existing! Use every and all available options to aid yourself in all areas of life to your own discretion.

The degree of momentum of limited thought caused by your attention to it and the degree that you **care** about any particular issue creates the degree of pain that you may feel which is now measurable biologically, and can thus then be manipulated biologically to some degree.

Of course it is hard to get your attention off where you don't want to be in life if you are living or experiencing something you do not want. In fact, it can **seem** impossible to do the mental gymnastics required in extreme cases because the momentum of thought relative to life experience may have built to such a degree that the awareness on a subject can seem like a runaway train, hence the intense feelings within can seem overwhelming and unstoppable. In which case this would be a good time to really begin the work of self in earnest. Learn how to truly relax your mind, learn to meditate, chill, breathe, let go whilst obviously also seeking medical and professional help as required. Do everything in your power to get back to an even keel.

At any rate, the negatively felt limitation of-self thoughts could be focused on one singular subject or a multitude of subjects this is the case within all degrees of negative emotion such as depression, anger or otherwise.

For example, jealousy has an awareness that somebody else has what you want and you are again aware of something missing in your own experience, in this case jealousy is evoked because of your awareness on what you don't have with some **limitation** in your thought and belief regarding you achieving similar results thus you feel jealousy. The common thread of **'limitation of self within the thought/belief regarding personal preference'** is active here in jealousy as it is in all negative emotions.

Of course we don't have to figure out the complexities of thought to this degree to feel better. Simply recognise the off feeling and reach for a lighter perspective or another subject to feel better however you can as we have discussed in Part Two of this book.

If you are one who is interested in the complexities of your mind and are keen to develop an awareness of where and what the limitation thoughts are in your mind, go easy about this as it really is a lifetimes journey understanding yourself to this degree. Use a curious discerning mind. Don't try and understand your thought process all at once, just quietly observe your thoughts relative to preference and feeling as you move through life.

A heavily depressed teenager will have all sorts of negative limitation bouncing around that they are often not even aware of nor able to readily see without more life experience to learn from. Understandable of course and in fairness it takes time to look at and adjust one's own thought patterns from this perspective of emotion described throughout. Plus, in the case of a teenager they have never been taught how to stay on an even keel through being led by example. Usually they have picked up the passed on negative thought pattern of self-criticism from authoritarian behaviours of those around them. Thus have often been brow beaten to behave in certain ways impeding feelings of freedom (empowerment), which in turn creates a lack in self-esteem thus the teenage rebellion is born as they fight for their inner empowerment or conversely the suppression, depression, fearfulness, self-loathing etc., which is common in far too many also.

Depression was good for me.

Strong states of depression are extremely hard to make a move out of **because of the strong mental momentum** just described. It appears to suck the will out of you, saps you of your energy and so much more. Hence the stronger the mental momentum is within a depressive state the more measurable the biology of the body is. A person who is susceptible to depression has to do the best they can to pivot off of or change their thought patterns however they can gradually over time, listen to your emotional friend and shift your habitual patterns gently quietly day by day. In heavy states of depression, I believe it is common for the awareness on the feeling in itself to have taken over the dominant thought. In other words, an awareness of the depression becomes an all-consuming and cyclic thought/awareness thus you become zombie like with no will to think or move, the body shuts down as such.

Getting out and being active is usually one of the best things you can do for yourself initially because activity aids you in getting your awareness off negatively focused subject(s) as has been discussed. Thus activity can help activate other more positive thinking patterns, especially if you are actively seeking to think differently, then the measurable biology can be seen as improving. Depression does not have to be a lifetimes struggle as it appears to be for many, as I thought it may have been for me before I learnt what is written here.

Depression was my go to default feeling, my set tone for the bulk of my life, this was really bugging me because it was hindering my quality of life. I **inaccurately** thought that the feeling of depression was the problem. When really my emotional friend was yelling at me to shift my thoughts and points of view to that of less limitation, eventually I listened.

Of course when you are depressed it appears depression is the problem or a condition especially if you have been declared clinically depressed and are walking around like a zombie! Yet it is not a condition from my perspective. Depression is simply a stronger emotional indicator in regards to what's going on between your ears due to not being more astute at the work of little niggles in the first place thus the momentum builds to such a degree. This is regardless of any life circumstance which may be evoking your mental activity. Stronger momentum equals stronger depression, lighter momentum equals less depression perhaps you could also call this low mood, which is really just a lighter degree of depression. When I finally understood that I was doing it to myself (creating my depression between the ears) and **therefore I could do something about it,** everything changed. This awareness is pure empowerment. Of course many look at this awareness as, 'it's my fault I'm depressed,' from a self-critical perspective, this is not helpful! Simply acknowledge that you now understand how to work towards a better state and take gentle steps. Stopping a freight train takes time. For me during the first couple of years of this work depression would come and go as my mind flicked and wandered around my old limiting perspectives. However, I have not had a case of depression in I don't know how long? In hind sight I can tell you that what once used to send me into depression in my reaction to it for days, weeks, and even months may now eventuate in a short period of time where I may feel angry, frustrated, grouchy, or impatient and these feelings are often worked past in **moments** as I continue the work of niggles. Before developing this improvement in my directed thinking I was pretty good at being depressed for weeks, months, in reality years! I no longer live on an emotional roller coaster with a default tone of 'flat depressive' to fall back on, of course it was a process of time and as part of that process there were occasional angry outbursts and dips backwards as I climbed the emotional scale by redeveloping my own limiting points of view. Remember anger is further up the scale than depression and is often a part of the growth process of moving higher hence angry outbursts are common place when climbing out of a horrible murky hole. Relax and empower yourself higher realising you are doing good work; anger is better than depression! My tone is much higher overall and will be even higher as time goes on as my experience is proving this to me, positive momentum is continuing to build.

In fact, the warmth of appreciation is a very real state of being for me now more often than not, whereas it was hard to get even a glimmer of that feeling at all in my earlier life, in fact I barely knew it existed! I can now truly resonate with the affirmation I learned in my early 20's whereas at the time these were cold empty words, *'I now choose to make my life light easy and joyful!'*

You **can** shift your emotional set points because they are never ever set, ever!

I can honestly say that depression is a thing of the past, and that I am very appreciative for having experienced it, because without having felt depression, I would not have eventually come to realise that I had some conscious work to do! Depression really is simply an emotional indicator proportionate to the degree of mental momentum you may carry, thus letting you know to seek lighter feeling, less limiting perspectives, truly that's all it is. Don't make such a big deal out of it. Just see it for what it is, your guiding light to make inner change for yourself. Of course it's hard to see that when we consider depression or any negative state as 'bad or a condition.' When really it is your inner guidance for conscious change which is always a good thing!

I can also emphatically say that the main habitual patterns of thought I was carrying were not so easy to move past. Firstly because of the momentum of them and secondly it was a challenge to embody new ideas that served me better than my old status quo mainstream and limiting beliefs. Hence, in my case it took two or three years before a sustainable emotional change was embodied. For me moving past depression required a process of making peace with several life subjects over time whilst continuing to build an overall **broader** perspective of life. This meant I had to learn everything I have written here and actually do it, actually embody it. Depression was always, always caused by my limited thought, my point of view, my opinion, my mental focus that generated the problem, there is simply no getting past this fact. Then when you are depressed you may become aware of the state of depression in and of itself and presume that it is a condition (it is not) which can perpetuate more of the same because what your awareness is on perpetuates more of what your awareness is on, as was discussed earlier.

Again depression is simply a stronger emotional indicator, your friend yelling at you, don't make such a big deal out of it.

This can be tricky to figure through sometimes, hence there were times I used to drive myself mad trying to figure it all out! (Unwittingly adding more negative momentum.)

There are many paths to overcoming any negative feeling state, there truly is a way through for all, and the three mental options can always be found within any path. It's important to realise there is only ever one path which is what do I give my attention to now, meaning what thought am

I thinking now. The power of now is always in your ability to pick better feeling thoughts now! The first step is **your eventual decision** to actually get over it and find a sustainable way through for yourself and the ongoing never ceasing work of niggles **IS a sustainable way.** Anyone who is heavily depressed will have moments of feeling better to some degree; you must recognize these improvements no matter how slight and milk them longer if this is you. Do the work and drag yourself out of the slumps any way you can and up that scale! **You are not helpless; you can do it!** Gently and surely the answers are within you. Make sure you take notice and recognize those moments that feel better to you, realise you are not actually depressed all of the time after all, therefore there must be a way through!

If you look around you will find people who have overcome all kinds of issues whether depression in all its differing degrees, horrific past traumas, mental health problems of various types and more beyond. Seek a higher state of being and you shall find a higher state of being, Seek!

Stress, anxiety and being overwhelmed.

Can you see how stress, anxiety, feeling overwhelmed and really every negative emotional state can be overcome with this ultimate inner behaviour regardless of your story because once you get a handle on your mind-emotion connection, you realise these feelings are simply your indicators busily trying to get your attention for inner conscious change. Meditate, relax, breathe, let go, reach for lighter perspectives. Of course if you have never done this work and you're just beginning to learn how to focus your mind relative to your emotional indicators within the heat of the moment it may be a bit of struggle. As this work becomes second nature with the deliberate use of it and you have actually lifted your tone sustainably you can usually readily work through all life issues that may have caused you great stress before. So again stress, a feeling of being overwhelmed, and anxiety really are **emotional indicators, your friend talking to you, that is all.** It does not pay to get nit-picky and catalogue, pigeon hole, or label emotions relative to life situations as that is really a futile effort. Simply recognize the off-ness you are feeling whatever feeling it is, and to whatever degree. Then strive beyond it. As I've mentioned before, anything less than appreciation leaves room for improvement.

There is an old lobster analogy regarding stress which goes like this: -

Lobster's shed their shells as they grow. Liken a Lobsters shell to the thoughts thus belief patterns of your mind, behaviours and preferences (values) as this is what you are presenting to the world. Often like a shield such as a lobster's shell, in a manner of speaking. You also perceive and interpret your experiences through your shell. The problem with a lobster's shell is as the lobster grows, his shell does not so he becomes uncomfortable, **he gets stressed** so he must shed his shell. (You must also shed your old ways, your out-dated beliefs, any limited perceptions etc.) He must grow a new shell to incorporate his expanded size (As you must find better feeling perspectives, meaning grow your new shell.) Life does this to us, we expand with experience but we often become overwhelmed or stressed within our experiences because of our current inability to deal with whatever situation is at hand mentally thus emotionally. We have to adjust and modify ourselves to accommodate the situation or event we are within; the work of niggles is the work of growing our shell. Of course life experience itself is the true teacher here so the feeling of stress is always your emotional indicator letting you know to shed your shell, in other words to find a lighter perspective within the current situation. Relax, let go, breathe. Grow yourself beyond your old shell. **Stress is a good thing like all negative emotion because without it you wouldn't know you have something to work through.** Of course many simply suppress, ignore or tolerate their stress, thus create a craggy old shell which becomes stiff and set in its ways, holding themselves back from a vibrant, free flowing expanding life. These people may truly struggle to deal with anything different to what their shell can accommodate. Their limiting beliefs cannot accommodate their own expansion and they refuse to shed their shell to their own determent. When the work of this book has become second nature to you in all areas of your life you will be constantly growing your new shell thus stress is less dominant in your overall experience!

Be careful what you focus on because that is all you will see.

Many believe the world is going to hell in a hand basket, they like to point out all the ill's in the world, the statistics regarding some topic or another, some science in a subject which may only be from a narrow perspective to begin with, the fighting in all its forms, climate change perhaps, and then say things like, "*Its buggered man can't you see?*"

Well when that is all you look at then that is all you will see and can thus then become your 'truth,' your 'belief,' yet you may have your blinkers on in a very big way. Your 'truth' your 'belief' may not be as accurate as you think it is, be prepared to bend and change as new information comes to light, be open. The negative slant in our media adds to negative bias which influences general public opinion, when someone offers a more positive opinion than general public opinion they may be labelled as naive. Yet those who focus on the negatives of life which often have become their 'truth' are often very naive in their own negative and narrow line of sight because they are blind to the **overwhelming** positives that exist! Isn't that interesting? **What you look at is all you will see. Broaden your vision.** I challenge you to spend time deliberately seeking out all positive aspects in every facet of your life, look for positivity, make an effort to truly look on the brightside. If it is an effort to look on the brightside then there truly is a lot of negative momentum in your current mental activity hence the effort. Don't give up, stick at it pluck away at it and in time see how every perspective you hold shifts for the better. In fact, your entire life begins to unfold for the better. Learning to focus on positives makes you wise because you now have a broader vision beyond a one sided often limiting negative and narrow vision.

So if you are one who is constantly fretting and worrying about big social and world issues, someone who is constantly looking at negative articles within any form of media, simply stop for a week and observe how you feel when you are not adding more snow to your snowballs. Take the time to notice how your fret and worry shifts and moulds relative to what's going on in your mind when you're not adding more thought to it in your incessant observation and thinking of such things. See how you are actually doing it to yourself, you are creating your state of being, choose thought with more discernment. In essence by not looking at negative media you would be using mental option one, which is a great tactic to steady your state of being just like meditation is. However, in time with your continuing conscious striving up the scale through your work of moulding thought relative to your niggles, you can come to a place of broader perspectives where you can observe such negative media and not be upset by it in the same way as before, if at all nor be de-sensitized either. **Not being upset by negative media does not mean that you don't care.** If you are one whom is negatively affected by subjects such as big social and environmental issues that are usually out of our individual control, then you need to find a way of making peace with whatever is going on for your own wellbeing. Again this does not mean you don't care or are naive; it means you are wisely trying to sort out your own inner world by removing all blame of outside circumstance for the way in which you feel! Unconditional love or sustainable happiness for that matter is precisely that, **unconditional and sustainable!** An appreciation for life is where it's at, not fear, anger, fret, worry or concern. This means in the early stages of this work we often have to turn the other cheek, sometimes we have to wear blinkers in the form of mental option one by getting our awareness off a subject long enough for us to gain control of our own state of being **first** before any real solution can come into our awareness. **There are solutions to all problems but whilst you continue to look at the problem, the problem is all you will see.** You must turn your attention off the problem and seek the solution and this is more effective from a higher emotional place. Solutions to problems cannot be found within the same consciousness that created them. So getting your attention off a problem for a while and reaching for a higher emotional state often helps you find a different perspective which aids in 'ah ha' moments and possible solutions of higher value. Also if you are one who is still highly sensitive in the early stages of this work hence are easily upset by negative subjects and you wish to help a situation in some way, be careful in associating these feelings as being a 'good thing' and that of 'caring.' Consider that you can find a place of appreciation for all life and thus therefore find solutions to your own inner issues first. Again love is the answer to all things and if you are feeling upset or sensitive in any way, is this a state of appreciation, of love? Of course not. I am very aware how hard this is to get your head around because of our emotional associations outside of-self, let alone embody, again life is a process for us all. If you can interpret life from a more appreciative state, then you will be shining a light for others to aspire to. Who wants to shine a worried light? Who wants to shine a fearful light? Who wants to shine a fretful light? Who wants to shine an angry light? Appreciation is the only strength worth developing, appreciation is the only weapon of any sustaining value anything else just adds fuel to the fire. Shine an appreciative light.

Lighter perspectives are everything.

Throughout this book I have painted a picture regarding a deeper aspect of human psychology and in so doing I have often talked about beliefs and how these directly affect individual states of being as and when the thought, the belief is **actually active** in the mind. When there is enough momentum in thought this results in an emotional indication, either positive or negative. However, I have neglected to really delve into too many individual beliefs in and of themselves and I can appreciate how that can be annoying if you are wanting to specifically pick apart a belief that is of interest to you. But consider thought and beliefs really are infinite **therefore it really is your job to reach for lighter perspectives yourself.** What angle would I pick a belief apart from? A religious angle, a spiritual angle, a scientific angle, a psychological angle, a medical angle, a nutritional angle, a because it happened in my life angle, all of these angles? And from whose perspective? The list goes on. Hence I have written this book from what I consider to be a general education of a deeper aspect of psychology thus of more benefit to more people. My intention was to offer enough information that anybody could begin to examine their own thoughts and beliefs relative to the ever present emotional link thus continue their life journey in a self-empowered way. Rather than pulling apart specific beliefs which would become quite arduous and of limited value because of the infinitely different beliefs people carry thus would only be of use to the few who have similar beliefs.

That said, I have said many things throughout this book which clearly challenge beliefs other people may hold, some of the statements made may be argued are not accurate or true because of another belief, point of view, or study of some sort which is then justified to those that think that way. Consider, from a scientific angle for every study done there is usually another that refutes it, adds to it, complicates it, makes an understanding more dynamic, and so on. This day and age almost everybody is quoting and citing science or research from this angle and that angle as I have done myself. But just because there has been research that says one thing and millions believe it, doesn't necessarily make it true or of any intrinsic value to self-empowerment. So, rather than arguing for your opinion, point of view, or belief whether you think it is true, or that you are right is irrelevant. Firstly, when you are arguing for your own point of view often you are not reaching to understand, and secondly how does it feel to you? Can you find peace in it? If not, then there will be some limitation within your belief relative to life preference somewhere. Stop fighting other people's points of view and relinquish your own that are no longer serving you, let go of the battle.

From my point of view, the more people that can get their head around full emotional responsibility to the degree that I am detailing, the better off our societies will progress because this is the root cause of all bickering, arguing, and fighting from the simplest of conversations to the most complex geopolitical situations.

For example, have you gotten your head around the statement I made earlier, "Nobody ever pisses you off, you piss yourself off each and every time?" This is a big ask to fully understand to begin with and until you do then you are still associating outside of self with limited emotional responsibility. This statement among many others I have made can feel counterintuitive, difficult, confusing and unpleasant in many differing situations. For example, in customer service, or staff management we are constantly standing on our heads to keep others happy for multiple reasons, more sales, staff retention etc. How does emotional responsibility fit in here when it is always another person's responsibility for how they feel? Simple, being kind to people coming from a place of agenda, obligation or appeasement is poles apart from being kind to people coming from a centred, emotionally secure, loving and appreciative position because that's just who you are! There are many reasons this level of inner responsibility can be challenging to understand and incorporate into life situations. However, when you do, when it clicks, you thrive in a way others may not even see in you and that's ok. No one else has to understand only you do. Shine your appreciative light anyway. Kindness, compassion and understanding goes along way and so does not disempowering others by teaching them their happiness depends on your behaviours or kindness! This is a powerful awareness to consider, although tricky to get your head around and embody. You can only do what is appropriate unto you as best as you are able, no one can ask more. Understanding others comes from truly understanding yourself first; many do not understand themselves that well, hence struggle to understand life and others.

I believe everybody has the right to, 'unlimited expectation for themselves,' meaning I am very aware that there are people in the midst of massive traumas, mental health issues of all kinds such as strong states of clinical depression, mental break downs, high anxiety, schizophrenia and so on. Also in some cases of mental health some things are deemed as a condition or believed by some to be incurable, or un-recoverable. Two things I wish to say about this.

Firstly, just because somebody is not quite right from your perspective for whatever reason, perhaps they have some serious physical condition or mental handicap, this does not make their being-ness wrong nor their experience of life wrong because they are experiencing such things. Yet again genuinely connected no agenda kindness goes along way!

Secondly, I flatly refuse to accept limitation on behalf of myself or anybody else ever! Therefore, I make zero apologies for expecting the best for all people (from their perspective) regardless of what study or belief structure may say otherwise about their particular circumstance. If you offer limitation such as 'no hope' often that belief is taken on board and becomes a self-fulfilling prophecy and I want no part in that type of limitation regardless of what other study or mainstream belief may say is, 'reality or the truth.'

You and the universe is a complex set of ever expanding harmonic vibration, meaning all energy is eternal and infinitely expanding of which we are all a part. This has been expressed spiritually for millennia and science is catching up to this awareness, where is there limitation in that? Whose reality or truth are you living? Choose your own nor impose your limitation on to others whom you perceive as having limitations. If you perceive limitation you are limited.

My thoughts ideas and opinions have been heavily influenced over the years by science, and personal spiritual experience. I see **absolutely no** separation between the two although I have endeavoured to keep most of that out of this, my first book. The laws of the universe are all encompassing and relate to all people, all life forms, all psychology, all math, all energy, all experience, all science, all religion, all spirituality and yet that is a big statement to make and what is meant by it? I am not about to try and answer that here. Seek for yourself.

A fair part of this book has been influenced from the education offered by Esther Hicks, I see Esther as one of the leading educators of true human psychology today, if you can hear what she has to say that is! (I am in deepest appreciation of your work Esther and you personally, thank you.) Yet I have clearly written this book from my interpretation of only part of the education she offers as well as only part of the education that I have to offer whilst keeping aspects of a spiritual and scientific nature mostly removed. This was mostly due to my intention of writing a book that many people could read and gain something from no matter their religious beliefs or whether of scientific or spiritual mind hence a bit of a challenge to write with no journalistic or writing training whatsoever. In writing this book, I have discovered through experience that writing is like a painting, you can keep coming back to it, adding to it, refining it, considering different angles etc. At this point I am reasonably happy with it even though I could continue the refining for at least another year or even add another two hundred thousand words in substantiating scientific and spiritual evidence, experience and ideas. But I haven't and here it is.

Thank you Sandra for your constant never ceasing support and encouragement in the writing of this book it was very much appreciated. Also thank you Debbie I truly appreciate your fresh eyes helping me to clarify what I was trying to say.

At any rate, I hope you enjoyed it and maybe I shall bump into you in passing one day, possibly on a hiking trail somewhere, then perhaps we can pull apart a specific belief to our hearts content. Or perhaps we can simply go fishing and appreciate good company, life and our surroundings.

Love Richard.

Printed in the United States
By Bookmasters